# Free Speech Madness

## A SAPIENT Being's Guide to the War Against Truth, Conservative Ideals & Freedom of Speech

By

Corey Lee Wilson

# Free Speech Madness

# Free Speech Madness

Fratire Publishing books can be purchased in bulk with special discounts for educational purposes, association gifts, sales promotions, and special editions can be created to specifications. All inquiries for such can be made below.

**FRATIRE PUBLISHING LLC**
4533 Temescal Canyon Rd. # 308
Corona, CA 92883 USA
www.FratirePublishing.com
FratirePublishing@att.net
1+ (951) 638-5502

Fratire Publishing is all about common sense and relevant books for sapient beings. If this sounds like you and you can never have enough common sense, wisdom, and relevancy, then visit us and learn more about the 50 *MADNESS* series of book titles at www.fratirepublishing.com/madnessbooks.

Printed paperback and eBook ePUB by Ingram Spark in La Vergne, Tennessee, USA
Copyright © 2021: First Edition December2021
ISBN 978-0-9847490-4-1 (Paperback)
ISBN 978-1-953319-35-7 (eBook)
FreeSpeechMadness-01-PDF (pdf)
LCCN 2021925671

Special thanks for the cover design by Jenny Barroso, J20Graphics, j20graphics@gmail.com and ebook conversion by Redeemer SoftTech, redeemer.softtech@gmail.com.

Thanks as well to the back cover synopsis comments, content, and suggestions from Paul Bates and Dave Henry.

Free Speech Madness

# Contents

# Acknowledgements

I owe a debt of gratitude to the following for "heavily" borrowing at times pieces of their and/or outright sections. I do this unashamedly to use the sapient phrase, "if it ain't broke—don't try to fix it." Most of the borrowed works and research cannot be improved upon—so why try? It's better to assemble these meaningful parts, profound messages, and eloquent arguments into a cohesive whole, told with high school and college students in mind, and that's what I've done and where my talent lies.

Below in alphabetical order are the major contributors to *Free Speech Madness* that I borrowed verbatim, quoted, and conceptualized much of their content from a little to a lot. Wherever this happened, I did my best to acknowledge my source. If I didn't at times within the 15 chapters, I did so intentionally because doing so would have distracted from their message. Nonetheless, they are more than acknowledged in the References and Index sections of this textbook.

**Dershowitz, Alan –** Is an American lawyer known for his work in U.S. constitutional law and American criminal law. He taught at Harvard Law School from 1964 through 2013, where he was appointed as the Felix Frankfurter Professor of Law in 1993. Dershowitz is a regular media contributor, political commentator, and legal analyst.

**Foundation for Individual Rights in Education (F.I.R.E**.): Is a non-profit organization that effectively and decisively defends the fundamental rights of tens of thousands of students and faculty members on our nation's campuses while simultaneously reaching millions on and off campus through education, outreach, and college reform efforts.

**Heterodox Academy (HxA):** Is a non-profit and nonpartisan collaborative of 5,000+ professors, educators, administrators, staff, and students who are committed to enhancing the quality of research and education by promoting open inquiry, viewpoint diversity, and constructive disagreement in institutions of higher learning.

*National Review*: is an American semi-monthly conservative editorial magazine, focusing on news and commentary pieces on political, social, and cultural affairs. The magazine was founded by the author William F. Buckley Jr. in 1955 and is currently edited by Rich Lowry.

**Pew Research Center:** Is a nonpartisan fact tank that informs the public about the issues, attitudes and trends shaping the world. They conduct public opinion polling, demographic research, content analysis and other data-driven social science research and do not take policy positions.

**Prager U:** Is an American nonprofit organization that creates videos on various political, economic, and philosophical topics from a conservative perspective. The university was created by conservative Dennis Prager, an American syndicated talk show host, to teach fundamental concepts. Its content is sapient and relevant, and they educate millions of Americans and young people about the values that make America great.

***The Epoch Times:*** Is the SAPIENT Being's most trusted and used news source and deserves special mention for their sapient editorials, timely articles, and in-depth reports and they're consistently the number one go-to-source for the MADNESS series of textbooks content for the depth and breadth of article and sapient contributors.

The remarkable American story unfolds under a protective umbrella of freedom of speech that is guaranteed by the First Amendment. However, these rights are under attack in unique and novel ways in the 21st century and this textbook is going to explore, expose, and analyze the reasons why with facts, figures, truth without bias, practical logic, viewpoint diversity, intellectual humility—and most importantly of all—freedom of speech and expression.

The most important thing about America is liberty and in particular the freedom of speech and expression that is guaranteed every American citizen from the First Amendment.

So many have sacrificed so much to secure our liberty and preserve it for future generations. How do we honor their sacrifice and that of so many others in our nation's 245-year history? We stand and fight to uphold liberty and our unalienable rights enshrined in America's founding documents. If liberty is to be lost, it won't be on our watch.

With these important points noted, we end this section with the words of John Adams, "wisdom, and knowledge … diffused generally among the body of the people [is] necessary for the preservation of [the people's] rights and liberties."

# A SAPIENT Being's Preface

Free speech in America is under attack and the primary targets are conservatives and their ideals, values, and organizations. Lacking in viewpoint diversity, intellectual humility, and critical thinking skills from decades of exposure to fake news and false narratives—impressionable young minds increasingly embrace illiberalism.

Illiberalism in popular usage describes an attitude that is close-minded, intolerant, and bigoted and it manifests itself with free speech suppression. It's increasingly prevalent in leftist, liberal and Democratic Party ideals, policies, and organizations and perpetuates itself in the form of cancel culture, social justice warriors, and the progressivism 'regressivism' movement.

Generations X Y Z have been denied many sapient conservative ideals and values and now view Antifa, BLM, OSF and SPLC as social justice warriors—whereas conservatives, whites, Republicans, and Trump supporters are seen as privileged racist fascists. It's a world gone mad and the inspiration for the SAPIENT Being's *MADNESS* series of sapient conservative textbooks.

Everyone is entitled to their own opinions—but they're not entitled to their own facts, logic, or truths. However, mainstream news, social media, and academia have avoided the telos of truth and are in many ways the media arm of the Democratic Party. Some are infected with various stages of Trump Derangement Syndrome (TDS).

So much so, a number of on-campus watchdog groups have shown how widespread TDS is by interviewing students as to what their opinions are on many of Trump's accomplishments by falsely claiming these were instead by progressives, Obama, Democrats, and so on. Repeatedly, the misinformed students are shocked when they learn they occurred under the Trump administration.

Every topic in *Free Speech Madness* provides a sapient point of view on the intellectual playing field—versus the 'so-called' progressive ones—and challenges all distractors to prove otherwise. For the close minded—this textbook will be a triggering event, denial of truth, and a painful intervention. For the open minded—it will be a revelation, an epiphany, a sapient being moment. Which one are you?

If you're the later, you'll be interested to know this textbook is a continuation of sorts of the first and essential sapient conservative textbook *Fake News Madness*. Why? Because when the overwhelming liberal, leftist, and Democrat Party aligned mainstream media, big tech, and academia (i.e., mediacrats) can influence, suppress, and censor the daily news cycle by utilizing a 21$^{st}$ century armory of illiberal tactic in the form of fake news journalism, false and biased narratives, and unproven non-truths due to their relative monopoly on the marketplace of ideas.

Like all MADNESS textbooks, *Free Speech Madness* offers an opportunity to be part of the solution to these many issues. Are you interested in learning about the war against truth, conservative Ideals and freedom of speech? If yes, please read on and if you also believe in the message of this book and willing to fight for it—please considering joining or participating in one of the three SAPIENT Being programs below.

**Make Free Speech Again On Campus (MFSAOC) Program**

Provide high school and college students the opportunity to start SAPIENT Being campus clubs, chapters, and alliances where independent, liberal, and conservative minded students can meet, discuss, and debate important issues and develop sapience in the process. Learn more about the process of practicing, protecting, and promoting viewpoint diversity, freedom of speech, and intellectual humility as part of the Make Free Speech Again On Campus (MFSAOC) program for on or off site campus groups at https://www.sapientbeing.org/programs.

**World Of Writing Warriors (WOWW) Program**

Return free speech, open dialogue and civil discourse to high school and college students and journalists without the cancel culture against those with differences in opinion, ideologies, and practices. Encourage open debate, dialogue, and the free expression of alternative and non-orthodox viewpoints with the goal of creating a World Of Writing Warriors (WOWW) program at https://www.sapientbeing.org/programs that upholds journalistic standards throughout all types of campus journalism and media.

**Sapient Conservative Textbooks (SCT) Program**

Relevant and current events textbooks program to help return conservative values, viewpoint diversity, and sapience to high school and college students and enlighten them on the many blessings to humankind that are the direct result of American exceptionalism, Western European culture, and Judeo-Christian values. The ethos for every textbook in the Sapient Conservative Textbooks (SCT) program is truth without bias and for more information on the 50 titles please visit the program website at https://www.fratirepublishing.com/madnessbooks.

# Are You a Sapient Being or Want to Be One?

Sapience, also known as wisdom, is the ability to think and act using knowledge, experience, understanding, common sense and insight. Sapience is associated with attributes such as intelligence, enlightenment, unbiased judgment, compassion, experiential self-knowledge, self-actualization, and virtues such as ethics and benevolence.

Being a sapient being is not about identity politics, it's about doing what is right and borrows many of the essential qualities of Centrism that supports strength, tradition, open mindedness, and policy based on evidence not ideology.

Sapient beings are independent minded thinkers that achieve common sense solutions that appropriately address America's and the world's most pressing issues. They gauge situations based on context and reason, consideration, and probability. They are open minded and exercise conviction and willing to fight for it on the intellectual battlefield. Sapient beings don't blindly and recklessly follow their feelings or emotions.

Their unifying ideology is based on the truth, reason, logic, scientific method, and pragmatism—and not necessarily defined by compromise, moderation, or any particular faith—but is considerate of them.

Most importantly, per a letter written by Princeton professor Robert George in 2017 and endorsed by 28 professors from three Ivy League universities for incoming freshmen, "Think for yourself!"

George's letter continues:

Thinking for yourself means questioning dominant ideas even when others insist on their being treated as unquestionable. It means deciding what one believes not by conforming to fashionable opinions, but by taking the trouble to learn and honestly consider the strongest arguments to be advanced on both or all sides of questions—including arguments for positions that others revile and want to stigmatize and against positions others seek to immunize from critical scrutiny.

The love of truth and the desire to attain it should motivate you to think for yourself. The central point of a college education is to seek truth and to learn the skills and acquire the virtues necessary to be a lifelong truth-seeker. Open-mindedness, critical thinking, and debate are essential to discovering the truth. Moreover, they are our best antidotes to bigotry.

Merriam-Webster's first definition of the word "bigot" is a person "who is obstinately or intolerantly devoted to his or her own opinions and prejudices." The only people who need fear open-minded inquiry and robust debate are the actual bigots, including those on campuses or in the broader society who seek to protect the hegemony of their opinions by claiming that to question those opinions is itself bigotry.

So, don't be tyrannized by public opinion. Don't get trapped in an echo chamber. Whether you in the end reject or embrace a view, make sure you decide where you stand by critically assessing the arguments for the competing positions. Think for yourself. Good luck to you in college!

Now, that might sound easy. But you will find—as you may have discovered already in high school—that thinking for yourself can be a challenge. It always demands self-discipline, and these days can require courage.

In today's climate, it's all-too-easy to allow your views and outlook to be shaped by dominant opinion on your campus or in the broader academic culture. The danger any student—or faculty member—faces today is falling into the vice of conformism, yielding to groupthink, the orthodoxy.

At many colleges and universities what John Stuart Mill called "the tyranny of public opinion" does more than merely discourage students from dissenting from prevailing views on moral, political, and other types of questions. It leads them to suppose that dominant views are so obviously correct that only a bigot or a crank could question them.

Since no one wants to be, or be thought of as, a bigot or a crank, the easy, lazy way to proceed is simply by falling into line with campus orthodoxies. Don't do it!

To be sure, our overly-politicized culture has a hard time viewing any "verbal cacophony" as a sign of strength and vibrancy. And perhaps nowhere is this truer than on many college campuses where political correctness is rampant, groupthink is common, and social media "mobs" arise in a flash to intimidate anyone who openly strays from the prevailing orthodoxy.

At the SAPIENT Being we're not intimidated—and our primary purpose is to seek the truth by enhancing viewpoint diversity, promoting intellectual humility, protecting freedom of speech and expression while developing sapience in the process—no matter what the cost on the intellectual battlefield, campus classroom, and marketplace of ideas. This is our ethos! Is it yours?

Best regards and sapiently yours,

Corey Lee Wilson

Corey Lee Wilson

S.A.P.I.E.N.T. Being

# 1 – The Demise of Civil Debate, Discourse & Freedom of Speech in the USA

Today, many people who claim to support freedom of expression regularly turn around to suppress the views of others. As noted by Allen C. Guelzo in his Autumn 2018 *City Journal* article titled "Free Speech and Its Present Crisis: In today's America, the right to express one's opinion is threatened by activists and authorities alike:"

In her Constitution Day lecture at Princeton University in September 2018, anthropology professor Carolyn Rouse called free speech a political illusion, a baseless ruse to enable people to "say whatever they want, in any context, with no social, economic, legal, or political repercussions."

There are, Rouse said, varieties of speech, and not all of them should be deemed deserving of the protections of freedom. What, then, serves to sort out the speech that does from the speech that does not deserve the shield of the First Amendment? Rouse's answer is culture: "culture is what helps us determine the appropriateness of speech by balancing our rights as enshrined in the Constitution with understandings of context."

And by culture, Rouse means her vision of culture. A climate-change skeptic, she explained, has no right to make "claims about climate change, as if all the science discovered over the last X-number of centuries were irrelevant." Climate change is not the only topic for which many are seeking to censor open debate.

In December 2016, Rouse organized a walkout of a lecture by sociologist Charles Murray, charging in a flyer that Murray represented the "normalization of racism and classism in academia." This is the same Charles Murray who was later shouted down and physically attacked by student activists at Middlebury College.

In an even more sensational confrontation, campus authorities at Evergreen State College refused to protect biology professor Bret Weinstein from physical threat by angry student activists after Weinstein, a self-avowed progressive in politics, questioned the wisdom of a day of racial "absence" that excluded white students from the Evergreen campus.

In a foreshadowing of Rouse's Constitution Day rationalization, the Evergreen activists insisted that Weinstein's questioning violated the norms of Evergreen's culture. "He has incited white supremacists and he has validated white supremacists and Nazis in our community and in the nation. And I don't think that should be protected by free speech," said one student in a Vice News interview on the protest.

## Majority of College Students Support Shouting Down Speakers They Don't Agree With

Furthermore, a majority of college students support shouting down speakers with whom they don't agree, according to a new survey from the Foundation for Individual Rights in Education (FIRE). Sixty-six percent of students said they supported speaker shout downs, an increase of 4 percentage points over last year, the study found. Meanwhile, 23 percent said they support going so far as to use violence to stop a speaker, an increase of 5 percentage points from last year.

As noted in the September 2021 National Review article "Support for Shouting Down Speakers on Campus Spikes after Political Chaos of 2020" by Brittany Berstein:

Wellesley College and Barnard College, both of which are elite women's colleges, had the highest number of students supporting the use of violence, at 45 percent and 43 percent, respectively. Sean Stevens, a senior research fellow in polling and analytics for FIRE, told National Review in a recent interview that the shift is likely reflective of the national political climate of the last year.

Stevens noted that the FIRE study results echoed findings from similar studies by the American National Election Studies and other outlets that have asked Americans about the acceptability of violence and have seen upticks in their data as well.

The results come as part of FIRE's 2021 college free speech rankings. FIRE, a non-partisan, non-profit group that focuses on protecting free speech rights on U.S. college campuses, worked alongside College Pulse and RealClearEducation to survey over 37,000 students at 159 of the country's largest and most prestigious campuses.

FIRE then compiled a list of free speech rankings assessing a school's free speech climate based on seven main components: openness to discussion of controversial topics, tolerance for liberal speakers, tolerance for conservative speakers, administrative support for free speech, comfort expressing ideas publicly, whether students support disruptive conduct during campus speeches, and FIRE's speech code rating.

He added that most students are "very tolerant of speakers they politically agree with" and are "intolerant of ones they politically disagree with, with almost equal potency." Students surveyed showed "much greater" intolerance for campus speakers with conservative positions.

## Universities Are Becoming Increasingly Hostile to Diverse Ideas

Sean Stevens pointed to a recent study published by the American Sociological Association that found that higher education liberalizes moral concerns for most students and promotes moral absolutism rather than relativism. While the study analyzed four waves of data from the National Study of Youth and Religion, the most recent of which was taken in 2013, Stevens hypothesized that the effects found then "are probably stronger today."

He said the results may support the argument that CRT and DEI efforts easily allow students to begin thinking that what they're learning is the truth, though it's simply one perspective, because the teachings portray a black-and-white view of the world without outside viewpoints.

Americans used to frequently quote Voltaire's declaration: "I disapprove of what you say, but I will defend to the death your right to say it." This is no longer the case at too many of our colleges and universities. We have entered the era of what has been called "the heckler's veto."

Nat Hentoff, a long-time eloquent advocate for free speech, said, "First Amendment law is clear that everyone has the right to picket a speaker, and go inside a hall and heckle him or her—but not to drown out the speaker, let alone rush the stage and stop the speech before it starts. That's called the 'heckler's veto.'"

A recent study by the Association of American Colleges and Universities of 24,000 college students and 9,000 faculty and staff members found that only eighteen per cent of the faculty and staff strongly agreed that it was "safe to hold unpopular positions on campus."

There is a difference between an opinion and an argument. An opinion is an expression of preference; it does not require any support (although it is stronger with support). An opinion is only the first part of an argument and to be complete, arguments should have three parts: an assertion, reasoning, and evidence (easily remembered with the mnemonic ARE).

We live in a climate ripe for noise: Media outlets and 24-hour news cycles mean that everyone with access to a computer has access to a megaphone to broadcast their views. Never before in human history has an opinion had the opportunity to reach so many so quickly regardless of its accuracy or appropriateness. This is a huge problem!

Educators are well positioned to provide a counterweight to this loudest-is-best approach. Speaking in a classroom or school environment is different from speaking in the outside world. Schools and classrooms strive to be safe places where students can exchange ideas, try out opinions and receive feedback on their ideas without fear or intimidation.

Children, of course, often come to school with opinions or prejudices they have learned in their homes or from the media. This means that it is also possible for schools to become places of intolerance and fear, especially for students who voice minority opinions.

Schools must work to be sites of social transformation where teachers and young people find ways to communicate effectively.

### The Heckler's Veto and Squelching Speech

The sad reality is that many college campuses today have become hotbeds of bullying and intimidation. Speech which challenges "politically correct" doctrine is often shouted down. Or relegated to tightly-restricted "free speech zones." Or deemed unworthy of respectful consideration.

The point here is that all of us (whether on the Left or the Right or in between) are capable of trampling on the freedoms of others. And the danger appears to be particularly great when one holds considerable power—as the white supremacists did in the Jim Crow South and as progressives do on today's college campuses.

Now, none of this would surprise our nation's founders (who had their own shortcomings, lest we forget). As James Madison famously said, "If men were angels, no government would be necessary." And part of the reason Madison penned the First Amendment is so that the public square could be filled with the vigorous exchange of (both popular and unpopular) ideas.

## Hate Speech and Political Correctness

Although 58% of students opined that "hate speech" should continue to receive First Amendment protection, 41% take the opposite view. Sixty percent of college women surveyed believe that efforts to promote and enforce an inclusive society are more important than fulfilling the First Amendment. Only 28% of men share this view, while 71% of college men support free speech over inclusion. A minority of women (41%) concur.

Women are not alone in this opinion. African-American college students, more than those of other races, are more inclined to believe that inclusion should trump free speech. More than six in ten African-American students believe that fostering inclusion and diversity should take priority over upholding the First Amendment. Forty-nine percent of Hispanic college students agree, whereas 42% of white students endorse this opinion. Fifty-eight percent of white students, and 50% of Hispanic students, place free speech as primary, with inclusion second.

There is also a religious dimension to the survey results: Eighty-one percent of Mormons, 71% of white evangelical Protestants, 64% of white mainline Protestants, and 62% of Catholic students believe that that upholding the First Amendment is more imperative than promoting inclusion. In contrast, 65% of Jewish students, 60% of students who profess Eastern faiths such Hinduism or Buddhism, and 54% of religiously unaffiliated students believe that inclusion is more critical.

### Most Students Appear to Agree With the Supreme Court's Rulings

Per the May 2019 "New Report: Most College Students Agree that Campus Free Speech is Waning" article by Tom Lindsay of *Forbes*:

When it comes to offensive or "hate speech," most students appear to agree with the Supreme Court's rulings declaring such speech to be protected by the First Amendment. The survey defined hate speech as "attacks (on) people based on their race, religion, gender identity or sexual orientation." Nearly 60% of surveyed college students say that such speech should be protected, whereas 41% disagree.

However, opinions vary on this according to gender: 53% of college women opine that offensive speech should not be protected free speech, whereas 74% of college men answered that such speech should be protected by the First Amendment.

There is also a racial gap on the question: 62% of white collegians believe that offensive speech should be protected by the First Amendment, whereas 48% of black students concur. Fifty-one percent of black students deny that hate speech should be protected. Fifty-two percent of Hispanic students affirm First-Amendment protection of hate speech, while 47% do not.

There is also a significant difference in opinion based on sexual orientation. Sixty-four percent of straight college students agree that hate speech should be protected, compared to 35% of gay and lesbian students.

Fifty-three percent of white students believe that it is never acceptable to attempt to bar speakers on campus from expressing their views while 41% of Hispanic, 38% of black, and 37% of Asian Pacific Islander students concur.

Sixty-five percent of white male students believe shouting down speakers (the "heckler's veto") is never acceptable; 45% of white female students agree.

Universities have not only failed to stand up to those who limit debate, they have played a part in encouraging them. The modish commitment to so-called diversity replaces the ideal of guaranteed equal treatment of individuals with guaranteed group preferences in hiring and curricular offerings.

## Something Very Strange is at Work on University Campuses

Most analyses of this new survey data pay insufficient attention to the one conclusion on which an overwhelming majority of college students agree: Sixty-eight percent of collegians "largely agree" that the campus climate today prevents some students from being able truly to speak their minds for fear of offending someone. Only 31% disagree.

Samantha Harris, director of policy research at the Foundation for Individual Rights in Education (FIRE), said censorship used to come primarily from the top down but now is coming from students. "Students increasingly seem to be arriving on campus believing that there is a generalized right not to be offended beyond the actual right to be free from harassment and threats, this amorphous right to emotional safety. It's a troubling trend," she said.

Most professors and campus administrators want an open environment where all members of the academic community can express their ideas honestly. But, in recent years reports that students and faculty have been self-censoring their views in the classroom and on campus in general, have increased and are concerning.

If this is going on in your classroom, or at your university, then it is vital to know: WHICH students are feeling intimidated, about WHICH topics, and WHY? Are students primarily afraid of the professors, or of other students? Is it happening in all departments, or only in a few? Heterodox Academy's Campus Expression Survey is an easy to administer tool for professors and administrators that provides a diagnosis, or X-ray, of what is going on in your classroom or on your campus.

## Civic Illiteracy in America is Partly to Blame

Through restoring genuine civic education, by which all students, regardless of political persuasion, would come to see that their rights, no less than others,' depend ineluctability on a content- or viewpoint-neutral First Amendment--we can reverse this illiberalism on campus and elsewhere.

"The electorate is largely ignorant, and there is an overall deficit of civic learning," said Charles Quigley, the executive director of the Center for Civic Education, a nonprofit group that advocates for civics learning. The political climate at the state, local and national levels, and the steady drumbeat of negative news, "has people wondering, 'How the hell could this have happened?' "

That our high school and college students are not receiving such an education is demonstrated irrefutably by recent polling drawn from questions on the USCIS Citizenship Test. This test is passed by 92% of immigrants applying for citizenship. Passage requires getting only six out of ten multiple-choice questions correct. However, only 36% of native-born Americans can get even six out of ten questions right.

Worse, and directly relevant to the free-speech poll under examination, there is a wide age gap in the civic knowledge of native-born Americans. Seventy-four percent of senior citizens can pass the Citizenship Test. But only 20% of native-born Americans under 45 can even get six out of ten questions correct. We expect immigrants in America to pass the USCIS test in order to become citizens. Yet four out of five native-born Americans under 45 cannot fulfill this minimal condition.

Think about that for a moment: Eighty percent of under-45 native-born Americans are strangers in their own country, bereft of needed knowledge regarding what their rights and duties are as citizens of a self-governing polity. They have been given no instruction in why all human beings are equal, in why we are born with the inalienable rights to life, liberty, and the pursuit of happiness, and in why and how we established a limited government.

A *Newsweek* survey from 2011 found that 70 percent of Americans didn't even know that the Constitution is the supreme law of the land. Sadly, this is not the only piece of evidence indicating that Americans are not as familiar with the Constitution and the Supreme Court as one might expect—a 2016 survey by the Annenberg Public Policy Center of the University of Pennsylvania found that only 26 percent of respondents could name all three branches of government, and only 33 percent knew that, in the case of a 4-4 Supreme Court tie, the decision of the lower court stands.

Recent studies demonstrate that two-thirds of Americans can't name all three branches of the government, yet three of four people can name all three stooges. Only 29 percent of eligible voters participated in the 2016 primary election. (And) less than half of the public can name a single Supreme Court Justice; yet two-thirds of Americans know at least one of the American Idol judges.

**Why Is American Public's Civic Literacy Is So Poor?**

The reality and importance of our civic literacy crisis is no longer subject to partisan debate. In 1983, the Reagan Administration published *A Nation at Risk*, which detailed the decline of American public education. The report was criticized for being "conservative." In 1987, when Allan Bloom's *Closing of the American Mind* argued that "higher education has failed democracy and impoverished the souls of today's students," it too was greeted by some as a "conservative" critique.

No more. Concern over Americans' civic illiteracy has gone bipartisan: The title of a CNN op-ed by Chris Cillizza screams its conclusion: "Americans know literally nothing about the Constitution." Cillizza draws evidence for his contention from the most recent poll from the University of Pennsylvania Annenberg Public Policy Center, the results of which constitute, in Cillizza's words, a "bouillabaisse of ignorance."

Among other things, the Annenberg Center survey found that 37% of those polled could not name even one right protected by the First Amendment. Worse, 33 percent of Americans surveyed were unable to name *even one* branch of government.

These dismal findings prompt another, broader question: why is it that the American public's civic literacy is so poor? The basic organization of American government is not overly complex, and the U.S. Constitution is a relatively short document. Americans should therefore have a much greater level of familiarity with the way their government operates. Schools, at both the K-12 and collegiate level, must make civic education a priority and should specifically ensure that students understand the Constitution and the Supreme Court.

And if that is the case, one possible remedy is this: Require all high-school as well as college students to spend a semester diving into our country's fundamental documents, which still define us today: the Declaration of Independence, U.S. Constitution, and the Bill of Rights.

We can't protect what we don't understand. So long as civic education in this country continues to decline, expect more assaults on our core principles of individual liberty and limited government. You cannot practice what you don't understand and if you don't have a basic civics knowledge of the United States then you'll never be able to fully appreciate freedom of speech and expression and why it's made America special.

**The Student Experience**

In addition to this analysis of state policy, the Brookings Institution in 2018 explored an important aspect of civics education: the student experience. Using data from the nationally representative 2010 National Assessment of Educational Progress (NAEP) student survey on civics education, the report looks at the types of activities students report engaging in through their civics coursework.

Similar to the policy inventory, students' self-reported experiences reflect an emphasis on in-class, discussion-based civics education. The below figure illustrates that discussion of current events occurs regularly, whereas opportunities for community engagement and participation in simulations of democratic procedures occur considerably less frequently.

Many of the failures in civic education seem to originate from a disagreement regarding what a civics education should include. Dr. Michael Poliakoff, president of the American Council of Trustees and Alumni (ACTA), believes that many schools have shifted away from traditional civics education. "I think there's been a very misguided trend towards ignoring the actual knowledge that a person needs to understand our institutions."

"What's happened is there's been a very good, a very wholesome, focus on civic obligations on community service; things that are really quite important for our duty to our communities, but are very different from the things that a school quintessentially is responsible for doing, which is exposing students to the knowledge and skills that they need."

Rebecca Burgess, who manages the American Enterprise Institute (AEI) Program on American Citizenship, provided another explanation for why there is little consensus surrounding the components of a thorough civics education in an interview with the HPR: "For a very long time, going back to say the 60s, the whole idea of a civics education kind of got subsumed within this idea of social studies, and that was just this big umbrella that covers sometimes everything from history to economics to geography to actual civics … And when you have an area that is so large, it's hard to know exactly what it is that you're going to do within that."

While it would be misleading to say that poor civics education is the predominant cause of America's current political division, it certainly has played a role. Burgess traced some of our political tensions to poor civic knowledge: "If a third of adult Americans don't even know what the three branches of government are, that there are three branches of government, that we have a separation of powers, then…our ideas of what government ought to be doing will be different from people who think that there are three branches of government."

The repercussions of failing to convey basic civic knowledge to students are not always immediately understood, but they are rather dire. To Poliakoff, the consequences of civic illiteracy are severe. "When our schools and our colleges and universities fail to set the kind of requirements that ensure that the students who leave their halls will be ready for engaged citizenship, they're really letting the nation down." In other words, we all suffer when civic education suffers.

### A Wake-up Call for Civic Literacy

Thomas Jefferson wrote that "wherever the people are well informed they can be trusted with their own government," implying that our democratic system rests on the assumption that citizens are civically literate. He also warned us that "no nation" can expect to be "both ignorant *and* free." If we are to believe Jefferson, surveys of Americans' civic knowledge indicate that "the people" currently cannot be trusted to govern.

While civic literacy as a whole is inadequate, it seems that Americans' knowledge of the Supreme Court and the Constitution is especially poor. A recent survey commissioned by C-SPAN found that 90 percent of likely voters agreed with the statement, "decisions made by the

U.S. Supreme Court have an impact on my everyday life as a citizen," yet 57 percent couldn't name a single justice on the court.

All available evidence suggests that the American education system fails to convey basic civic knowledge to students. Despite civics being a common requirement in schools, only 24 percent of 12th grade students scored "proficient" on the 2010 National Assessment of Educational Progress civics test. Even among college graduates, civic literacy is startlingly poor. A 2016 report by the ACTA found that almost a tenth of college graduates thought Judith Sheindlin—more commonly known as Judge Judy—was a member of the Supreme Court.

**What Happened to Civics Education?**

To understand why civic literacy is so poor, it is necessary to consider the various pressures that have caused civics education to fall by the wayside. In a 2015 report on the state of professional development for civics teachers. Burgess argues that the focus on STEM—science, technology, engineering, and math—has limited federal and state funding for civics education.

The emphasis on standardized test scores in subjects other than civics has also taken a toll on students' knowledge. Burgess explains that while "civics teachers themselves are immensely dedicated to the field … they're just not given much time by their own districts. And so, they might be the one … class of teachers … who would like more testing, because that seems to be the only way where you can get attention."

Despite the numerous problems that come with excessive testing, Burgess argues that a standardized civics test would be beneficial. Poliakoff agreed, suggesting that a good "baseline" would be if "all the students that leave high school can at least pass the same test that a new citizen would have to pass."

It is worth noting that the deterioration of civics education is not limited to K-12 schools; it has also been seen at the collegiate level. The 2016 ACTA report found that of more than 1,100 liberal arts colleges and universities surveyed, only eighteen  percent required students to take a course in American history or government. Considering this statistic, it is unsurprising that many college students graduate civically illiterate.

"What's happened in higher education is a retreat from addressing the core question of any institution," Poliakoff explained, "which is what does it mean to be a graduate of our institution, what does it mean to have a college or university degree? What's happened is that departments have splintered and fragmented into their own little silos."

**How College History Departments Leave the United States out of the Major**

The American Council of Trustees and Alumni (ACTA) released the second edition of *No U.S. History? How College History Departments Leave the United States out of the Major*. Using the 2020–21 U.S. News and World Report's rankings, we identified the top 25 liberal arts colleges, top 25 national universities, and top 25 public universities. Examining university catalogs going back nearly 70 years, we asked whether the baccalaureate major, as well as the core curriculum, required all students to complete a course in U.S. history in 1952, 1976, 2000, and 2020.

The troubling results reveal the extent of America's crisis in civic education. Only 18% of colleges and universities nationwide require the study of U.S. history and government in their general educational programs. National surveys have documented the consequences of failing to graduate students who understand their nation's history and institutions of government. In a multiple-choice question, for example, more than 50% of respondents failed to identify the correct term lengths for Members of Congress; 18% of American adults selected New York congresswoman Alexandria Ocasio-Cortez, as the architect of President Franklin Roosevelt's New Deal.

Our coarsening public discourse is traceable to the erosion of a common sense of purpose in the citizenry which stems, in large part, from ignorance. For much of our nation's past, America's institutions took seriously the profound responsibility to educate students about their country's history and cultivate civic virtues. When American history vanishes from the curriculum, so does a shared basis for informed civil debate.

Top universities have neglected to teach America's history and, worse, they have politicized it. As such, institutions essential to building civic literacy have become engines of division. Take the controversy surrounding the *New York Times'* 1619 Project, which aims to "reframe" America's Founding instead of aspiring to historical objectivity. Schools should work to teach a common history rooted in historical fact, not opinion.

**Better Ways to Teach Civics**

While the level of civic ignorance may be frightening, there are numerous efforts underway to reinvigorate American civics education. A number of programs assist civics teachers by offering free teaching materials. For example, the Civics Renewal Network (CRN), run by the Annenberg Public Policy Center, is a group of nonprofit organizations that offer free, online civics education teaching resources.

The CRN seeks to "bring together the many, many civics education organizations that are out there, to collaborate, to start talking to each other … to make more efficient use of our resources," Ellen Iwamoto, the director of research support services at the Annenberg Center, told the HPR. The goal is to "help teachers by creating a website where they go and find great resources that they may not have known about."

One of the most promising programs is iCivics, which was founded by former Supreme Court Justice Sandra Day O'Connor in 2009 with the mission to improve civic education throughout the country. iCivics hosts free games and lessons plans that can be used by teachers and students to "make the subject come alive."

In an interview with the HPR, iCivics Executive Director Louise Dubé said that the platform currently has over five million student users, over halfway to its goal of reaching ten million citizens. "The original idea was to reinvent, or reimagine, civics, by putting kids at the center of the action," Dubé said. "So, in iCivics games you play as the president of the United States. We think that's the only way to make it relevant to you."

By making knowledge about our constitutional system more accessible to the average student, this kind of innovation has the potential to drastically change the way civics is taught and to increase the number of Americans who are civically literate.

As proof of iCivics' teaching model, Dubé points to Florida, which in 2010 passed the Sandra Day O'Connor Education Act to require a semester of civics education in seventh grade. According to Dubé, at least 80 percent of these seventh grade teachers are using iCivics, and last year their students had a remarkable 68 percent proficiency. When compared to the 23 percent of eighth graders who were proficient on the 2014 NAEP civics test, it is clear that iCivics is indeed making a significant difference.

**Hope for the Future?**

While programs like CRN and iCivics offer free, high quality resources to teachers and students, their success depends on whether people actually access those resources. Every school must make civics education a priority, rather than simply a minor graduation requirement. In today's highly politicized environment, civics may be confused with politics, but they are not at all the same.

According to Burgess, "a large part of the civics problem, is that as soon you start to talk about what is a good citizen, or what does citizenship mean, you start to rub up against values." As a result, teachers "either retreat from inviting more controversy in the classroom, or just try and talk about it in the vaguest, largest way possible." Requiring students to learn basic information about our government is not a partisan endeavor; it simply ensures that our democracy can function.

Despite the promising efforts being made to improve civic education, there is much more work to do. As Burgess puts it, "Everyone nods and says, 'oh my goodness, (civic illiteracy) is an immensely … troubling problem' and then they move on, immediately. Part of that is just because it's not an immensely sexy issue; it's a long-term project."

Admittedly, there is no easy solution to the civic illiteracy our country faces, but it is a problem worth solving. The costs of an uninformed public are simply too great for us not to address the current deficits in civic knowledge.

## A Look at Civics Education in the United States

The policy solution that has garnered the most momentum to improve civics in recent years is a standard that requires high school students to pass the U.S. citizenship exam before graduation.

According to our analysis, seventeen states have taken this path. Yet, critics of a mandatory civics exam argue that the citizenship test does nothing to measure comprehension of the material and creates an additional barrier to high school graduation.

Other states have adopted civics as a requirement for high school graduation, provided teachers with detailed civics curricula, provided community service as a part of a graduation requirement, and increased the availability of Advanced Placement (AP) United States Government and Politics classes.

When civics education is taught effectively, it can equip students with the knowledge, skills, and dispositions necessary to become informed and engaged citizens. Educators must also remember that civics is not synonymous with history. While increasing history courses and community service requirements are potential steps to augment students' background knowledge and skill sets, civics is a narrow and instrumental instruction that provides students with the agency to apply these skills.

A recent report on civics education in high schools across the country, *The State of Civics Education,* from which this section is drawn, finds a wide variation in state requirements and levels of youth engagement. While this research highlights that no state currently provides sufficient and comprehensive civics education, there is reason to be optimistic that high-quality civics education can impact civic behavior.

As noted by Dr. April Kelly-Woessner, Professor of Political Science and Chair of the Department of Politics, Philosophy and Legal Studies at Elizabethtown College, "What we find is that confidence in civic knowledge correlates pretty strongly and is a good predictor of political tolerance.

So, if you think you know a lot relative to other people, if you think you can hold your own in a political conversation, you're more tolerant than people who are insecure about their civic knowledge. The perception of these college students protestors is that they're ideological radicals who have these strong opinions, and yet what the data shows is wanting to shut down other voices reflects an insecurity to defend your own. The decline in civic knowledge is a big factor in political intolerance."

# 2 – The Rise of Academia, Mainstream & Social Media Illiberalism & Intolerance

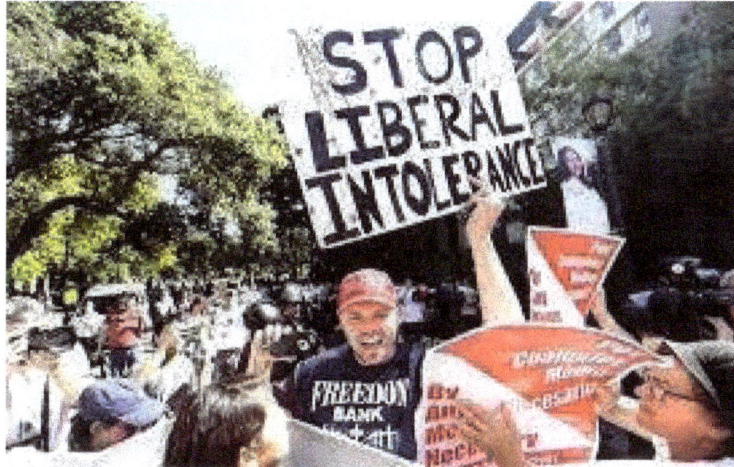

*Credit: Reuters.*

Our present ideological circumstances and point of views should not prevent us from engaging with a variety of conservative, religious, and libertarian modes of thinking, just as they shouldn't prevent us from engaging with modes of thinking organized under the banner of progressivism or critical theory.

Such engagement might actually lead to greater understanding among those who disagree politically, and it might also allow for more robust critical and creative thinking about our histories, our present and the possibilities for the future.

K12 schools, community colleges and 4-year universities—and their principals, superintendents, presidents, boards of trustees, faculties, parents, and alumni—must maximize support for free expression, intellectual pluralism, and most of all viewpoint diversity.

Instead, they more frequently practiced "illiberalism" which is a 21st century term used to describe an attitude that is close-minded, intolerant, and bigoted.

A 2016 Gallup survey found that more than one in four college students felt colleges should be able to restrict students from "expressing political views that are upsetting or offensive to certain groups," while nearly half were open to restricting press access to public events.

Furthermore, intellectual humility is the key to questioning our beliefs, lowering our defense mechanisms, and finding the truth—and canceling out illiberalism. Consider watching the short an imaginative "The Joy of Being Wrong" video by the John Templeton Foundation found in the Appendix where this principle is nicely summarized.

## Consider These Disturbing Trends

Given the current undergraduate tendency toward intellectual orthodoxy, one wonders: Would the advances of the feminist movement even have happened, had the campus conformists of a half-century ago had their way?

- A recent study found that 68 percent of college students "largely agree" the campus climate today prevents some of them from speaking their minds for fear of offending someone.

- In a 2016 Gallup survey, one in four college students felt their schools should be able to restrict students from "expressing political views that are upsetting or offensive to certain groups."

- Shockingly, the Foundation for Individual Rights in Education (FIRE, for short) rated the level of freedom of speech permitted at 466 major universities in America. They found that 19 percent received a "red light' rating, 68 percent a "yellow light" rating, and only 13 percent received a "green light" rating.

Regarding the lack of viewpoint diversity needed to burst the prevailing ideological bubbles on campus, consider these alarming statistics:

- More than 50 percent of students surveyed reported that they do not think their college frequently encourages students to consider a wide variety of viewpoints and perspectives.

- UCLA's Higher Education Institute shows that the faculty has moved considerably leftward since the late 1980s, especially in the Arts and Humanities. In New England alone, liberal professors outnumber conservative ones by an astonishing ratio of 28:1.

- A large student and faculty sampling by the American Association of Colleges and Universities reported only 18 percent of the faculty and staff strongly agreed that it was "safe to hold unpopular positions on campus."

And the third major concern is a lack of intellectual humility from students, administrators, and faculty. Consider these examples:

- The first is the rise of Intolerance: Since 2000, the FIRE has recorded 379 instances of disinvitations, with nearly a quarter of those occurring between 2016 to 2018. In those two years, 82 percent of these disinvitations have been because of the Left's doing.

- The second is the lack of Constructive Disagreement: The concept centers around creating a dynamic where key stakeholders in the faculty and student body are compelled to disagree. The word "constructive" alludes to the need to raise issues, debate, and resolve them reasonably. In the academy, this rarely happens--but it does so in the corporate world—successfully.

- And the third concerns the prevalence of Confirmation Bias: The 2008 paper, "Estimating the reproducibility of psychological science" describes the replication failure rate being as high as one-half to two-thirds of 100 sampled experiments published in 2008 in three high-ranking psychology journals.

## The New Campus Illiberalism Is More Than Intolerance

The pursuit of knowledge and the maintenance of a free and democratic society require the cultivation and practice of the virtues of intellectual humility, openness of mind, and, above all, love of truth. These virtues will manifest themselves and be strengthened by one's willingness to listen attentively and respectfully to intelligent people who challenge one's beliefs and who represent causes one disagrees with and points of view one does not share.

That's why all of us should seek respectfully to engage with people who challenge our views. And we should oppose efforts to silence those with whom we disagree—especially on college and university campuses. As John Stuart Mill taught, a recognition of the possibility that we may be in error is a good reason to listen to and honestly consider—and not merely to tolerate grudgingly—points of view that we do not share, and even perspectives that we find shocking or scandalous.

None of us is infallible. Whether you are a person of the left, the right, or the center, there are reasonable people of goodwill who do not share your fundamental convictions. This does not mean that all opinions are equally valid or that all speakers are equally worth listening to. It certainly does not mean that there is no truth to be discovered. Nor does it mean that you are necessarily wrong. But they are not necessarily wrong either.

"The person you are now only exists because the person you were was willing to grow into something new." - John Templeton.

All of us should be willing—even eager—to engage with anyone who is prepared to do business in the currency of truth-seeking discourse by offering reasons, marshaling evidence, and making arguments. The more important the subject under discussion, the more willing we should be to listen and engage—especially if the person with whom we are in conversation will challenge our deeply held—even our most cherished and identity-forming—beliefs.

## Is There "Viewpoint" Diversity On Your Campus?

K12 schools, colleges, and universities—and their principals, superintendents, presidents, boards of trustees, faculties, parents, and alumni—must maximize support for free expression, intellectual pluralism, and most of all viewpoint diversity.

A 2016 Gallup survey found that more than one in four college students felt colleges should be able to restrict students from "expressing political views that are upsetting or offensive to certain groups," while nearly half were open to restricting press access to public events.

Given the current undergraduate tendency toward intellectual orthodoxy, one wonders: Would the advances of the feminist movement even have happened, had the campus conformists of a half-century ago had their way?

Respect for freedom of speech and diversity of thought are essential for achieving civil and thoughtful discourse, but also for enabling societal progress itself. Progress relies on early agitators, who are willing to speak out and press forward, no matter the backlash they engender. Many ideas once considered heretical have become accepted wisdom, thanks to early dissenters challenging the tide.

Real change relied on the courage of young women during the 1960s and 1970s, who stood up for equal opportunity in higher education and the workforce. They faced vocal opposition from many college alumni, professors, and fellow students. Nevertheless, these women persisted, no matter how "problematic" their efforts may have been considered. Their determined activism paved the way for the generations to come.

Today's campus conformists are in danger of squandering this legacy. How can students learn, think, and grow without exposure to unexpected, challenging ideas? How can any campus fulfill its mission of preparing tough-minded and capable students if it instills in them a desire to squelch opposing views rather than a willingness to consider and confront them?

Perhaps some unwise ideas will be presented with which students will vociferously disagree, but this debate will strengthen campus discourse and help students become independent thinkers. In the end, students—and society—can only benefit from embracing intellectual humility and the free marketplace of ideas.

## The 'Heckler's Veto' on America's University and High School Campuses

There is a George Orwell statue at the headquarters of the BBC and the Orwell quote on the wall reads: "If liberty means anything at all, it means the right to tell people what they do not want to hear."

The *Economist* reports, "People as different as Condoleezza Rice, a former secretary of state, and Bill Maher, a satirist, have been dissuaded from giving speeches on campuses, sometimes on grounds of safety … Fifty years ago, student radicals agitated for academic freedom and the right to engage in political activities on campus. Now some of their successors are campaigning for censorship and increased policing by universities of student activities. The supporters of these ideas on campus are usually described as radicals. They are, in fact, the opposite."

Our society, it seems, has failed to transmit our values, in particular free speech, to the next generation. According to a new survey by the Pew Research Center, 40 per cent of Millennials support government censorship of speech offensive to minority groups. The poll found that Millennials were the most likely of any age group to agree that government should have the authority to stop people from saying things that offend minorities.

There can be little doubt that our society is not doing a particularly good job in transmitting our history and values to the next generation. A recent survey of 1,100 colleges and universities found that only eighteen  percent require American history or government, where the foundations of our society, such as the First Amendment, can be explained.

The survey, by the American Council of Trustees and Alumni (ACTA), found that at the universities where free speech is now under attack, such as the University Missouri, Amherst, and Yale, very little is being done to transmit our history and values.

## Those in Charge Tend to Recoil From the Defense of Free Speech

With few defenders in today's academic world, the future of academic freedom looks increasingly bleak. Hopefully, alumni will rally to restore the universities they once knew, a genuine marketplace of ideas where "political correctness," "safe zones" and "microaggression," were terms yet to be coined. But if they and others in positions of influence prove unwilling or unable to address this growing problem, "academic freedom" will begin to reflect with what the SAPIENT Being has pointed out.

The seriousness of freedom of speech suppression was recently investigated in 2017 by the House of Representatives Joint Hearing Before the Subcommittee on Healthcare, Benefits and Administrative Rules and the Subcommittee on Intergovernmental Affairs of the Committee on Oversight and Government Reform titled *Challenges to Freedom of Speech on College Campuses*.

The issues with trigger warnings, safe spaces, safe zones, shout-downs, microaggressions, bias response teams, and riots on campuses were discussed and debated regarding their impact of campus freedom of speech suppression.

## Herbert Marcuse Wrote That Conservative Ideas Should be Repressed

Indeed, in 1968, Critical Theorist Herbert Marcuse wrote that society should only be tolerant of the ideas from oppressed groups, and that conservative ideas should be repressed. Marcuse wrote:

It should be evident by now that the exercise of civil rights by those who don't have them presupposes the withdrawal of civil rights from those who prevent their exercise, and that liberation of the Damned of the Earth presupposes suppression not only of their old but also of their new masters….Withdrawal of tolerance from regressive movements before they can become active; intolerance even toward thought, opinion, and word, and finally, intolerance in the opposite direction, that is, toward the self-styled conservatives, to the political Right—these anti-democratic notions respond to the actual development of the democratic society which has destroyed the basis for universal tolerance.

CRT writers applied this idea to their area of study. Richard Delgado wrote in 1994, "We are raising the possibility that the correct argument may sometimes be: the First Amendment condemns [the suppression of speech, even hate speech], therefore the First Amendment (or the way we understand it) is wrong."

Still more pointedly, Delgado and Jean Stefancic write in Critical Race Theory: An Introduction, "If one is an idealist, campus speech codes, tort remedies for racist speech, diversity seminars, and increasing the representation of black, brown, and Asian actors on television shows will be high on one's list of priorities."

Again, remember CRT founder Derrick Bell's comment cited earlier in this Backgrounder that CRT scholarship should incite rebellion and "most critical race theorists are committed to a program of scholarly resistance, and most hope scholarly resistance will lay the groundwork for wide-scale resistance."

In addition to CRT's central tenets of disrupting systems of power and destabilizing classical liberal civil and political structures, CRT and Critical Theory object to free speech as a cornerstone of society. The themes and logical responses from CRT proponents are echoed by students who shout down professors, guest speakers, and even other students at colleges across the country.

## Support for Controversial Speakers

Would you support or oppose your school ALLOWING a speaker on campus who promotes the following idea:

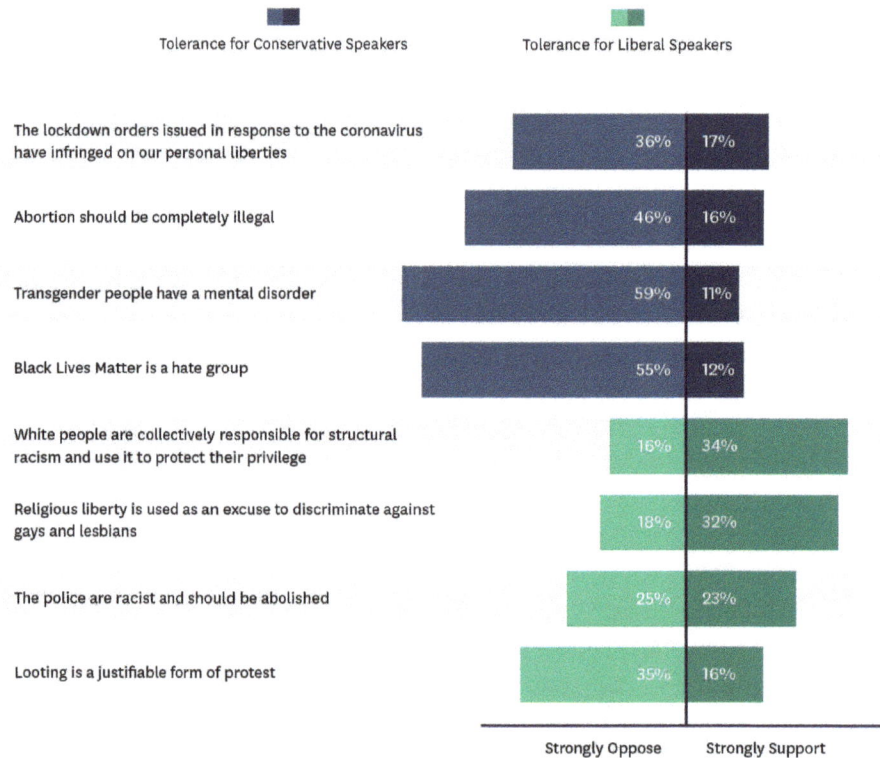

■ Tolerance for Conservative Speakers      ■ Tolerance for Liberal Speakers

| Idea | Oppose | Support |
|------|--------|---------|
| The lockdown orders issued in response to the coronavirus have infringed on our personal liberties | 36% | 17% |
| Abortion should be completely illegal | 46% | 16% |
| Transgender people have a mental disorder | 59% | 11% |
| Black Lives Matter is a hate group | 55% | 12% |
| White people are collectively responsible for structural racism and use it to protect their privilege | 16% | 34% |
| Religious liberty is used as an excuse to discriminate against gays and lesbians | 18% | 32% |
| The police are racist and should be abolished | 25% | 23% |
| Looting is a justifiable form of protest | 35% | 16% |

Strongly Oppose        Strongly Support

*Credit: 2021 College Free Speech Rankings.*

## Spotlight on Speech Codes 2022: Major Findings

From the Spotlight on Speech Codes F.I.R.E. 2022 report from the Foundation for Individual Rights in Education (FIRE):

The percentage of colleges and universities earning an overall "red light" rating in FIRE's Spotlight database has gone down for the fourteenth year in a row—this year to 19%. This is approximately a three percentage point drop from last year, and is more than 50 percentage points lower than the percentage of red light institutions in FIRE's 2009 report.

- 68% of institutions now earn an overall "yellow light" rating. Though less restrictive than red light policies, yellow light policies still restrict expression that is protected under First Amendment standards and invite administrative abuse.

- 13 %, or a total of 58 colleges and universities now earn an overall "green light" rating, up from 56 schools as of last year's report. Policies earn a green light rating when they do not seriously threaten protected expression. Significantly, there are now more public schools earning a green light rating (54) than there are earning a red light rating (45).

- 5.2% of institutions surveyed maintain "free speech zone" policies, which limit student demonstrations and other expressive activities to small and/or out-of-the-way areas on campus. A 2013 FIRE survey of these institutions found roughly triple that percentage.

- Eighty-two university administrations or faculty bodies have now adopted policy statements in support of free speech modeled after the "Report of the Committee on Freedom of Expression" at the University of Chicago (the "Chicago Statement"), released in January 2015.

**Executive Summary**

Most college students in the United States should be able to expect that freedom of expression will be upheld on their campuses. After all, public institutions are legally bound by the First Amendment, and the vast majority of private colleges and universities promise their students commensurate free speech rights.

Nevertheless, far too many colleges across the country fail to live up to their free speech obligations in policy and in practice. Often, this occurs through the implementation of speech codes: university policies that restrict expression protected by the First Amendment.

For our 2022 report, FIRE surveyed the written policies of 481 colleges and universities, evaluating their compliance with First Amendment standards. Overall, 18.5% of surveyed colleges maintained at least one severely restrictive policy that earned FIRE's worst, "red light" rating, meaning that the policy both clearly and substantially restricts protected speech. This is the fourteenth year in a row that the percentage of schools earning a red light rating has gone down; last year, 21.3% of schools earned a red light rating.

The majority of institutions surveyed (68%) earned an overall "yellow light" rating, meaning they maintained at least one yellow light policy. Yellow light policies are either clear restrictions on a narrower range of expression or policies that, by virtue of vague wording, could too easily be applied to restrict protected expression. While the steady decline in red light institutions is cause for optimism, FIRE will continue to work with colleges and universities to ensure that yellow light institutions improve to earn our highest, "green light" rating.

A green light rating indicates that none of a university's written policies seriously imperil protected expression. A total of 58 colleges and universities (12.1% of those surveyed) earned an overall green light rating, up from 56 schools as of last year's report.

In further good news, a growing number colleges and universities are adopting policy statements in support of free speech modeled after the "Report of the Committee on Freedom of Expression" at the University of Chicago (the "Chicago Statement"). As of this writing, 82 universities, university systems, or faculty bodies have endorsed a version of the "Chicago Statement," with seven adoptions since last year's report.

Though these improvements in policy are heartening, free speech on campus remains under threat. Demands for censorship of student and faculty speech—whether originating on or off campus—are common, and universities continue to investigate and punish students and faculty over protected expression.

This year, schools across the country continued to grapple with challenges presented by the COVID-19 pandemic. During the spring semester, and before COVID-19 vaccines became widely available, many classes continued to be conducted remotely, making the concerns presented by policies that govern online speech that much greater.

It is imperative that those who care about free speech on campus stay vigilant. The decrease in restrictive speech codes and the proliferation of free speech policy statements are the result of the tireless work of free speech advocates at FIRE and elsewhere. But we must ensure that new national and global challenges do not result in such progress being lost. We must continue to work to ensure that students have the opportunity to pursue their education and that faculty are able to teach with the greatest possible foundation for free expression in place.

**Methodology**

For this report, FIRE surveyed publicly available policies at 374 four-year public institutions and 107 of the nation's most prestigious private institutions. Our research focuses in particular on public universities because, as explained in detail below, public universities are legally bound to protect students' right to free speech and can be successfully sued in court when they do not.

FIRE rates colleges and universities as "red light," "yellow light," or "green light" institutions based on how much, if any, protected expression their written policies governing student conduct restrict. The speech code ratings do not take into account a university's "as-applied" violations of student speech rights or other cases of censorship, student- or faculty-led calls for punishment of protected speech, and related incidents and controversies. Monitoring and rating such incidents consistently across 481 institutions with accuracy is not feasible and is beyond the scope of this report.

The speech code ratings are defined as follows:

**Red Light:** A red light institution maintains at least one policy that both clearly and substantially restricts freedom of speech, or bars public access to its speech-related policies by requiring a university login and password for access.

A "clear" restriction unambiguously infringes on protected expression. In other words, the threat to free speech at a red light institution is obvious on the face of the policy and does not depend on how the policy is applied. A "substantial" restriction on free speech is one that is broadly applicable to campus expression. For example, a ban on "offensive speech" would be a clear violation (in that it is unambiguous) as well as a substantial violation (in that it covers a great deal of what is protected under First Amendment standards). Such a policy would earn a university a red light.

When a university restricts access to its speech-related policies by requiring a login and password, it denies prospective students and their parents the ability to weigh this crucial information prior to matriculation. At FIRE, we consider this denial to be so deceptive and serious that it alone warrants an overall red light rating.

**Yellow Light:** A yellow light institution maintains policies that could be interpreted to suppress protected speech or policies that, while clearly restricting freedom of speech, restrict relatively narrow categories of speech.

For example, a policy banning "verbal abuse" has broad applicability and poses a substantial threat to free speech, but is not a clear violation because "abuse" might refer to unprotected speech and conduct, such as threats of violence or unlawful harassment. Similarly, while a policy banning "profanity on residence hall door whiteboards" clearly restricts speech, it is relatively limited in scope. Yellow light policies are typically unconstitutional when maintained by public universities, and a rating of yellow light rather than red light in no way means that FIRE condones a university's restrictions on speech. Rather, it means that in FIRE's judgment, those restrictions do not clearly and substantially restrict speech in the manner necessary to warrant a red light rating.

**Green Light:** If FIRE finds that a university's policies do not seriously threaten campus expression, that college or university receives a green light rating. A green light rating does not necessarily indicate that a school actively supports free expression in practice; it simply means that the school's written policies do not pose a serious threat to free speech.

Warning: FIRE believes that free speech is not only a moral imperative, but an essential element of a college education. However, private universities, as private associations, possess their own right to free association, which allows them to prioritize other values above the right to free speech if they wish to do so. Therefore, when a private university clearly and consistently states that it holds a certain set of values above a commitment to freedom of speech, FIRE gives it a Warning rating in order to warn prospective students and faculty members of this fact. Seven schools surveyed for this report meet these criteria

Overall ratings: To determine overall ratings, FIRE does not produce an "average" of an institution's policy ratings; a school with five yellow light policies and one red light policy earns an overall red light rating, just as a school with one yellow light policy and five red light policies earns an overall red light rating.

### Findings

Of the 481 schools reviewed by FIRE, 89, or 18.5%, received a red light rating. 327 schools received a yellow light rating (68%), and 58 received a green light rating (12.1%). Seven schools earned a Warning rating (1.5%).

This marks the fourteenth year in a row that the percentage of universities with an overall red light rating has fallen, this year from 21.3% to 18.5%. The continued reduction in red light institutions is encouraging: Just over a decade ago, red light schools encompassed about 75% of the report's findings.

However, this year's numbers also reveal an increase in yellow light institutions, as 65.3% of schools earned an overall yellow light last year, compared to 68% this year. While yellow light policies are not as clearly and substantially restrictive as red light policies on their face, they nevertheless impose impermissible restrictions on expression.

The number of green light institutions has continued to rise this year, though only slightly, from 56 institutions last year to 58 now. At 12.1%, the percentage of green light schools is at an all-time high, with more than one million students across the country enrolled at green light colleges and universities.

In total, 20 schools improved their overall ratings this year.

### Public Colleges and Universities

The percentage of public schools with a red light rating dropped again, from 14.5% last year to 12% this year. Overall, of the 374 public universities reviewed for this report, 45 received a red light rating (12%), 273 received a yellow light rating (73%), and 54 received a green light rating (14.4%). As a result, public colleges and universities have reached a significant turning point: There are now more public institutions earning an overall green light rating than an overall red light rating. As just nine public schools earned the green light rating a decade ago, this milestone reveals significant progress.

This year, FIRE was pleased to welcome Elizabeth City State University and the University of North Carolina School of the Arts to the list of green light institutions.

Notably, 13 of the 16 institutions in the University of North Carolina System currently earn an overall green light rating, making North Carolina the state in the country with the greatest number of green light schools. We hope to use North Carolina as a model, working with governing bodies of other public university systems across the country to adopt similar, sweeping reform in other states.

### Private Colleges and Universities

Of the 107 private colleges and universities reviewed, 44 received a red light rating (41.1%). 54 received a yellow light rating (50.5%), four received a green light rating (3.7%), and five earned a Warning rating (4.7%).

The percentage of private universities earning a red light rating, which stood at 44.3% last year, continued to decrease, coming in at 41.1% this year. This progress, albeit slight, is hard-earned, given that private universities are not legally bound by the First Amendment, which regulates only government actors. For this reason, it is gratifying that these colleges are closer to fulfilling their institutional commitments to free expression.

FIRE will continue to work with private colleges and universities to improve policies so that they better meet institutional commitments to protecting students' free speech rights.

## Speech Codes on Campus: Background and Legal Challenges

Speech codes—university regulations prohibiting expression that would be constitutionally protected in society at large—gained popularity with college administrators in the 1980s and 1990s. As discriminatory barriers to education declined, female and minority enrollment increased. Concerned that these changes would cause tension and that students who finally had full educational access would arrive at institutions only to be offended by other students, college administrators enacted speech codes.

In the mid-1990s, the phenomenon of campus speech codes converged with the expansion of Title IX, the federal law prohibiting sex discrimination in educational institutions receiving federal funds. Under the rationale of the obligation to prohibit discriminatory harassment, unconstitutionally overbroad harassment policies banning subjectively offensive conduct proliferated.

In enacting speech codes, administrators ignored or did not fully consider the philosophical, social, and legal ramifications of placing restrictions on speech, particularly at public universities. As a result, federal courts have overturned speech codes at numerous colleges and universities over the past several decades.

Despite the overwhelming weight of legal authority against speech codes, a large number of institutions—including some of those that have been successfully sued on First Amendment grounds—still maintain unconstitutional and illiberal speech codes. It is with this unfortunate fact in mind that we turn to a more detailed discussion of the ways in which campus speech codes violate individual rights and what can be done to challenge them.

## Public Universities vs. Private Universities

With limited, narrowly defined exceptions, the First Amendment prohibits the government—including governmental entities such as state universities—from restricting freedom of speech. A good rule of thumb is that if a state law would be declared unconstitutional for violating the First Amendment, a similar regulation at a state college or university is likewise unconstitutional.

The guarantees of the First Amendment generally do not apply to students at private colleges because the First Amendment regulates only government conduct. Moreover, although acceptance of federal funding does confer some obligations upon private colleges (such as compliance with federal anti-discrimination laws), compliance with the First Amendment is not one of them.

This does not mean, however, that students and faculty at all private schools are not entitled to free expression. In fact, most private universities explicitly promise freedom of speech and academic freedom in their official policy materials.

Howard University, for example, provides in its student handbook that "all students are guaranteed freedom of expression, inquiry and assembly." Likewise, the University of Tulsa states that "[t]he rights of free inquiry and free expression, both public and private, are essential to the learning process," and that these rights "shall not be infringed upon."

Yet both of these institutions, along with most other private colleges and universities, maintain policies that prohibit the very speech they promise to protect.

This year, both private and public institutions, including statewide systems, have continued to adopt policy statements in support of free speech modeled after the one produced in January 2015 by the Committee on Freedom of Expression at the University of Chicago. Since our last report, seven more institutions have adopted policy statements in support of free speech modeled after the "Chicago Statement." Notably, earlier this year the University of Virginia convened a Committee on Free Speech and Inquiry, tasked with drafting a statement of principles affirming the university's strong commitment to freedom of expression. Following significant community engagement, the Board of Visitors officially adopted the Committee's statement over the summer, becoming the sixteenth green light institution to adopt a version of the Chicago Statement.

FIRE will continue to encourage institutions, private and public alike, to adopt a similar policy statement over the course of the next year.

What does FIRE mean when we say that a university restricts "free speech"? Do people have the right to say absolutely anything, or are certain types of expression unprotected?

**Overwhelming Majority of Speech is Protected by the First Amendment**

Over the years, the Supreme Court has carved out a limited number of narrow exceptions to the First Amendment, including speech that incites reasonable people to immediate violence; so-called "fighting words" (face-to-face confrontations that lead to physical altercations); harassment; true threats and intimidation; obscenity; and defamation. If the speech in question does not fall within one of these exceptions, it most likely is protected.

The exceptions are often misapplied and abused by universities to punish constitutionally protected speech. There are instances where the written policy at issue may be constitutional— for example, a prohibition on "incitement"—but its application may not be. In other instances, a written policy will purport to be a legitimate ban on a category of unprotected speech like harassment or true threats, but (either deliberately or through poor drafting) will encompass protected speech as well. Therefore, it is important to understand what these narrow exceptions to free speech actually mean in order to recognize when they are being misapplied.

**Speech Codes**—university regulations prohibiting expression that would be constitutionally protected in society at large—gained popularity with college administrators in the 1980s and 1990s. Utilizing the Foundation for Individual Rights in Education's (FIRE) extensive website, reports, and statistics, most of the content for this chapter is borrowed from these ground breaking resources in the arena of free speech rights and protections.

As discriminatory barriers to education declined in the Sixties and Seventies, female and minority enrollment increased substantially starting in the Eighties. Concerned that these changes would cause tension and that students who finally had full educational access would arrive at institutions only to be offended by other students, college administrators enacted speech codes.

In the mid-1990s, the phenomenon of campus speech codes converged with the expansion of Title IX, the federal law prohibiting sex discrimination in educational institutions receiving federal funds. Under the guise of the obligation to prohibit discriminatory harassment, unconstitutionally overbroad harassment policies banning subjectively offensive conduct proliferated. Given the current undergraduate tendency toward intellectual orthodoxy, one wonders: Would the advances of the feminist movement even have happened, had the campus conformists of a half-century ago had their way?

Respect for freedom of speech and diversity of thought are essential for achieving civil and thoughtful discourse, but also for enabling societal progress itself. Progress relies on early agitators, who are willing to speak out and press forward, no matter the backlash they engender. Many ideas once considered heretical have become accepted wisdom, thanks to early dissenters challenging the tide.

Real change relied on the courage of young women during the 1960s and 1970s, who stood up for equal opportunity in higher education and the workforce. They faced vocal opposition from many college alumni, professors, and fellow students. Nevertheless, these women persisted, no matter how "problematic" their efforts may have been considered. Their determined activism paved the way for the generations to come.

## What Exactly Is "Free Speech," And How Do Universities Curtail It?

With limited, narrowly defined exceptions, the First Amendment prohibits the government—including governmental entities such as state universities—from restricting freedom of speech. A good rule of thumb is that if a state law would be declared unconstitutional for violating the First Amendment, a similar regulation at a state college or university is likewise unconstitutional.

The guarantees of the First Amendment generally do not apply to students at private colleges because the First Amendment regulates only government conduct. Moreover, although acceptance of federal funding does confer some obligations upon private colleges (such as compliance with federal anti-discrimination laws), compliance with the First Amendment is not one of them.

This does not mean, however, that students and faculty at all private schools are not entitled to free expression. In fact, most private universities explicitly promise freedom of speech and academic freedom in their official policy materials. Lehigh University, for example, promises students "free inquiry and free speech and expression, including the right to open dissent."

Similarly, according to Middlebury College's student handbook, students "are free to examine and discuss all questions of interest to them and to express opinions publicly and privately." Yet both of these institutions, along with most other private colleges and universities, maintain policies that prohibit the very speech they promise to protect.

Encouragingly, more colleges than ever before, including private institutions, have adopted policy statements in support of free speech modeled after the one produced in January 2015 by the Committee on Freedom of Expression at the University of Chicago.

# 3 – How Fake News Thrives With Illiberal Journalists, Social Justice Warriors & Multi-Media

*Credit: Vern Bender.*

From Mark R. Levin in his 2019 best-selling book *Unfreedom of the Press* he shows how those entrusted with news reporting today are destroying freedom of the press from within: "not government oppression or suppression," he writes, but self-censorship, group-think, bias by omission, and passing off opinion, propaganda, pseudo-events, and outright lies as news.

It's a paradox states Levin: Misinformation has become so pervasive in the information age that some say we're living in a 'post-truth' world. The Oxford Dictionary defines post-truth as "Relating to or denoting circumstances in which objective facts are less influential in shaping public opinion than appeals to emotion and personal belief."

The constant flow of media that is carefully crafted from multibillion-dollar corporate conglomerates has gotten constructing a post-truth world down to a science. Millions of people are mesmerized by an endless amount of information that bombards us constantly; wanting our attention, wanting us to believe something, wanting us to buy something, and wanting us to be something. It's hard to tune it out and think for ourselves sometimes, and it seems that fewer people are even thinking at all.

Thankfully, however, many are waking up to this mass manipulation and have seen the new systems of media production and distribution as they were constructed, and remember what society was like before this information overload engulfed our world. The many victims of fake news are taking a stand like Nick Sandmann.

In January 2020, the cable news network CNN reached a settlement with Nick Sandmann, a Covington Catholic High School student who sued the news outlet for $275 million saying it defamed him over coverage of a viral video that took place in January 2019 when he was filmed with Nathan Phillips, a Native American in Washington D.C. A video shows Sandmann and Phillips standing close to each other in a crowd. Nick stares at Phillips as Phillips plays the drum. The situation unfolded after the March for Life on January 18 which Sandmann and his classmates attended. Phillips was attending the Indigenous Peoples March.

As reported by Julia Fair of the *Cincinnati Enquirer* in August 2020, the Sandmann lawsuit against CNN stated: "CNN brought down the full force of its corporate power, influence, and wealth on Nicholas by falsely attacking, vilifying, and bullying him despite the fact that he was a minor child."

In January 2020, CNN settled for an undisclosed account and so did the *Washington Post* in July 2020. More lawsuits like this one might be filed but most never see a courtroom because the odds of winning are seen as insurmountable due to the financial resources mainstream and social media have to squash, or in this rare case, settle. A David versus a Goliath scenario is extremely intimidating.

## Influencing People Instead of Informing Them

Owners of major media companies see the power their empires hold and often choose to use their outlets to influence people instead of informing them. From activist journalists to senior editors to CEOs, many in the big media companies can't help but impose their personal political ideology on the world by using the infrastructure they have at their disposal.

By building mountains out of molehills, through lying by omission, agenda-setting, framing stories and issues in a certain light, and by manipulating what is spread through social media by either limiting its reach or artificially amplifying it—the major media and tech companies influence the way people think and tell us how to act.

Fake news stories have been around for centuries, although they had usually just been called disinformation, propaganda, yellow journalism, conspiracy theories, or hoaxes; but this modern incarnation was different. All of a sudden it was supposedly everywhere, and just cost Hillary Clinton the election.

As Mark Dice points out in *The True Story of Fake News: How Mainstream Media Manipulates Millions*: Just one week after the 2016 presidential election, when tens of millions of Hillary supporters were still in absolute shock that Donald Trump actually beat her—and while many Trump supporters were in a similar state of surprise since he was the long-awaited anti-establishment underdog and populist—the term "fake news" became the talk of the town and quickly turned into one of the most loaded and controversial labels in America.

The mainstream media often steers the public conversation by giving constant coverage to certain stories which reinforce the ideologies they are trying to promote, which fits within The SAPIENT Being's definition of fake news. They'll often choose an isolated incident that's making news in the local community where it happened, and while it has no real national significance, the major networks will 'coincidentally' determine it should be one of the top stories in the country and then sensationalize it, so the incident then becomes a widely talked about topic.

## Agenda Setting by Fake News Media

These stories often include rare police brutality incidents involving a white police officer and a black suspect. But when it's a white officer and a white victim, or a black officer and a white victim, the incidents remain local stories and don't get national attention. Similarly, if a celebrity happens to call a gay or transgender person a derogatory name, then the big networks all have panels of pundits complain about it for hours, days, or even weeks on end to emphasize how 'hateful' and 'dangerous' such language is.

When these mountains out of molehills are turned into the top stories on the evening news of the Big Three broadcast networks (ABC, NBC, CBS) it doesn't take a professional media analyst to see a pattern and realize there is coordination among these companies behind the scenes to decide which topics will be the "top stories."

It's statistically impossible that the Big Three would regularly choose the same little-known local stories from the newswires to all report on nationally. Many events of the day warrant being the top stories on all networks, but most do not and shouldn't make it any further than their local news channels, yet they regularly get the national spotlight, and always when they fit the current agenda of the time.

The technical term for what they're doing is called agenda-setting. They magnify selected stories and topics through their constant coverage and endless panel discussions about every little detail. Talking for hours on end about the stories creates a self-fulfilling prophecy by building certain instances into major issues, and by treating them as if they are major issues when they are not and getting people to talk and think about them so much, they then become major issues.

As television became part of everyone's lives, a study was conducted during the 1968 presidential election called the Chapel Hill Study, which showed the strong correlation between what people thought were the most important election issues and what the national news media repeatedly reported were the most important issues.

It basically showed that instead of just reporting on the news, the networks were actually influencing what people thought was news. Since then, hundreds of studies into the agenda-setting power of the mainstream media have been conducted which consistently show the immense power the industry has to shape public opinion and not only influence what people think about, but how they think about it.

Aside from agenda-setting, the major networks also frame topics in a certain light trying to influence how they are perceived. Through their carefully selected panelists and pointed questions, they can easily paint a person or issue in a positive light or a negative one.

For example, during the height of the Black Lives Matter protests in 2016 and 2020, the liberal media always portrayed the protests (and riots) as a civil rights movement on par with Martin Luther King of the 1950s and 60s, consisting of people who were fighting against an 'epidemic 'of white police officers shooting 'innocent' black men. In reality, the vast majority of black men shot and killed by police are armed and dangerous thugs with criminal histories, but those facts are ignored, and the incidents are always framed as another 'innocent' black man who has been 'murdered' by police because 'they're all racists.'

The media likes to take rare and isolated instances of officer involved shootings and magnify them to give the appearance that there is a nation-wide epidemic of 'racist' police officers who are gunning down innocent young black men, thus adding fuel to the fire of black power groups and further straining race relations in America.

People like Trayvon Martin, Michael Brown and George Floyd are turned into celebrities from the nonstop coverage. Their names even trend on Twitter on the birthdays and the anniversaries of their deaths. Leftist organizations had signs, T-shirts, and murals made with their faces on them which people wore to protests and they are revered as if they're Martin Luther King or Tupac Shakur.

CNN and MSNBC love to give airtime to any Republican who expresses sympathy for a liberal cause. Congressmen who are completely unknown outside of their own small districts are held up as examples of a "growing trend" of "resistance " against conservatives when they speak out against members of their own party, when in reality, most of the time they're just an eccentric member of the House of Representatives with no national influence at all.

## Top Fake News Statistics and Trends: 2021

In today's pluralistic democracy, every voice counts. Behind every vote, there's an opinion. This opinion is formed when people interpret the information that reaches them. But what happens when this information is inaccurate or fake? How does one make a valid conclusion based on false premises? How does fake news affect public opinion?

From the April 2021 "27 Alarming Fake News Statistics on the Effects of False Reporting [The 2021 Edition]" post by Milos Djordjevic in LETTER.LY:

As these fake news statistics below will show, this is one of our society's biggest plights. We can see its adverse effects everywhere. Political occurrences and oscillations, mass hysteria, and global trends can all be shaped by falsified information. This is why it's vital to delve deeper into the concept of false reporting and the misinformation it creates:

- Media trust worldwide has dropped by 8% between 2020 and 2021.

- In 2020, only 29% of US adults said they mostly trust news media.

- 52% of Americans say they regularly encounter fake news online.

- 67% of US adults say they've come across false information on social media.

- 35.5% of millennials read political news on Facebook.

- Social media is the least trusted news source worldwide, fake news statistics show.

- 56% of Facebook users can't recognize fake news that aligns with their beliefs.

- In Q3 of 2020, there were 1.8 billion fake news engagements on Facebook.

Each year, more and more people are losing trust in mainstream media, statistics show. According to a 2021 survey, 53% of people worldwide still trust the media. While this is more than half the world's population, it's a significant decrease from 61% in 2020. Most people (61%) cite the lack of objectivity as the main reason for their loss of trust. Furthermore, 59% say that news organizations exaggerate or entirely fabricate information to support their ideology.

## Viewpoint Diversity Can Get You Fired

*The Atlantic* faced a campaign to fire Kevin Williamson shortly after he was hired away from *National Review*. Writers at the *New Republic*, the *New York Times*, Slate, Vox, the Daily Beast, and other outlets called him unfit for the job. They were particularly appalled by an earlier podcast in which Williamson, in a spirit of provocation, said that women who have abortions deserved the same punishment as those who commit first-degree murder, even if that meant hanging.

*The Atlantic* initially stood by him, and Ta-Nehisi Coates, one of its star progressive writers, even praised Williamson's work and said that he'd advised hiring him. But the online dragging and internal discontent soon led to his exit. At a staff meeting (a video of which was leaked to *HuffPost*) after Williamson's firing, Coates apologized to his colleagues. "I feel like I kind of failed you guys," he said.

A more immediate danger is self-censorship by writers fearful of being fired or blacklisted and by editors fearful of online rage, staff revolts, and advertising boycotts. After the cowardly firing of Kevin Williamson, *The Atlantic* (to its credit) published a dissent from that decision by Conor Friedersdorf, in which he worried about the chilling effect it would have on the magazine's writers and editors, and how their fear of taking chances would ultimately hurt readers.

But all editors and publishers can take a couple of basic steps. One is to concentrate on hiring journalists committed to the most important kind of diversity—viewpoint diversity with a wide range of ideas open for vigorous debate. The other step is even simpler: stop capitulating.

Ignore the online speech police, and don't reward the staff censors, either. Instead of feeling their pain or acceding to their demands, give them a copy of Nat Hentoff's *Free Speech for Me—but Not for Thee.*

These are just some of the dangers at every unsapient publication that bows to the new censors. Resisting them won't be easy if journalism keeps going the way of a *1984* type fake news scenario, but in the 21st century setting. If they still don't get it—if they still don't see that free speech is their profession's paramount principle—tactfully suggest that their talents would be better suited to another line of work.

## Republican Ideas Are Frequently Caricatured and Rarely Presented Fairly

From the July 2009 *Christian Science Monitor* article "Republican Ideas Are Frequently Caricatured and Rarely Presented Fairly," below is a relevant article about what happened when freelance journalist and journalism student Dan Lawton at the University of Oregon posed a simple question. In his own words, Lawton explains:

Nearly all my professors are Democrats. Isn't that a problem? That's a sure sign that universities should address the lack of ideological diversity. When I began examining the political affiliation of faculty at the University of Oregon, the lone conservative professor I spoke with cautioned that I would "make a lot of people unhappy."

Though I mostly brushed off his warning—assuming that academia would be interested in such discourse—I was careful to frame my research for a column for the school newspaper diplomatically.

The University of Oregon (UO), where I study journalism, invested millions annually in a diversity program that explicitly included "political affiliation" as a component. Yet, out of the 111 registered Oregon voters in the departments of journalism, law, political science, economics, and sociology, there were only *two* registered Republicans.

A number of conservative students told me they felt Republican ideas were frequently caricatured and rarely presented fairly. Did the dearth of conservative professors on campus and apparent marginalization of ideas on the right belie the university's commitment to providing a marketplace of ideas?

In my column, published in the campus newspaper *The Oregon Daily Emerald* June 1, I suggested that such a disparity hurt UO. I argued that the lifeblood of higher education was subjecting students to diverse viewpoints and the university needed to work on attracting more conservative professors.

I also suggested that students working on right-leaning ideas may have difficulty finding faculty mentors. I couldn't imagine, for instance, that journalism that supported the Iraq war or gun rights would be met with much enthusiasm.

What I didn't realize is that journalism that examined the dominance of liberal ideas on campus would be addressed with hostility.

**The Marketplace of Ideas on Campus is Closed**

A professor who confronted me declared that he was "personally offended" by my column. He railed that his political viewpoints never affected his teaching and suggested that if I wanted a faculty with Republicans I should have attended a university in the South. "If you like conservatism you can certainly attend the University of Texas and you can walk past the statue of Jefferson Davis every day on your way to class," he wrote in an e-mail.

Lawton was shocked by such a comment, which seemed an attempt to link Republicans with racist orthodoxy. When he wrote back expressing his offense, the professor neither apologized nor clarified his remarks. Instead, he reiterated them on the record. Was such a brazen expression of partisanship representative of the faculty as a whole?

Lawton continues: I decided to speak with him in person in the hope of finding common ground. He was eager to chat, and after five minutes our dialogue bloomed into a lively discussion. As we hammered away at the issue, one of his colleagues with whom he shared an office grew visibly agitated. Then, while I was in mid-sentence, she exploded:

"You think you're so [expletive] cute with your little column," she told me. "I read your piece and all you want is attention. You're just like Bill O'Reilly. You just want to get up on your [expletive] soapbox and have people look at you!" she screamed.

Lawton continues: From the disgust with which she attacked me; you would have thought I had advocated Nazism. She quickly grew so emotional that she had to leave the room. But before she departed, he added: "You understand that my column was basically a prophesy."

And so, by simply suggesting right-leaning ideas weren't welcome on campus and in response to the faculty tying Lawton's viewpoints to racism and addressing him with profanity-laced insults, the ideological bubble on campus is a tough one to penetrate with sapience.

Per Lawton: "What's so remarkable is that I hadn't actually advocated Republican ideas or conservative ideas. In fact, I'm not a conservative, nor a Republican. I simply believe in the concept of diversity—a primarily liberal idea—and think that we suffer when we don't include ideas we find unappealing."

## So Called 'Impartial' Algorithms Disproportionately Impact Conservative Material

Borrowing the politics and policy article "Viewpoint Discrimination with Algorithms" written in March 7, 2018 by Ben Shapiro for the *National Review*, it's becoming more evident that media companies' so called 'impartial' algorithms disproportionately impact conservative material. Ben Shapiro is the editor in chief of the Daily Wire and writes the following.

The biggest names in social media are cracking down on news. In particular, they're cracking down disproportionately on conservative news. That's not necessarily out of malice; it's probably due to the fact that our major social-media sites are staffed thoroughly with non-conservatives who have no objective frame of reference when it comes to the news business.

Thus, Google biases its algorithm to prevent people from searching for guns online in shopping; temporarily attached fact-checks from leftist sites like Snopes and PolitiFact to conservative websites but not leftist ones; showed more pro-Clinton results than pro-Trump results in news searches; and, of course, fired tech James Damore for the sin of examining social science in the debate over the wage gap. Google's bias is as obvious as the "doodles" it chooses for its logos, which routinely feature left-wing icons and issues.

YouTube has demonetized videos from conservatives while leaving similar videos up for members of the Left. Prager University has watched innocuous videos titled "Why America Must Lead," "The Ten Commandments: Do Not Murder," and "Why Did America Fight the Korean War" demonetized (i.e., barred from accepting advertisements) at YouTube's hands. Prager's lawyer explains, "Google and YouTube use restricted mode filtering not to protect younger or sensitive viewers from 'inappropriate' video content, but as a political gag mechanism to silence Prager U."

Facebook was slammed for ignoring conservative stories and outlets in its trending news; now Facebook has shifted its algorithm to downgrade supposedly "partisan" news, which has the effect of undercutting newer sites that are perceived as more partisan, while leaving brand names with greater public knowledge relatively unscathed.

Facebook's tactics haven't just hit conservative Web brands—they've destroyed the profit margins for smaller start-ups like LittleThings, a four-year-old site that fired 100 employees this week after the algorithm shift reportedly destroyed 75 percent of the site's organic reach (the number of people who see a site's content without paid distribution).

And Twitter has banned nasty accounts perceived as right-wing while ignoring similar activity from the Left. James O'Keefe recently exposed the practice of "shadowbanning," in which Twitter hides particular content or mutes particular hashtags for political purposes. That's no coincidence: Twitter head Jack Dorsey is an ardent leftist who has campaigned with radicals like DeRay Mckesson, and whose company relies on the input of an Orwellian Trust and Safety Council staffed thoroughly with left-wing interest groups.

## The Fact Checkers' Fact Checker is Real Clear Politics

News media fact checkers were once a rarity, but according to a report titled "Who Is Fact Checking The Fact Checkers?" by *Investor's Business Daily* in August 2018, they're now in a position to determine what people can read online, despite their own checkered past. So, who keeps the fact checkers honest? Thankfully, Real Clear Politics has stepped into the breach by creating what it calls Fact Check Review.

If a fact-checking outfit deems a story not entirely true, for example, Facebook can limit its reach on its News Feed. Google now includes a "fact check" box on its main search results page to help "people make more informed judgments."

The problem is that fact checkers themselves can be unreliable sources for what's true or not. Fact checkers make their own mistakes. They sometimes change ratings based on new information. Or they make determinations based on arbitrary standards that can change from one review to the next.

Per a report titled "Facebook Censors Pro-Trump Ad After Fact-Checker Admits Claim May Be True" by John Bickley in a September 2020 edition of the Daily Wire, amid pressure from left-wing activists and media outlets to clamp down on "misinformation" from the right, Facebook has begun censoring political ads that receive negative fact-checks—fact-checks that are produced by mostly left-leaning fact-checkers and that mostly target right-leaning ads.

In at least two new cases, these fact-checks do not actually check facts—they instead merely state that factually true claims are "missing context," then downgrade the ads.

The danger of this political speech-silencing policy by the social media giant—which nearly 70% of Americans use and where more than 40% read their news—is on full display in the case of the censoring of the pro-Trump 30-second political ad "Too Risky."

The ad launched on August 4, 2020 before getting slapped with a "mostly false" rating by PolitiFact and subsequently blocked by Facebook the next month. The ad directly quotes Biden declaring, "If you elect me, your taxes are going to be raised, not cut," and warns that his plan will raise taxes "on all income groups."

## Fact Checkers Often "Check" Opinions

Fact checkers also often "check" opinions, rather than factual claims, even though two people can form diametrically opposed opinions based on the same facts.

Worse, many media "fact checks" use other media sources to check facts, apparently forgetting that journalists get their facts wrong almost as often as politicians. (Take a look at the list of corrections on any given day in *The New York Times*.)

On top of this are legitimate complaints of political bias among fact checkers, who often seem to spend most of their time trying to debunk claims made by conservatives rather than liberals.

Thankfully, Real Clear Politics has stepped into the breach by creating what it calls Fact Check Review.

Not only does the site regularly review problematic "fact checks," it constantly updates a database on fact checks published by Snopes, FactCheck.org, PolitiFact, *New York Times*, *Washington Post* and the *Weekly Standard*.

41

It then rates them based on how often each site checks opinions rather than facts. In July 2020, for example, a quarter of the *Post's* "fact" checks were of opinions, as were 18% of PolitiFact's. It also looks at how often fact checkers rely on other news outlets to verify claims. In July, 90% of Snopes fact checks used other media sources.

There's a bigger problem with this fact-checking trend, however. As the *Weekly Standard's* Mark Hemingway explained: "It's basically a way for a bunch of reporters with no particular expertise to render pseudoscientific judgments on statements from public figures that are obviously argumentative or otherwise unverifiable. Then there's the matter of them weighing in with thundering certitude—pants on fire!—on complex policy debates they frequently misunderstand."

## Media Biased Against Conservative Research & Think Tanks

A new study in the *Journal of Media Economics* shows the media is biased against right-leaning think tanks. Wayne Dunham, an economist in the Anti-Trust Division of the Department of Justice, concluded that the media "had a much higher propensity to associate ideological frames with think tanks associated with the right or conservative side of the political spectrum."

For example, an article may cite a study from the "conservative Heritage Foundation" while citing another study from the "Urban Institute" with no ideological qualifier indicating the Urban Institute is a "liberal" think tank.

The study measured 25,000 references to think tanks by six major newspapers and the Associated Press over an 18-year period. Dunham used 12 think tanks in his measurement, including the Heritage Foundation and American Enterprise Institute on the right, and the Brookings Institution, RAND Corporation and the Urban Institute on the left.

"This data show that conservative think tanks are ideologically framed 10 times more frequently than liberal think tanks," said Dunham. There are several factors that "suggest a liberal media bias."

Attaching an ideological label to a think tank is a subtle way of making its conclusion seem less credible. By doing this selectively, journalists have a powerful influence on the public perception of conservative think tanks.

## The Southern Poverty Law Center Bullies and Silences Conservatives

One of the most sinister ways tech companies have stifled conservative speech has been by caving to pressure from anti-conservative groups, especially the Southern Poverty Law Center (SPLC) as MRC's *"CENSORED! How Online Media Companies Are Suppressing Conservative Speech"* guidebook points out.

The SPLC claims to fight "hate and bigotry" and promote "justice for the most vulnerable members of our society." In reality, it has used its position to attack conservative groups like the American Family Association (AFA) and the Family Research Council (FRC) alongside Ku Klux Klan and Black Panther groups. Most conservative groups targeted by the SPLC were categorized as being "Anti-Muslim" or "Anti-LGBT" for either criticizing Islamic terrorism or promoting traditional marriage.

The SPLC has a disturbing history with the conservative movement. In August 2012, a gunman entered the FRC headquarters to "kill as many people as possible" and wounded a security guard before being disarmed. The man told investigators he targeted FRC after finding it listed as an anti-LGBT "hate group" on the SPLC's "Hate Map," a literal map pinpointing the location of supposed "hate groups."

Despite the shooting and conservative complaints, FRC and other conservative groups remain on the SPLC's dangerous hate map.

News outlets and companies continue to trust SPLC claims in spite of the group's history. Social media organizations not only refuse to stand up to the SPLC's bullying, but they also consult the anti-conservative group for data and recommendations about so-called hate groups.

The SPLC's hate list is the impetus behind actions at companies including Facebook and Google too.

## The New Media Pandemic: Trump Derangement Syndrome (TDS)

Documenting the severe reactions many people have to Donald Trump, a new medical term has emerged to describe it as noted in Joseph Epstein's humorous May 2020 *WSJ* Opinion section article titled "The New Pandemic: Trump Derangement Syndrome."

Symptoms include obsession with the president's hair and comparing him to Mao. It's been going around for some time and now appears to be in danger of spreading widely. I refer not to COVID-19, but to Donald-20, or, to use its pseudoscientific name, Trump Derangement Syndrome (TDS). Research has shown that TDS appears in five stages, each of advanced intensity. Perhaps there will be some value, if not promise of diminishment, in setting these parameters out for public awareness.

The cause of TDS is clear enough—Donald Trump, his looks, his manner, his nearly every utterance. So far there is no known cure. Ventilators are unnecessary in TDS, for people who progress beyond the first stage tend to vent quite vigorously on their own.

In Stage One, the afflicted has decided before 2016 that Donald Trump has serious, even strenuous, character flaws that disqualified him for the presidency or any other public office. Voting for him was never possible. For Stage One sufferers, a second Trump term could have effects that are frightening to contemplate. Stage One patients view the Trump presidency as a blotch in American political history.

In Stage Two, one dwells upon Donald Trump's looks. One has put a fair amount of thought into the architecture of his hairdo, wondering how much time each morning he must devote to its re-creation and whether he employs a stylist to help. One notices that the length of his neckties covers up his ample alderman as does the way he sits, leaning forward in his chair. Photographs of him in golf apparel are studied for what they reveal of the impressive breadth of his backside. The smugness of his smile is registered, the smallness of his hands always noted.

In Stage Three, one is ready to believe anything—anything pernicious or salacious, that is—about Mr. Trump and to reject anything he has done that might be good for the country, if only because he is the man who did it. One is ready to believe that he diets exclusively on the meat of endangered species, that there is something weirdly illicit about his relationship with Vladimir Putin, that he secretly admires Kim Jong Un's wardrobe. For Stage Three sufferers, nothing about President Trump can be totally disbelieved.

As for those of Donald Trump's policies that, coming from another president, one might be pleased about, these are rejected in Stage Three derangement syndrome. Israel shouldn't count on the allegiance of Mr. Trump. The revival of the American economy, before COVID-19 sent it cratering, was owing not to Mr. Trump but to President Obama. The lowering of black and Hispanic unemployment figures under the Trump administration is scarcely to be believed. Nor is the utility of his legislation reforming prisons or of his creating opportunity areas in black neighborhoods, if only because it happened under Donald Trump, who is, patients say, clearly a racist. In Stage Three derangement syndrome, if Donald Trump is for any specific policy, one is automatically against it; if he is against it, one is for it. Case not so much closed as never really opened.

In Stage Four, one imputes evil to Mr. Trump. One believes he became president of the United States to boost his hotel business. One is certain he has it in mind to create a dynasty, with Don Jr. and Jared Kushner waiting to succeed him as president-emperor. Even should Mr. Trump lose the forthcoming presidential election, Stage Four derangement syndrome sufferers believe he is unlikely to depart the White House willingly and is not beyond using military force to keep himself in power. Mussolini, Hitler, Stalin, Mao—for people with Stage Four derangement syndrome, Donald Trump is clearly a figure in their line.

In Stage Five TDS, one is weighted down with all the symptoms of the first four stages but brings to them an added choleric intensity of anger. At the mere mention of the name Donald Trump, unprintable expletives issue out of one's foam-flecked lips. One's skin flushes, veins appear on one's forehead, one's hands tremble, one loses all powers of speech.

Still, the nice thing about Trump Derangement Syndrome is that to prevent catching or spreading it, you don't have to wear a mask or always be washing your hands or practice social distancing. All you have to do is turn off your television set, social media, and .radio.

And that begs the question: What stage of TDS are you in?

# 4 – The Mediacrats Collusion Is the Essence of Anti-Conservative Bias & Censorship

*Credit: MarketWatch - 2020 presidential debate Fox News moderator Chris Wallace (mediacrat) slammed by critics for anti-Trump and pro-Biden biases as moderator.*

As John Tierney explains in his November 2019 *City Journal* article "Journalists Against Free Speech" the once unswerving defenders of the First Amendment, members of the press increasingly support restricting expression. Free speech is no longer sacred among young journalists who have absorbed the campus lessons about "hate speech"—defined more and more broadly—and they're breaking long-standing taboos as they bring "cancel culture" into professional newsrooms.

They're not yet in charge, but many of their editors are reacting like beleaguered college presidents, terrified of seeming insufficiently "woke." Most professional journalists, young and old, still pay lip service to the First Amendment, and they certainly believe that it protects *their* work, but they're increasingly eager for others to be "de-platformed" or "no-platformed," as today's censors like to put it—effectively silenced.

Even journalists are adopting these attitudes, as Robby Soave observed while reporting on young radicals in his book *Panic Attack*. A decade ago, when Soave was an undergraduate on the University of Michigan's student paper, his fellow editors stood in the Hentoff tradition: devout leftists but also free-speech absolutists.

Starting around 2013, though, Soave saw a change at Michigan and other schools. "The power dynamic switched on campus so that the anti-speech activists began dominating the discourse while those who believed in free speech became afraid to speak up," says Soave, now a writer for *Reason*.

"Campus newspapers, especially at elite institutions, have become increasingly sympathetic to the notion that speech isn't protected if it makes students feel unsafe. And now you're seeing these graduates going into professional journalism and demanding that their editors provide a safe workplace by not employing people whose views make them uncomfortable."

## Journalists Are Becoming Zealous to Silence Their Ideological Rivals

Today, journalists are becoming zealous to silence their ideological rivals—and the fervor is mainly on the left. During the 1960s, the left-wing activists leading Berkeley's Free Speech Movement fought for the rights of conservatives to speak on campus, but today's activists embrace the New Left's intellectual rationalizations for censorship.

To justify the protection of an ever-expanding array of victimized groups, theorists of intersectionality—the idea that subgroup identities, such as race, gender, and sexuality, overlap to make people more oppressed—have adapted Herbert Marcuse's neo-Marxist and Critical Theory notions of "repressive" and "liberating" tolerance."

In the essay "Repressive Tolerance" (1965), the German born American critical theorist Herbert Marcuse (1898-1979) of the Frankfurt School of political theorists argued that, under the conditions of advanced industrial capitalism, the only hope for realizing the original objectives of "liberalist" or "pure" toleration (as articulated by the British philosopher John Stuart Mill [1806-1873])—freeing the mind to rationally pursue the truth—was to practice a deliberately selective "liberating tolerance" that both targeted and enacted the repression alluded to in the essay's paradoxical title.

Simplified, this "liberating tolerance" would involve "the withdrawal of toleration of speech and assembly from groups and movements" on the Right, as opposed to the aggressive partisan promotion of speech, groups, and progressive movements on the Left. Younger journalists and the "so-called" progressive BLM and Antifa movements (whether they know it or not) practice liberating tolerance. That's why the term liberating tolerance is referred to by the SAPIENT Being as an oxymoron and illiberal because it represents *intolerance of the right* in favor of *tolerance of the left* and that by itself, suppresses First Amendment rights, and is also unsapient.

Dr. Greg Lukianoff, who has fought free-speech wars on campus for two decades as the head of the Foundation for Individual Rights in Education (FIRE), dates the ascendancy of the new censors to 2013, when student protesters at Brown University forced the cancellation of a speech by Raymond Kelly, the New York City police commissioner.

"For the first time, rather than being ashamed of this assault on free speech, most people on campus seemed to rally around the protesters," says Lukianoff, coauthor of *The Coddling of the American Mind*. "That's when we started hearing the language of medicalization, that free speech would cause medical harm. Outsiders dismissed this as a college phenomenon and predicted that these intolerant fragile kids would have to change when they hit the real world. But instead, they're changing the world."

## 'Progressive' Journalists Lead Campaigns to Get Conservative Journalists Fired

These mostly younger progressive journalists lead campaigns to get conservative journalists fired, banned from Twitter, and "de-monetized" on YouTube. They don't burn books, but they've successfully pressured Amazon to stop selling titles that they deem offensive. They encourage advertising boycotts designed to put ideological rivals out of business. They're loath to report forthrightly on left-wing censorship and violence, even when fellow journalists get attacked. They equate conservatives' speech with violence and rationalize leftists' actual violence as…speech.

It's a strange new world for those who remember liberal journalists like Nat Hentoff, the *Village Voice* writer who stood with the ACLU in defending the free-speech rights of Nazis, Klansmen, and others whose views he deplored—or who recall the days when the *Columbia Journalism Review* stood as an unswerving advocate for press freedom. While America has seen its share of politicians eager to limit speech, from John Adams and Woodrow Wilson (who both had journalists prosecuted for "sedition") to Donald Trump (who has made various unconstitutional threats), journalists on the left and the right have long shared a reverence for the First Amendment, if only out of self-interest.

When liberals supported campaign-finance laws restricting corporations' political messages during election campaigns, they insisted on exemptions for news organizations. One could fault them for being self-serving in this selective censorship, which the Supreme Court declared unconstitutional in its Citizens United decision, but at least they stood up for their profession's freedom.

*Citizens United v. Federal Election Commission, 558 U.S. 310 (2010),* was a landmark decision of the Supreme Court of the United States concerning campaign finance. The Court held that the free speech clause of the First Amendment prohibits the government from restricting independent expenditures for political communications by corporations, including nonprofit corporations, labor unions, and other associations.

## A Generational Divide in Newsrooms and Social Media

The result is what Dean Baquet, the *New York Times* executive editor, recently called a "generational divide" in newsrooms. The progressive activism of younger journalists often leaves their older colleagues exasperated. "The paper is now written by 25-year-old gender studies majors," said one *Washington Post* veteran. She wouldn't speak for the record, though: as fragile and marginalized as these young progressives claim to be, they know how to make life miserable for unwoke colleagues.

If their publication is considering hiring a conservative, or if a colleague writes or tweets something that offends them, young progressives express their outrage on social media—sometimes publicly on Twitter, sometimes in internal chat rooms. The internal chat is supposed to be confidential, but comments often get leaked, stoking online outrage.

It takes remarkably little to start the cycle, as *New York Times* opinion writer Bari Weiss discovered. Weiss, already in disfavor among progressives for criticizing aspects of the #MeToo movement, got into trouble for celebrating the Olympic performance of gymnast Mirai Nagasu, the American-born daughter of Japanese immigrants. Weiss adapted a line from the Hamilton musical to tweet: "Immigrants: They get the job done." Weiss was promptly attacked for describing Nagasu as an immigrant, making her guilty of a progressive offense known as "othering."

"Today, journalists are becoming zealous to silence their ideological rivals with illiberalism—and the fervor is mainly on the left." Illiberalism describes an attitude that is close-minded, intolerant, and bigoted.

## Social Justice Warriors Taking Over and Purging Newsrooms

In the wake of the protests and riots that erupted following the killing of George Floyd by a Minneapolis police officer, MRC's CNS News site Jarrett Stepman reports in June 2020 on "Social Justice Warriors Taking Over and Purging Newsrooms."

Stepman provides a revealing transformation has been occurring in the country's media landscape. This is now the message coming from the media: The narrative about how society should look at these police shooting incidents shall remain in accordance with the most radical, "woke" voices. Deviating opinions will not be tolerated. Words are violence!

That attitude was on full display in a dustup at America's leading liberal newspaper. Chaos at *The New York Times* began after it published an editorial by Sen. Tom Cotton, R-Ark., who argued that cities with police forces overwhelmed by looting and violence have the option, under the Federal Insurrection Act, to request aid from the military.

The article's headline was "Call in the Troops," which had been selected by *New York Times* editors. In it, Cotton explained how military force has been used to quell domestic unrest in the past, including those who attempted to obstruct desegregation at Little Rock's Central High School in Arkansas in 1957. Following the article's publication on June 3, *New York Times* reporters and editors protested publicly en masse. Many claimed that Cotton's opinions put their colleagues "in danger."

The same *New York Times* has also published Russian leader Vladimir Putin, a member of the Taliban, a long symposium glorifying the communist Russian Revolution of 1917, and even an excerpt of "Mein Kampf" in the 1940s (to demonstrate the philosophy of Hitler as the nation entered World War II).

Yet, an editorial by a U.S. senator, articulating views shared by more than half of registered voters and 37 percent of black voters, according to a Morning Consult poll, is beyond the pale and a literal threat to fellow Americans?

Instead of standing by the practice of publishing diverse opinions, *The New York Times* appended a lengthy editor's note to Cotton's column, saying that the piece "fell short of our standards and should not have been published."

However, the note didn't list any serious fact-based inaccuracies and only nitpicked at Cotton's characterizations of the protests. It concluded by saying that the tone of the piece was "needlessly harsh."

I challenge anyone reading the piece to check out this week's lineup of *New York Times* editorials and columns and not find one that's harsh. A recent Paul Krugman editorial column, for instance, insinuated that President Donald Trump is provoking a race war and that the president is "clearly itching for an excuse to use force." It didn't end there, however. The editorial-page editor, James Bennet, was effectively forced to step down and resigned from the position.

Whatever else can be said of the merits of Cotton's piece or of whatever else is published generally in *The New York Times*, it's increasingly clear that newsrooms of the most prominent liberal publications are being taken over by the most radical voices, who demand that they maintain an increasingly rigid ideological line in how they cover—and comment on—the news of the day.

## Most of America's Leading "Mainstream" Media Outlets Lean to the Left

The fact is, most of America's leading "mainstream" media outlets have leaned to the left—in some cases, the far left—of the average American for a long time. Generations, really.

The difference, however, is that in the past they at least attempted to thread the needle of nudging the country leftward without outright devolving into cheerleading for the Democratic Party or leading with activism at the expense of at least some measure of objectivity.

Wesley Lowery—a correspondent for "60 in 6," a short-form spinoff of CBS' "60 Minutes" for the Quibi short-form streaming service—wrote of this turning point in journalism on Twitter:

"American view-from-nowhere, 'objectivity'-obsessed, both-sides journalism is a failed experiment. We need to fundamentally reset the norms of our field. The old way must go. We need to rebuild our industry as one that operates from a place of moral clarity."

That old dynamic of objectivity is crumbling, as newsrooms are now being turned entirely over to the whims of the most activist social justice warriors, who demand political conformity with a strident push toward the left's current cultural and political aims.

It's a process that has already taken place on America's college campuses for several generations, as aggressive left-wing activists push the mostly liberal faculty and staff to be more aggressively left-wing. But campus politics are spilling over into the rest of society.

Nikole Hannah-Jones, the lead architect of the Pulitzer Prize-winning—but factually challenged—"1619 Project," actually did a good job of revealing and elucidating what's happening in our leading newspapers' newsrooms.

She said in an interview with CNN on Sunday that outlets need to abandon the adherence to "evenhandedness, both-sideism," and that an article offering the views of someone like Cotton should only occur in a news piece "where we can check the facts, where we can push back," so readers wouldn't receive what she called "misinformation."

We can't let people decide for themselves what to believe, after all, without social justice warriors—I mean, reporters—guiding the way and leading us along. People might start to form opinions of their own. The horror and free speech madness!

Hannah-Jones then said, "Our role as journalists is to give people correct information so they can make decisions," but clearly demonstrated that she thinks the role of journalists is subtle and not-so-subtle activism, rather than simply reporting the news.

So, the mask is coming off for media outlets, big and small, that are now revealing that they are ultimately tools of the political left, rather than objective guardians of truth, as they often portray themselves.

The recent actions of many prominent media outlets simply reveal and highlight what many Americans already know; namely, that they have an agenda beyond simply publishing "all the news that's fit to print," as the *Times'* motto insists.

It's a clarifying moment—or at least it should be—for Americans who have been under the illusion that they can simply trust, without question, what they see in even the most prominent and established publications.

Furthermore, the media and Democrats are so close in association and so close in their philosophical views that we might as well use one word to describe both, and that's Mediacrats.

## Biden Revokes Trump Order Protecting Users From Censorship on Social Media

As reported in Janita Kan's May 2021 *Epoch Times* article "Biden Revokes Trump Order Protecting Users From Censorship on Social Media Epoch Times:" President Joe Biden this week revoked an order from the previous Trump administration that sought to protect users from unfair or deceptive content restriction practices by Big Tech companies.

The effect of the revocation would require the Director of the Office of Management and Budget and the heads of executive departments to take steps to rescind any regulations or policies that enforced former President Donald Trump's executive order entitled "Preventing Online Censorship," which was signed in May 2020.

Trump's order sought to prevent social media companies such as Twitter, Facebook, and YouTube from moderating users' content in what his administration said was being done in an unbalanced and inconsistent way. The order cited examples from Twitter that added "fact-checking labels" to certain tweets in a manner that the administration said clearly reflects political bias.

Twitter added a "fact-checking" label on two of Trump's tweets two days before the president issued his executive order. Trump accused Twitter of "selectively applying" its warning labels, arguing such action amounted to political activism.

Biden's order also seeks to roll back liability protections under Section 230 of the 1996 Communications Decency Act. That law largely exempts online platforms from liability for content posted by their users, although they can be held liable for content that violates anti-sex trafficking or intellectual property laws.

The law allows companies to block or screen content "in good faith" if they consider it "obscene, lewd, lascivious, filthy, excessively violent, harassing, or otherwise objectionable." The protections, however, weren't intended to apply to services that act more like publishers than online platforms, then-Attorney General William Barr said in a speech in May.

Trump's order directs the Federal Communications Commission (FCC) to develop regulations for what is and isn't "good faith" in terms of what content companies can remove or restrict.

The order has been challenged in the courts by several advocacy groups claiming that Trump was seeking to punish social-media companies for fact-checking the president's posts. The groups asked the court to declare the order "unconstitutional and invalid," and to block its implementation or enforcement.

The lawsuit, filed on behalf of Common Cause, Free Press, Maplight, Rock the Vote, and Vote Latino, argues that social media platforms "have First Amendment rights to ensure that accurate information … is not undermined by misinformation on their platforms."

Barr had warned last year that Section 230 was no longer doing what it was intended to do, adding that there was a need to update the federal law.

He said the internet and tech industry has evolved since Section 230 was adopted 25 years ago. At the time, it was used to protect websites that served as bulletin boards for third-party content and to give protection to companies from liability for removing content such as child pornography or human trafficking advertising, he said.

But now, he said that Section 230 was been interpreted in such a broad manner that online platforms are left "unaccountable for a variety of harms flowing from content on their platforms and with virtually unfettered discretion to censor third-party content with little transparency or accountability."

Biden didn't explain his move to revoke his predecessor's order and the decision was announced along with the revocation of several other Trump orders made in 2020, including the order on Protecting American Monuments, Memorials, and Statues, and Combating Recent Criminal Violence and Building the National Garden of American Heroes.

## Research on Media Bias: It's Real and the Data Don't Lie

Since the 1980s, studies have consistently shown that the professionals who constitute America's mainstream news media—reporters, editors, anchors, publishers, correspondents, bureau chiefs, and executives at the nation's major newspapers, magazines, and broadcast networks—are preponderantly left-oriented and Democrat.

These studies have excluded commentators, editorialists, and opinion columnists—all of whom make it clear that they are giving their opinions and analyses of the news as they view it. Rather, the focus of the research has been on those individuals whose ostensible duty is to present the relevant facts impartially and comprehensively to the readers, listeners, and viewers.

### What Media Believe About a Wide Array of Social, Ethical, and Political Issues

A useful way of gauging the news media's political and ideological makeup is to examine what the professionals in that industry believe about a wide array of social, ethical, and political issues. For example, research shows that:

- Fully 81% of news media professionals favor affirmative action in employment and academia.

- Some 71% agree that the "government should work to ensure that everyone has a job."

- 75% agree that the "government should work to reduce the income gap between rich and poor."

- 56% say that the United States has exploited the nations of the Third World.

- 57% say that America's disproportionate consumption of the world's natural resources is "immoral."

- Nearly half agree that "the very structure of our society causes people to feel alienated."

- Only 30% agree that "private enterprise is fair to workers."

### How Media Have Supported Democrat or Liberal/Left Candidates and Causes

It is equally illuminating to examine the degree to which members of the news media have supported Democrat or liberal/left candidates and causes, both at the ballot box and with their checkbooks:

- In 1964, 94% of media professionals voted for Democrat Lyndon Johnson over Republican Barry Goldwater.

- In 1968, 86% voted for Democrat Hubert Humphrey over Republican Richard Nixon.

- In 1972, 81% voted for Democrat George McGovern over the incumbent Nixon.

- In 1976, 81% voted for Democrat Jimmy Carter over Republican Gerald Ford.

- In 1980, twice as many cast their ballots for Carter rather than for Republican Ronald Reagan.

- In 1984, 58% supported Democrat Walter Mondale, whom Reagan defeated in the biggest landslide in presidential election history.

- In 1988, White House correspondents from various major newspapers, television networks, magazines, and news services supported Democrat Michael Dukakis over Republican George H.W. Bush by a ratio of 12-to-1.

- In 1992, those same correspondents supported Democrat Bill Clinton over the incumbent Bush by a ratio of 9 to 2.

- Among Washington bureau chiefs and congressional correspondents, the disparity was 89% vs. 7%, in Clinton's favor.

- In a 2004 poll of campaign journalists, those based outside of Washington, DC supported Democrat John Kerry over Republican George W. Bush by a ratio of 3-to-1. Those based inside the Beltway favored Kerry by a 12-to-1 ratio.

- In a 2008 survey of 144 journalists nationwide, journalists were 8 times likelier to make campaign contributions to Democrats than to Republicans.

- A 2008 *Investor's Business Daily* study put the campaign donation ratio at 11.5-to-1, in favor of Democrats. In terms of total dollars given, the ratio was 15-to-1.

It is exceedingly rare to find, even in the most heavily partisan voting districts in the United States, such pronounced imbalances in terms of votes cast or dollars earmarked for one party or the other.

## How News-Media Professionals Identify Themselves

The figures cited above are entirely consistent with how news-media professionals identify themselves in terms of their political party affiliations and ideological leanings:

- In a 1988 survey of business reporters, 54% of respondents identified themselves as Democrats, 9% as Republicans.

- In a 1992 poll of journalists working for newspapers, magazines, radio, and television, 44% called themselves Democrats, 16% Republicans.

- In a 1996 poll of 1,037 reporters at 61 newspapers, 61% identified themselves as Democrats, 15% as Republicans.

- In a 2001 Kaiser Family Foundation poll, media professionals were nearly 7 times likelier to call themselves Democrats rather than Republicans.

- A 2014 study by Indiana University's School of Journalism found that just 7.1% of all journalists identified themselves as Republicans, vs, 28.1% who self-identified as Democrats and 50.2% who said they were Independents.

**How News-Media Professionals Rate Themselves on the Left-to-Right Political Spectrum**

We see similar ratios in studies where news people are asked to rate themselves on the left-to-right political spectrum:

- In a 1981 study of 240 journalists nationwide, 65% identified themselves as liberals, 17% as conservatives.

- In a 1983 study of news reporters, executives, and staffers, 32% identified themselves as liberals, 11% as conservatives.

- In a 1992 study of more than 1,400 journalists, 44% identified themselves as liberals, 22% as conservatives.

- In a 1996 study of Washington bureau chiefs and congressional correspondents, 61% identified themselves as liberals, 9% as conservatives.

- In a 1996 study of 1,037 journalists, the respondents identified themselves as liberals 4 times more frequently than as conservatives. Among journalists working for newspapers with circulations exceeding 50,000, the ratio of liberals to conservatives was 5.4 to 1.

- In a 2004 Pew Research Center study of journalists and media executives, the ratio of self-identified liberals to conservatives was 4.9 to 1.

- In a 2007 Pew Research Center study of journalists and news executives, the ratio was 4 liberals for each conservative.

Bias in the news media manifests itself most powerfully not in the form of outright, intentional lies, but is most often a function of what reporters choose *not* to tell their audience, i.e., the facts they purposely omit so as to avoid contradicting the political narrative they wish to advance. As media researchers Tim Groseclose and Jeffrey Milo put it: "For every sin of commission...we believe that there are hundreds, and maybe thousands, of sins of omission—cases where a journalist chose facts or stories that only one side of the political spectrum is likely to mention."

By no means is such activity the result of an organized campaign or conspiracy. Media expert Bernard Goldberg says: "No, we don't sit around in dark corners and plan strategies on how we're going to slant the news. We don't have to. It comes naturally to most reporters." Goldberg explains that "a lot of news people … got into journalism in the first place" so they could: (a) "change the world and make it a better place," and (b) use their positions as platforms from which to "show compassion," which "makes us feel good about ourselves."

Expanding further upon this point, Goldberg quotes researcher Robert Lichter of the nonpartisan Center for Media and Public Affairs, who said that journalists increasingly "see themselves as society's designated saviors," striving to "awaken the national conscience and force public action." Or as ABC News anchor Peter Jennings admitted to the *Boston Globe* in July 2001: "Those of us who went into journalism in the '50s or '60s, it was sort of a liberal thing to do: Save the world."

## The Mainstream Media Is at the Point of No Return

A recent 2020 landmark poll of 20,000 citizens undertaken by the Knight Foundation and Gallup found that Americans' hope for and trust in an objective media is all but lost. They see not only an ever-growing partisanship in news reporting but a determination by the mainstream media to push a political agenda instead of honestly disseminating the news.

While generic faith in the media has been gradually declining over recent decades, the precipitous drop in trust and questions about what motivates the mainstream media can be traced to June 2015 and Donald Trump's entry into the presidential sweepstakes.

This latest poll is the most devastating indictment of the media in polling history. Some highlights:

- 84% of surveyed Americans lay either a moderate or a great deal of the blame for today's partisan hostility at the feet of the media.

- Further, 82% believe news outlets are either deliberately "misrepresenting the facts" or are "making them up entirely".

- This is further amplified as 79% of those surveyed say media outlets are trying to persuade people to adopt a certain opinion about an issue or an individual.

- Similarly, while the respondents in the poll believe that the media is "critical" or "very important" to democracy, 86% say they have witnessed either a fair amount or a great deal of bias in news reporting. Damningly, 78% feel that this bias is reflected in the spread of fake news which "is a major" problem" that exceeds all other in the mainstream media environment.

- By contrast, in 2007 62% of respondents in a Pew Research poll claimed to have witnessed either a fair amount or a great deal of bias in news reporting; in another Pew

Research poll in 2012, that result increased slightly to 67% as compared to 86% today. How did the mainstream media sink to this abysmal level of distrust and disdain?

Donald Trump's entry into the presidential field in 2015 was a godsend to the mainstream media that had been hemorrhaging red ink for many years. The denizens of the mainstream media hierarchies knew that unremitting coverage of Trump, a global celebrity, would dramatically increase viewership, clicks on the internet and newspaper readership and thus their bottom line.

However, Donald Trump, during the campaign, continuously pointed out the left-wing bias and misreporting in the mainstream media and popularized a phrase that is now part of the American lexicon: fake news. With ridicule and mockery, he succeeded in making the media a potent campaign issue and a focal point of voter resentment.

While the vast majority of those in the mainstream media seethed at this disparagement, they, certain in the final outcome of the election, continued their unrestrained reporting and coverage of his every movement and utterance as their ratings and readership went through the roof.

### First Annual Media Fibbys

To memorialize all of the fake news, false narratives, and blatant lies spewed forth from the mediacrats in 2021 Ben Shapiro provides sapient viewers (in tux and bow tie red carpet fashion) with a diversity/equity/inclusion (DEI) spectrum of award categories.

The Daily Wire's "Ben Shapiro Breaks Down the Top Mainstream Media Fails of 2021" Dec. 23, 2021 episode covers the CNN/Cuomo debacle, to Stephen Colbert's 'Vax-Scene' song, to the infamous 'Let's Go Brandon' moment—the mainstream media had no shortage of lowlights this year and he eloquently breaks them all down in the First Annual Media Fibbys!

Ben Shapiro is a graduate of UCLA, Harvard Law School, editor-in-chief of The Daily Wire, columnist with *National Review*, and nationally syndicated columnist with Creators Syndicate. Author of many bestselling books including *Bullies: How The Left's Culture of Fear and Intimidation Silences America*, Shapiro is the host of the most listened-to conservative podcast in America, "The Ben Shapiro Show." His quick wit and words deliver more persuasion in 5 minutes than most others accomplish in an hour.

Without further ado—the award categories are—"the envelope please": Who is the Dumbest Cuomo?; Most Spin; Let's Go Brandon; Biggest Lie; Furthest Reach; Most Nationally-Damaging 'Fake News' Story; Lifetime Achievement in Hackery; Most Overpriced TV Host; Worst Co-Opted Influencer; Most Hysterical; Dying in Darkness; Starving Polar Bear; Worst Host; Worst Show; and Most Likely To Cry On Air.

The Annual Media Fibbys award categories is a fitting end to this chapter and the YouTube video with an Oscar awards ceremony setup that goes with it can be seen in the Appendix link.

## 5 – Illiberal Journalists Defy Facts, Logic & Universal Truths in the 'Name of Free Speech'

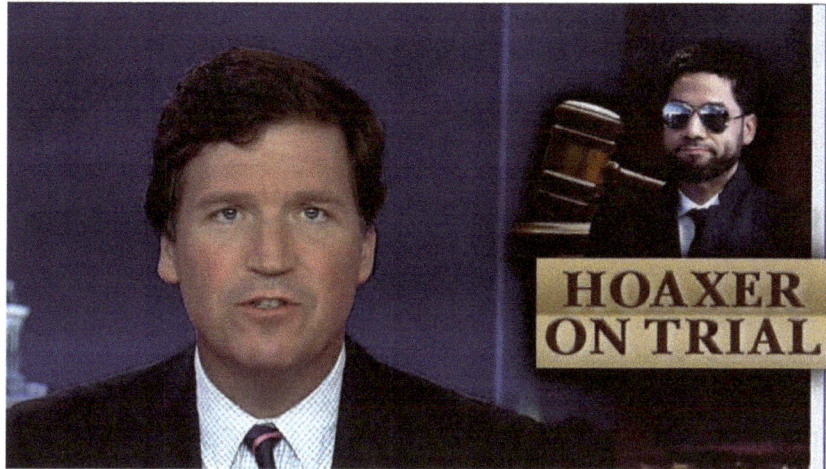

*Credit: Fox News – Provocative Fox newscaster Tucker Carlson calls out the mediacrats and fake news journalists for believing in the Jussie Smollett hoax-story from day one.*

After a century of journalism based on the ethos of fairness, objectivity, and balance, the news media, generally speaking, have abandoned their venerable values. According to Dr. Tobe Berkovitz and his November 2016 *Newsmax* piece titled "The Biggest Loser: Mainstream Media" mainstream media has become obsessed with an internal debate over the concept of "false equivalency," also called "false balance."

The false equivalency theory holds that once a candidate 's rhetoric ventures beyond the accepted mainstream paradigm and proves offensive to the sensibilities of elite gatekeepers (i.e., the media), that balance, objectivity, and fairness become moot.

Stories that rely on these classic journalistic principles become "false" because they do not treat a candidate who espouses potentially offensive ideas—building a wall and "extreme vetting" of Muslims—the same way they treat a candidate who does not hold those views.

In the current election cycle, the sacrificial lamb to false equivalency was NBC's Matt Lauer. He was vilified by his media brethren for daring to pose follow-up questions to the former secretary of state over her homebrew email server, and for not jumping on Trump every time he made a dubious statement. *New York Times* columnist Nicholas Kristof branded Lauer's performance "an embarrassment to journalism." Lauer's offense? He treated Trump and Clinton equally.

The 24-hour news cycle, the rise of social media, and the turn to overtly partisan journalism from both ends of the political spectrum are aggravating the social disruption and undermining the business of journalism in the 21st century. Today, "balance" has come to mean competing, uber-partisan talking heads who provide grist for the cable programming mill.

## Can We Trust the Media: Are They Fair and Balanced?

The profession of news sharing involves the presentation of facts. Opinion related topics should present multiple views. Unfortunately, editorial bias has become increasingly prevalent, with news often leaning to one side as noted in D.J. Wilson's Association of Mature American Citizens (AMAC) article "Is the Media Fair?" When media bias prevails, whether left or right, or somewhere in between, journalistic objectivity is lost and the ability for audiences to decide issues for themselves falls to the wayside.

An examination of Trump's first 100 days in office reflects forward progress for his administration. Trump, at a historic pace, enacted more legislation and signed more executive orders than any other president in half a century. Trump's assertive stance on immigration has worked to decrease the flow of illegal entry into the United States through Mexico. The President's swift response to Syria's dictator Bashar al-Assad's use of chemical weapons on innocent civilians was a step to prevent and deter the end of chemical weapons.

Trump promotes America's energy independence, restoration of economic optimism, create jobs, rebuild the military, and to repeal and replace failing Obamacare.

Meanwhile, the media remained adversarial. Using Twitter as a forum, Trump singled out *The New York Times*, CNN, NBC, "and many more" in a February 2017 tweet which read, "The FAKE NEWS media is not my enemy, it is the enemy of the American people. SICK!"

A revised version deleted the word "sick" and added ABC and CBS to the list. Preceding the tweet, Trump openly criticized press coverage during a 77-minute news conference. One of the biggest things Trump says he learned in his first 100 days in office is the extent of dishonesty in the news media.

It's widely accepted that politicians, such as Trump, who do not subscribe to mainstream media's left leaning ideologies, become targets of the press.

A study, conducted by the Harvard Kennedy School's Shorenstein Center on Media, Politics, and Public Policy, analyzed Trump's first 100 days in office. The study found that "Trump received unsparing coverage for most weeks of his presidency, without a single major topic where Trump's coverage, on balance, was more positive than negative, setting a new standard for unfavorable press coverage of a President."

It was concluded that Fox was the only news outlet in the study that came close to giving Trump positive coverage overall. The study noted a variation in the tone of Fox's coverage, depending upon the topic. Media Research Center (MRC), conducted a study in April that showed that Trump received "by far the most hostile press treatment of any incoming American President."

The study also concluded that TV news pushed a relentlessly negative agenda (see chart on next page).

**The 'Mediacrats' Are Everywhere!**

Congressman Lamar Smith, U.S. Representative for Texas' 21st congressional district and founder of the House Media Fairness Caucus, called for the media to adhere to the highest standards of reporting to provide the American people with facts, balanced stories, and fair coverage of the news. Smith stated, "The media and Democrats are so close in association and so close in their philosophical views that we might as well use one word to describe both, and that's Mediacrats."

Due to extreme negative coverage, Trump labeled the media as the "opposition party" to his administration, and he encouraged his supporters to "...do your part to fight back against the media's attacks and deceptions."

In an unusual break of protocol, Trump barred some reporters from attending his daily off-camera briefing. When speaking at the Coast Guard commencement in May 2017, Trump directly addressed his negative treatment by the media. "No politician in history, and I say this with great surety, has been treated worse or more unfairly."

Controversial Civil Rights Activist Malcolm X once said, "The media's the most powerful entity on earth. They have the power to make the innocent guilty and to make the guilty innocent, and that's power.

Because they control the masses." The press has slammed Trump for many things; the controversy surrounding former National Security Advisor Mike Flynn, allegations of a Russian-Trump interference in the 2016 election, the timing of the firing of FBI Director James Comey, Trump's relationship with German Chancellor Angela Merkel, legality of the travel ban, and withdrawal from the Paris Climate Accord.

Trump is sometimes criticized for the contents of his tweets, but the 45th President has an advantage: he can bypass the press and bring his voice directly to the people. According to Twitter, Trump has 80.3 million followers and counting as of May 28, 2020, before they cancelled his account.

## Pew Study: Media Bias Against Trump is Real and Extreme

The President and his supporters have often lamented unfair coverage from sources they dub 'fake news,' and this study below reported by Rusty Weiss in the October 2017 Liberty Unyielding, titled "Pew Study: Media Bias Against Trump is Real and Extreme," confirms their suspicions.

While the fact that the media has been unfair to Trump should come as no surprise to anyone paying attention, the rate of negative coverage might raise an eyebrow. The Pew study indicates that 62 percent of the media coverage of this President has been negative, while a scant 5 percent has been positive.

Compare that to two other presidents who were somewhat polarizing in their initial days in the White House—Bill Clinton and George W. Bush. Both had more negative coverage than positive, but the numbers were relatively close. According to the research, Clinton had 28 percent negative media stories to 27 percent positive, while Bush had 28 percent negative to 22 percent positive.

That's nothing like what former President Obama received from a media that practically fawned over him on a daily basis. His coverage—42 percent *positive* to 20 percent negative.

"Compared with the first 60 days of the Clinton, Bush and Obama presidencies, news outlets' evaluations of Trump's start in office were far more negative and less positive," a summary of the report states. "About six-in-ten news stories about Trump's first 60 days (62%) carried an overall negative assessment of his words or actions."

"That is about three times more negative than for Obama (20%) and roughly twice that of Bush and Clinton (28% each)."

"Coverage was also far less positive, with just 5% of stories conveying an overall positive assessment of the president and the administration," the study continues. "This is in sharp contrast to Obama's first days in 2009, when 42% of the stories offered an overall positive assessment."

Another recent study out of Harvard indicated that during his first 100 days in office, 93 percent of the mainstream media's coverage toward President Trump was negative. Next time Trump is complaining about unfair media coverage, understand this—he's absolutely right.

### Can Any Sapient Being Deny Trump Labeling Fake News as "Fake News?"

"No!" they cannot, and the majority of content outlined by the Media Research Center (MRC) shows why.

Going back to the 2016 presidential election fake news that Bozell and Graham captured, CNN commentator Sally Kohn lit some warning flares of her own. Even if you couldn't vote for Hillary, "the woman who's running with the impeccable and vast record of experience, if that's not enough for people, at least stopping us from being Nazi Germany would hopefully get Democrats and others to turn out." CNN anchor Alisyn Camerota left the Nazi smear unchallenged. Three days later on CNN, Kohn drove the hyperbole into Fantasyland. She worried: "When Trump institutes internment camps and suspends habeas; we'll all look back and feel pretty bad."

The Nazi smears were all the rage for the outraged! *New York Times* columnist David Brooks cracked on Meet the Press: "If we're going to get Trump, we might as well get the Nuremberg rallies to go with it!"

CNN host Erin Burnett badgered Florida's Republican governor, Rick Scott. "The current president of Mexico—two former presidents of Mexico—have compared him to Hitler," she said. "Vicente Fox, former president, specifically said, 'He reminds me of Hitler.' It's direct. It's not an allusion. It's a direct thing. 'He reminds me of Hitler.' Do they have a point?"

By March 15, 2016, Trump had won nineteen of the first twenty-nine state primaries or caucuses and his opponents were dropping like flies.

By May 13, as Trump closed in on the Republican nomination, NPR's On the Media host Bob Garfield lost control of his metaphors and, for a moment, his mind. Trump's "supposedly courageous candor is contaminated with the most cowardly hate speech—racism, xenophobia, misogyny, incitement, breathtaking ignorance on issues, both foreign and domestic, and a nuclear recklessness, reminiscent of a raving meth-head, with a machete on an episode of Cops."

Trump was no longer a joke. He was a threat, and once the leftists convinced themselves Trump was a national menace, it wasn't long before some of them started talking up violence. The *Huffington Post* published an article by Jesse Benn on June 6, 2016, headlined "Sorry, Liberals, a Violent Response to Trump Is as Logical as Any." Benn argued: "In the face of media, politicians, and GOP primary voters normalizing Trump as a presidential candidate—whatever your personal beliefs regarding violent resistance—there's an inherent value in forestalling Trump's normalization. Violent resistance accomplishes this."

Benn wasn't kidding. After a radical leftist gunned down Congressman Steve Scalise and several others in June 2017, Benn tweeted the shooter some advice: "For violent resistance to work, it'd need to be organized. Individual acts can be understandable, but likely counterproductive ineffective."

Then there was the army of amateur psychiatrists. On June 8, 2016, CBS contributor Nancy Giles insisted to MSNBC host Lawrence O'Donnell that Trump was "clinically insane." O'Donnell agreed. "You're not alone," he responded. "There's a lot of clinicians who have been speculating about that." Unsurprisingly for O'Donnell, he didn't produce a single name.

Legendary *Washington Post* reporter Carl Bernstein kept dropping the political F-word on Trump, as in this CNN interview snippet on October 21, 2016: "This campaign is now about a neo-fascist—I keep coming back to that—sociopath... He is setting himself up as the head of ... a real neo-fascist movement... Is there going to be remnants of a neo-fascist movement that he leads in this country after this election? It's a dangerous thing. We're in a dangerous place."

## Multi-Media Bias Basics

Over the years, the Media Research Center has catalogued the views of journalists on the subject of bias. A number of journalists have admitted that the majority of their brethren approach the news from a liberal angle.

Surveys of journalists' self-reported voting habits show them backing the Democratic candidate in every presidential election since 1964, including landslide losers George McGovern, Walter Mondale and Michael Dukakis. In 2004, a poll conducted by the University of Connecticut found journalists backed John Kerry over George W. Bush by a greater than two-to-one margin.

Compared to their audiences, journalists are far more likely to say they are Democrats or liberals, and they espouse liberal positions on a wide variety of issues. A 2004 poll by the Pew Research Center for The People & The Press found five times more journalists described themselves as "liberal" as said they were "conservative."

Many journalists continue to deny the liberal bias that taints their profession. During the height of CBS's forged memo scandal during the 2004 campaign, Dan Rather insisted that the problem wasn't his bias, it was his anybody who criticized him. "People who are so passionately partisan politically or ideologically committed basically say, 'Because he won't report it our way, we're going to hang something bad around his neck and choke him with it, check him out of existence if we can, if not make him feel great pain,'" Rather told *USA Today* in September 2004. "They know that I'm fiercely independent and that's what drives them up a wall."

The Media Research Center (MRC) continuously reports on instances of the liberal bias in the mainstream media. Daily Bias Alerts offer a regular roundup of the latest instances of biased reporting, their NewsBusters blog allows Web users to post their own reactions. MRC's Media Reality Check reports showcase important stories that the news media have distorted or ignored, and several times each year the MRC publishes its Special Reports offering in-depth documentation of the media's bias on specific issues.

They also have the Chris Cuomo Memorial Award for Worst Quote of the Year and in 2021 it was a challenging task but an esteemed panel of NewsBusters editors led by MRC President L. Brent Bozell and MRC's Vice President for Research and Publications Brent Baker boiled down all the biased outbursts from lefty hack hosts, anchors, reporters and pundits in 2021 and declared a winner(s):

This year we had a tie. The two quotes reflect the stark double-standard seen in the coverage between President Joe Biden and Donald Trump. During his first three months in office, the broadcast evening newscasts showered President Joe Biden with 59% positive press. Four years ago, those same programs were hammering Trump with 89% negative press.

The bias was so strong at CNN they produced not one but two contenders who earned the dubious honor of worst quote of the year, as previously mentioned the Chris Cuomo Memorial Award For Worst Quote of The Year. MRC President Bozell announced: "This explains why CNN is now unwelcome even in airports. CNN is to news what Cuomo was to integrity."

Without further ado here are the winners:

"If you voted for Trump, you voted for the person who the Klan supported. You voted for the person who Nazis support. You voted for the person who the alt-right supports. That's the crowd that you are in."—*Host Don Lemon on CNN Tonight with Don Lemon, January 14.*

"Those lights that are, that are just shooting out from the Lincoln Memorial along the reflecting pool....It's like almost extensions of Joe Biden's arms embracing America. It was a moment where the new President came to town and sort of convened the country in this moment of remembrance, outstretching his arms." —*CNN Political Director David Chalian during CNN's Inauguration coverage, January 19.*

## The Media Bubble is Real—And Worse Than You Think

Heterodox Academy leader Musa al-Gharbi shared his April 2017 viewpoint diverse report "The Media Bubble is Real—And Worse Than You Think" with Heterodox Academy's 3,000 plus academic membership as follows:

Journalistic outlets face many of the same challenges as academic institutions. Like the academy (especially social research fields), most newsrooms skew decisively left. According to the American Journalism Project—one of the longest-running and most comprehensive studies of U.S. journalists (conducted every ten years since 1972)—only about 7% of contemporary journalists are Republicans.

This is a major decrease as compared to previous studies, suggesting that much like U.S. institutions of higher learning, there has been a significant and fairly rapid ideological shift in newsrooms since the 90s. The American Journalism report also shows that, like the academy, journalism is also suffering a legitimacy crisis driven, in part, by the perceived distance between reporters and the publics they are supposed to serve.

### Americans' Trust in Mass Media, by Political Party

In general, how much trust and confidence do you have in the mass media -- such as newspapers, TV and radio -- when it comes to reporting the news fully, accurately and fairly -- a great deal, a fair amount, not very much or none at all?

% Great deal/Fair amount

— Republicans — Independents — Democrats

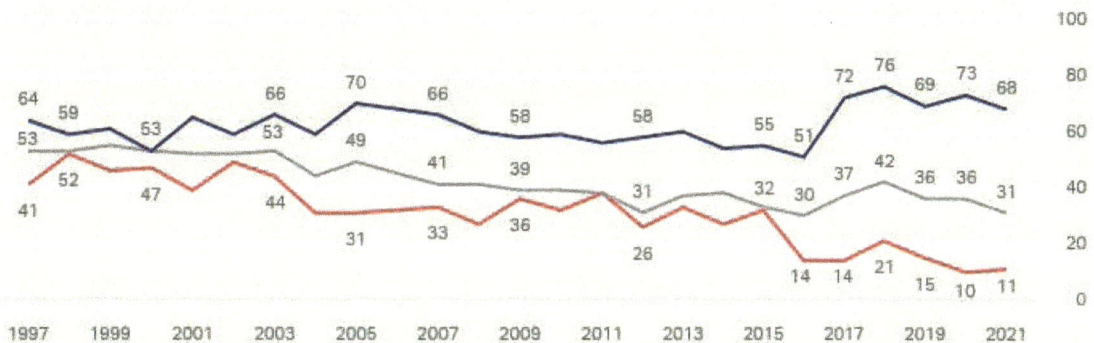

Data from 1972, 1974 and 1976 not shown

GALLUP

A recent study by Jack Shafer and Tucker Doherty, published by Politico, demonstrates just how vast this divide has grown:

Where do journalists work, and how much has that changed in recent years? To determine this, Doherty excavated labor statistics and cross-referenced them against voting patterns and Census data to figure out just what the American media landscape looks like, and how much it has changed.

### The Results Read Like a Revelation

The national media really does work in a bubble, something that wasn't true as recently as 2008. And the bubble is growing more extreme. Concentrated heavily along the coasts, the bubble is both geographic and political. If you're a working journalist, odds aren't just that you work in a pro-Clinton county—odds are that you reside in one of the nation's most pro-Clinton counties…

…The "media bubble" trope might feel overused by critics of journalism who want to sneer at reporters who live in Brooklyn or California and don't get the "real America" of southern Ohio or rural Kansas. But these numbers suggest it's no exaggeration: Not only is the bubble real, but it's more extreme than you might realize. And it's driven by deep industry trends.

The authors then go on to explain why the shift is happening. It turns out, the trend seems to be driven overwhelmingly by structural changes to the industry itself rather than by any type of overt or intentional bias on the part of reporters. Internet publishers are now adding workers at nearly twice the rate newspaper publishers are losing them.

This isn't just a shift in medium. It's also a shift in sociopolitics, and a radical one. Where newspaper jobs are spread nationwide, internet jobs are not: Today, 73 percent of all internet publishing jobs are concentrated in either the Boston-New York-Washington-Richmond corridor or the West Coast crescent that runs from Seattle to San Diego and on to Phoenix. The Chicago area, a traditional media center, captures 5 percent of the jobs, with a paltry 22 percent going to the rest of the country. And almost all the real growth of internet publishing is happening outside the heartland, in just a few urban counties, all places that voted for Clinton. So, when your conservative friends use "media" as a synonym for "coastal" and "liberal," they're not far off the mark.

Something akin to the *Times* ethos thrives in most major national newsrooms found on the Clinton coasts—CNN, CBS, the *Washington Post*, BuzzFeed, Politico and the rest. Their reporters, an admirable lot, can parachute into Appalachia or the rural Midwest on a monthly basis and still not shake their provincial sensibilities: Reporters tote their bubbles with them.

Unfortunately, as the authors explain in great detail, the structural changes driving these bubbles are likely to persist, or even accelerate, in coming years. So, what can be done to mitigate the sociocultural and epistemic costs of these changes?

The best medicine for journalistic myopia isn't re-education camps or a splurge of diversity hiring, though tiny doses of those two remedies wouldn't hurt. Journalists respond to their failings best when their vanity is punctured with proof that they blew a story that was right in front of them. If the burning humiliation of missing the biggest political story in a generation won't change newsrooms, nothing will.

Overall, this seems like a constructive approach—one also advocated in the *Times Higher Education* piece. However, one point of concern remains, namely, the extent to which most reporters actually perceive or acknowledge they did in fact, "blow the story."

## Understanding the Liberal vs. Conservative Imbalance in Journalism

To get an idea of the imbalance, consider the cases of Quinn Norton, a libertarian technology writer, and Sarah Jeong, a progressive technology writer. After the *New York Times* announced that it was hiring Norton for its editorial page, it took just seven hours for progressives to get her fired. On Twitter and in an internal *Times* chat room (as HuffPost reported), Norton was attacked for having tweeted that she was friends with a neo-Nazi hacker whom she had covered.

She had always repudiated his ideology, calling him a "terrible person," but that wasn't enough to save her job. Six months later, in August 2018, when the *Times* hired Jeong for the editorial page, conservative activists unearthed tweets from Jeong, an Asian-American, denigrating white men as well as whites as a race. One used a hashtag "#CancelWhitePeople;" another predicted that whites would soon go extinct and said, "This was my plan all along." The *Times* stuck with its decision to hire her. (The paper recently announced that Jeong would no longer be part of its editorial board, though she will continue as a contributing writer.)

Conservative journalists criticized the *Times* for its double standard, but they didn't unite with the online activists demanding that Jeong be fired. The *Times*'s Bret Stephens wrote a column urging the paper to overlook the offensive tweets. Andrew Sullivan lambasted Jeong's bigotry and the progressive dogma that it's impossible to be racist against whites, but he, too, urged the *Times* not to fire her because media companies should not succumb to online mobs.

You might think that Sullivan's forbearance would win him some points with progressives, and perhaps even make them question their own enthusiasm for purges, but the column didn't play well even with Sullivan's colleagues at the *Times*. Brian Feldman, an associate editor, tweeted: "Andrew Sullivan's newest column is complete garbage and I'm embarrassed to be even tangentially associated with it." Not exactly collegial, but again, that's where we are.

### Media Conservatives: An Endangered Species

When you add it up, 58.47% admit to being left of center. Along with that, another 37.12% claim to be "moderate."

What about the mythic "conservative" financial journalist? In fact, a mere 0.46% of financial journalists called themselves "very conservative," while just 3.94% said they were "somewhat conservative." That's a whopping 4.4% of the total that lean right-of-center.

That's a ratio of 13 "liberals" for every one "conservative." Whatever happened to ideological diversity? Please remember this as you watch the business news or read a financial story in the paper. You might want to take its message with a grain of salt. That's especially true if the piece seems unduly harsh on the free-market system and its many proven benefits. Or if it lauds socialism as an "answer" to society's ills.

This is an enormous problem for the media—perhaps bigger than they realize. A Rasmussen Reports survey in late October 2018 found that 45% of all likely voters in the midterm elections believed "that when most reporters write about a congressional race, they are trying to help the Democratic candidate."

Just 11% said the media would try to help the Republican. And only 35% said they thought reporters simply try to report the news in an unbiased way.

Rasumussen notes that this "helps explain why Democratic voters are much bigger fans of election news coverage" than others. They see it as favorable to their own beliefs. Perhaps that's why the 2016 presidential election results triggered an epic snowflake meltdown and liberal madness.

## What Journalists Think/How Journalists Vote

Reporters should keep their personal opinions from influencing the news stories they write and produce. But journalists are only human. A reporter's political outlook is bound to sway the judgments he or she makes each day, such as what events are newsworthy, and on whom to rely for trustworthy information. It is therefore essential to know if the media truly represent a diverse range of viewpoints or are dominated by just one political philosophy.

Surveys over the past 50 years have consistently found that journalists—especially those at the highest ranks of their profession—are much more liberal than rest of America. They are more likely to vote liberal, more likely to describe themselves as liberal, and more likely to agree with the liberal position on policy matters than members of the general public. The Media Research Center has compiled the relevant data on journalist attitudes, as well as polling showing how the American public's recognition of the media's liberal bias has grown over the years.

These surveys of journalists were conducted by professional pollsters, academics, or news organizations, not by conservatives trying to score a political point against the press. That fact, along with the remarkable consistency of their findings, is powerful proof that liberals are far over-represented in the American media.

**Adding Insult to Injury: Social Media**

The conservative movement is facing a threat to its very existence—a new, insidious form of media censorship. Media bias has always been an enemy of the right. Liberal journalists relied on talking points and talking heads they agreed with for their stories. Conservatives were typically ignored or even targeted by old-school media monopolies.

But while conservatives were excluded, their organizations were still allowed to function and even flourish. The internet gave the right new tools to go around traditional media—websites, email, video, and social media. Conservatives' power online continued to grow as groups expanded their base of supporters and were even able to fundraise online.

Now, all of that is under threat by social media, also known as Big Tech.

The left has become more radicalized, more obsessed with political correctness. They have taken the tools honed by the left for years on college campuses into the tech world. Disagreement is discouraged. Opponents are to be silenced or even banned. Opinions they don't like are termed "hate speech" and those they disagree with are called "bigots." The goal is to deny their opponents the chance to speak, also known as "deplatforming."

Tech companies awash in these so-called progressive worldviews are eager to placate the left. They push diversity initiatives internally that care little for opinion diversity. As a result, their workforces are filled with social justice activists promoting everything from the LGBT agenda to a war on gun rights. Conservatives in that world either go along to get along or find themselves marginalized and even fired.

Furthermore, as latter discussed in this book, anti-conservative bias using deplatforming is coming from major social media services such as Facebook and Twitter, as well as those platforms outright silencing important news that harms Democrats, like the Biden family influence peddling scandal.

Twitter and Facebook regularly place notices and/or restrictions on Trump's tweet and news of voter fraud on the allegation that the opinions and/or evidence expressed and presented are disputed or not yet confirmed. In the four years Trump has been the subject of dishonest and malicious conspiracy claims, particularly the Russia collusion (and so much more), far fewer restrictions, or none at all, are placed on Adam Schiff, other Democrat politicians, or mainstream media outlets peddling their own and/or unrestricted disinformation.

These double standards exist as you will see and are mostly the left's doing.

## CRT Has Seeped Into American Media and Into Americans' Collective Consciousness

The jargon of CRT had seeped into American media, and thus into Americans' collective consciousness, years before the Trump presidency, long before Floyd's death. Goldberg explains:

Starting well before Donald Trump's rise to power, while President Obama was still in office, terms like 'microaggression' and 'white privilege' were picked up by liberal journalists. These terms went from being obscure fragments of academic jargon to commonplace journalistic language in only a few years.... During this same period, while exotic new phrases were entering the discourse, universally recognizable words like 'racism' were being radically redefined. Along with the new language came ideas and beliefs animating a new moral-political framework to apply to public life and American society.

All the beliefs that are espoused today by the three founders of the Black Lives Matter organizations (Alicia Garza, Patrisse Cullors, and Opal Tometi)—that America is institutionally/structurally/systemically racist, that its legal system protects the powerful and amounts to racism codified in statutes, that neutrality and objectivity are impossible to obtain, that "objectivity and individuality are privileges," that the gauge by which to judge America is equality of outcome, that speech and other rights must be suppressed in order to protect the marginalized—come straight from the CRT canon.

Writing about the impact that Michael Brown's death in August 2014 had on the nation, the academic James A. Lindsay observed:

Brown's death mainstreamed Black Lives Matter and, in many respects, many of the core claims and assumptions of critical race theory throughout 2015 and 2016.... Its fundamental claim was that America was systemically racist and that this could be seen most clearly in the American police, criminal justice, and penal systems....

## 'Lived Experience' and 'Lived Realities' Are More Important Arbiters of 'Truth' Than Truth Itself

That none of this was true was irrelevant as Black Lives Matter mainstreamed the idea that 'lived experience' and 'lived realities' are more important arbiters of 'truth' than truth itself. These beliefs are central to the core assumption of critical race theory that 'counter stories' and narratives are more important than facts and truth where systemic racism (and other systemic oppression) is concerned. (This—storytelling, counter story, and narrative related in service to 'politically Black' identity political goals should be forwarded over truth—is usually listed in the top five cornerstone assumptions of critical race theory.)

A September 2020 report from the U.S. Crisis Monitor, which receives support from Princeton University, revealed that BLM activists were involved in 95 percent of the riots between June 2020 and September 2020 for which the identity of the perpetrator was known.57

When the Claremont Review's Charles Kesler called the disturbances "the 1619 riots" (after the CRT-influenced New York Times project that places slavery at the center of everything in America), the architect of the project, Nikole Hannah-Jones tweeted, "It would be an honor. Thank You."

# 6 – Progressivism's Multiculturalism + Wokeness + Cancel Culture = Free Speech Intolerance

*Credit: The Economist.*

The term "cancel culture" has hurtled into popular use as a way of identifying instances of social justice mobbing—essentially, the attack on a person, place, or thing that is perceived as inconsonant with "woke" ideological narratives. When a "cancel culture" event takes place the complainants demand—and often get—offenders fired, shut down, silenced, or otherwise removed from the public eye.

In *Cancel Culture: The Latest Attack on Free Speech and Due Process*, Alan Dershowitz—*New York Times* bestselling author and one of America's most respected legal scholars—makes an argument for free speech, due process, and restraint against the often overeager impulse to completely cancel individuals and institutions at the ever-changing whims of social media-driven crowds.

Alan Dershowitz has been called "one of the most prominent and consistent defenders of civil liberties in America" by Politico and "the nation's most peripatetic civil liberties lawyer and one of its most distinguished defenders of individual rights" by *Newsweek*. Yet he has come under intense criticism for his steadfast and consistent championing of those same principles, and his famed "shoe-on-the-other-foot test," to those who have been "cancelled" for any number of faults, both real and imagined.

Cancel Culture is a defense of due process, free speech, and even-handedness in the application of judgment. It makes the case for restraint and care in decisions about whom and what to cancel, boycott, deplatform, and bar from public life, and offers recommendations for when, why, and to what degree these steps may be appropriate, as long as objective, fair-minded criteria can be determined and met.

While Dershowitz argues against the worst excesses of cancel culture—the rush to judgment and the devastating results it can have on those who may be innocent, the power of social media to effect punishment without a thorough examination of evidence, the idea that historical events can be viewed through the same lens as actions in the present day—he also acknowledges that its defenders ostensibly try to use it to create meaningful, positive change, and notes that cancelling may itself be a constitutionally protected form of free speech.

In the end, Cancel Culture represents an icon in the defense of free speech and due process reckoning with the greatest challenge and threat to these rights since the rise of McCarthyism. It is essential reading for anyone interested in or concerned about cancel culture, its effects on our society, and its significance in a greater historical and political context.

## Taking on the 'Wokeism' Movement

John McWhorter, an African-American, teaches at Columbia University and has been published in the nation's leading left-wing journals. But he is not your typical liberal. The Woke antiracism "we're being sold," he believes, "isn't the path to a more just and equitable world for all. It's the barrier."

McWhorter's thesis: Wokeism "has come to excite a grievous amount of influence over American institutions to the point that we are beginning to accept, as normal, the kinds of language, policies, and actions that Orwell wrote of as fiction."

He argues that Woke ideology "is one under which white people calling themselves our saviors make Black people look like the dumbest, weakest, most self-indulgent human beings in the history of our species, and teach Black people to revel in the status and cherish it as making us special."

The Woke movement has morphed into a modern secular religion that does not tolerate dissent. Dissenting is a form of "environmental pollution" for disciples. Hence, Woke inquisitors, or the "Elect," as McWhorter calls them, demand white people submit to self-mortification because of their "original sin," namely white privilege.

According to their catechism, for a white person to say "I don't see color" is racist. To assert one is not racist proves one is racist. Racism is "what makes one white." And for black kids to "embrace school" is bad because it is "acting white." To hold a contrary view is "heresy" and any black thinkers who dare to "question the Elect orthodoxy are traitorous Judases out to make a buck."

Elect ideology, McWhorter concludes, …teaches black people that cries of weakness are a form of strength. It teaches us that in the richness of this thing called life, the most interesting thing about you is that the ruling class doesn't like you enough. It teaches us that to insist that black people can achieve under less than perfect conditions is ignorant slander. It teaches us that we are the first people in the history of the species for whom it is a form of heroism to embrace the slogan "Yes, we can't!" Elect philosophy is, in all innocence, a form of racism in itself. Black America has met nothing so disempowering—including the cops—since Jim Crow.

McWhorter calls for the Elect "anti-white" ideology to be exorcised from school curriculums and calls for commonsense programs to tackle black America's problem.

These include making sure kids "not from book-lined homes" learn to read via phonics, ending the war on drugs, and advocating "vocational training for poor people," and battling "the idea that 'real' people go to college."

Such modest proposals may put the nation on the road to "saving Black America for real." McWhorter concedes that if a white man wrote Woke Racism, he would be dismissed as racist. He also expects to be labeled a traitor and self-hating. Nevertheless, the fearless McWhorter dedicates his book "to each who find it within themselves to take a stand against the detour in humanity's intellectual, cultural, and moral development."

During the fall campaign, we witnessed the beginning of a movement dedicated to taking a stand against Woke's disordered ideology that divides us as a people. And touting Professor McWhorter's prescriptions may help in the battle to restore unity and the cogency of our Nation's original motto, "E pluribus unum"—"Out of many, one."

## The Woke Crowd Took a Beating on Election Day 2021

Per John McWhorter's November 2021 *Newsmax* article "Taking on the Woke Movement," the "Woke" crowd took a beating on Election Day 2021. Voters of every race and creed came out to express opposition to defunding the police, teaching critical race theory, and classroom mask mandates. Here's why:

- In Virginia, Democrat Terry McAuliffe's statement, "I don't think parents should be telling schools what they should teach," backfired. Enraged parents — many who voted for Biden last year — turned against him and elected the first Republican governor in a dozen years.

- In Buffalo, New York, the Woke candidate for mayor, Socialist-Democrat, India Walton, lost to a write-in campaign for incumbent Byron Brown.

- In Minneapolis, Minnesota, voters rejected a ballot measure that called for the elimination of the police department in favor of a Woke-style department of Public Safety.

- MSNBC's Joy Reid called governor-elect Youngkin of Virginia a "soft white racist."

- Over at CNN, Brianna Keller, claimed Youngkin was elected because of "dog whistle racism." Anthony Van Jones, described Youngkin's victory as "the emergence of the Delta variant of Trumpism."

- The ever-delusional Congresswoman Alexandria Ocasio-Cortex made the ludicrous claim that McAuliffe lost in Virginia because he dared to run as a moderate.

- At the White House, Deputy Press Secretary Karine Jean-Pierre, accused Republicans of "lying" and stuck to the Woke party line that kids "should learn about critical race theory."

With the left in denial, the anti-Woke movement has an opportunity to build on their ballot box success. And to prepare for the 2022 elections, must reading is John McWhorter's new book, *Woke Racism: How a New Religion has Betrayed Black America.*

## Progressivism Isn't Progressive: It's Recycled Marxism

According to historian William Leuchtenburg: The Progressives believed in the Hamiltonian concept of positive government, of a national government directing the destinies of the nation at home and abroad. They had little but contempt for the strict construction of the Constitution by conservative judges, who would restrict the power of the national government to act against social evils and to extend the blessings of democracy to less favored lands. The real enemy was particularism, state rights, limited government.

However, an entrenched and growing bureaucracy, without drastic measures, becomes an entrenched and immovable force, whether it's in American government or our educational systems. And because the intellectual capital of our educational institutions is so heavily weighted with liberal and leftist ideals, it appears they've become a safe haven for today's progressivism movement, starting with the Frankfort School at Columbia established in 1934 during the midst of the Great Depression.

The Frankfurt School's biggest intellectual creation was Critical Theory, an approach to cultural analysis that focuses on criticizing existing social structures. To counter Critical Theory, Social Justice, and Progressivism, I argue that the message, goals, and sapience from organizations like the Heterodox Academy, FIRE, and the Templeton Foundation and their "progressive" programs, trump critical theory as you will see clearly in Chapter 13.

Along with sapience, they are creating a reasonable and illuminating path for second age of enlightenment on campus to follow that promotes viewpoint diversity, cherishes intellectual humility and fights for freedom of speech. To understand and appreciate this second age of campus enlightenment, we need to first understand and identify Critical Theory, New Modernism, and Progressivism.

### Understanding Critical Theory and the Frankfurt School

Critical Theory is a social theory oriented toward critiquing and changing society as a whole. It differs from traditional theory, which focuses only on understanding or explaining society. Critical theories aim to dig beneath the surface of social life and uncover the assumptions that keep human beings from a full and true understanding of how the world works.

Over the years, many social scientists and philosophers who rose to prominence after the Frankfurt School have adopted the goals and tenets of critical theory. We can recognize critical theory today in many feminist theories and approaches to conducting social science. It is also found in critical race theory, cultural theory, gender, and queer theory, as well as in media theory and media studies.

Critical theory as it is known today can be traced to Karl Marx's critiques of the economy and society. It is inspired greatly by Marx's theoretical formulation of the relationship between economic base and ideological superstructure and focuses on how power and domination operate.

Following in Marx's critical footsteps, Hungarian György Lukács and Italian Antonio Gramsci developed theories that explored the cultural and ideological sides of power and domination. After seeing that wealth and quality of life for workers was increasing after his imprisonment from the Italian fascist regime, Gramsci theorized from his many letters published in his *Prison Notebooks* written between 1929 and 1935, that traditional Western values must be destroyed in order to promote Communism, because old Marxist economic arguments could no longer be made.

In other words, workers were no longer poor enough and desperate enough for Communism to appeal to them. For these ideas to take hold, cultural structures such as religion (Christianity), the family, and traditional values of personal responsibility must be broken down.

Shortly after Lukács and Gramsci published their ideas, the Institute for Social Research was founded at the University of Frankfurt, and the Frankfurt School of critical theorists took shape. The work of the Frankfurt School members, including Max Horkheimer, Theodor Adorno, Erich Fromm, Walter Benjamin, Jürgen Habermas, and Herbert Marcuse (whom I already introduced), is considered the heart of critical theory.

One of the most influential members of the Frankfurt School, Herbert Marcuse fled to Columbia University in New York in 1934 following Hitler's rise to power where the new Frankfurt School of Columbia was started. The Frankfurt School, known more appropriately as Critical Theory, is a philosophical and sociological movement spread across many universities around the world.

During the civil rights and antiwar movements against the Vietnam conflict in the 1960s, Marcuse's *One-Dimensional Man: Studies in the Ideology of Advanced Industrial Society*, a 1964 best seller by the philosopher, primarily known by the "power of negative thinking" became the standard for revolutionary speech in the movement he called the "Great Refusal."

His devotees included campus radical Angela Davis, from Brandeis University. Countless students read his books. New Left marchers carried posters of his face, along with images of the Chinese communist leader Mao Tse Tung, the Argentinean guerrilla leader Che Guevara, and the Vietnamese president Ho Chi Minh.

In contrast to orthodox Marxism, Marcuse champions non-integrated forces of minorities, outsiders, and radical intelligentsia, attempting to nourish oppositional thought and behavior through promoting radical thinking and opposition. *One-Dimensional Man* made Marcuse famous for this.

## Today's Progressivism as the New Marxism

As in Marx's older drama, the moral imperative of progressives is to once again "set things right." In Marx's time this was the task of revolutionaries. Today this task falls to progressive politicians and activists, social justice reformers, civil rights workers, cultural appropriation enforcers, diversity, and inclusion warriors and the like who have spread into the media, government, college campuses, neighborhood organizations and workplaces.

Marxist revolutionaries sought to set things right by leading a revolution to overthrow the capitalist system and replace it with a just economic system. Progressives want to set things right through social change in order to create a just society. In a just society everyone is equal: men and women, immigrants and native-born, persons of various racial and ethnic groups, heterosexuals, and homosexuals, first and third world people, disabled and able-bodied. This will be a society free from the "isms" of sexism, nativism, racism, heterosexism, colonialism, and ableism.

To the progressive, the success of the newly liberated oppressed person must not be limited by the extent of his talent or effort. Success is merited by the very existence of his membership in an oppressed group. As in Marxist theory—"from each according to his ability, to each according to his needs"—even people of lesser abilities and efforts deserve equal outcomes. The progressive sees anything less than this as failure.

Undergirding all this is the assumption that a just society will be gained through the intervention of government. Only government can force the needed changes. This is achieved through a complex and extensive web of government mechanisms: civil rights laws; affirmative action programs; minimum wage laws; housing assistance; guaranteed income; income maintenance programs that seamlessly transfer wealth from haves to have nots; block grants to states; guaranteed health care for all; national disaster relief...and more.

Per Berger, "In the progressive view there is little tolerance for government that cannot deliver equal outcomes for all. However, every human being is unique and not standardized widgets, so ultimately, government is incapable of creating a society of equals (which is impossible)."

### The Critical Method of the Frankfurt School Fuels Progressivism

Some of the key issues and philosophical preoccupations of the Frankfurt School's Critical Theory and methods involve the critique of modernity and capitalist society, the definition of social emancipation, as well as the detection of the pathologies of society. The academic influence of Critical Theory throughout America's academia provides the foundation for today's progressivism thought, issues, and actions.

These foundations were influenced by Marxism and/or inherently Marxist in nature.

For a sapient being and follower of the Scientific Method—Critical Theory is a far-left social philosophy pertaining to the reflective assessment and critique of society and culture in order to reveal and challenge power structures. A primary criticism of the theory is that it is anti-scientific, both for its lack of the use of the scientific method, and for its overt criticism of science as a tool used for oppression of marginalized groups of people.

The first generation of Marxist Frankfurt School philosophers, particularly Herbert Marcuse and Jurgen Habermas, have influenced generations within the American academy and its students throughout, and turned global, influencing methodological approaches in other European academic contexts and disciplines after World War II.

It was during this phase that Richard Bernstein, a second generation Frankfurt School philosopher and contemporary of Habermas, embraced the research agenda of Critical Theory and significantly helped its development in American universities (after the initial influence of Marcuse) when he joined in 1989 the graduate faculty at the New School for Social Research in New York.

This first taste of Critical Theory is only a brief intro to set the table for an in depth analysis of CT and CCT and CRT.

## Marxism and Progressivism: A Play in Two Acts

From Dr. Raymond M. Berger, "Marxism and Progressivism: A Play in Two Acts" published 2018 in *The Times of Israel*, about why every Marxist government in history has been a repressive nightmare, the section is drawn from.

Today's progressives believe they are onto something new. But the progressive script is an old theatrical play with the same drama as the earlier communist play. It stars the same protagonists dressed up with different names. And despite the hype of the performance, when the curtain comes down after the finale, both plays are equally unsatisfying.

**Yesterday's Communism**

Communist theory was first expounded by the nineteenth century philosopher, Karl Marx. Marx crafted a morality play. He observed economic changes wrought by the early industrial revolution in Western Europe, and he correctly perceived the inherent injustice in the evolving economic system.

This was high drama, complete with villains and downtrodden heroes. The villains were the bourgeoisie, the owners of industry or what Marx called the "means of production." The downtrodden heroes were the proletariat or workers.

When the enclosure movement threw the serfs off the manor and into the towns and cities, they were robbed of their former dignity and means of livelihood. Forced to resort to selling their labor as their only means of survival, they became wage slaves. Gone was the pride of craftsmanship and the stability of manor life. As the bourgeoisie exploited the "surplus labor"—that is, the money value created by proletariat labor—the proletarian was robbed of the fruits of his labor.

Even worse, he was now subject to the wild swings of economic expansion and contraction and hence to misery and insecurity. At the same time, societal wealth became increasingly concentrated in the hands of the small bourgeoisie class while the proletariat remained impoverished.

The system was maintained by a false consciousness in which the proletariat failed to recognize the "class structure" of society and the exploitive nature of the bourgeois class and the system of capitalism.

The play's drama was advanced by revolutionaries—like Marx—who alerted the proletariat to their exploitation and encouraged them to overthrow the capitalist system. The workers would inevitably open their eyes. According to Marx, this would lead to a revolution and a "dictatorship of the proletariat."

But despite the dictatorial nature of this transitional phase, the new paradigm would result in a just society in which each contributed according to his ability and took according to his need. Thus, the unjust capitalist society would be replaced by a just and classless society.

The central purpose of twentieth century communism was to "set things right."

**Today's Progressivism**

Berger continues that today's progressive movement—different from the American Progressive movement of the late nineteenth century—repackaged this Marxist theory with new actors and injustices but the same old drama.

The epic struggle between bourgeoisie and proletariat is replaced by the morally laden struggles between privileged and oppressed actors with new names. In this contemporary version of Marxist drama, people of color are pitted against a white male power structure supported by a mysterious but powerful force of institutional racism. Women are pitted against a male patriarchy that invades not only the workplace but intrudes into the very intimacy of the home to wreak injustice.

As the blinders of the new false consciousness fall from the eyes of the oppressed, new oppressed groups emerge. Some are based on "sexual minority status"—gay people, transsexuals, intersex, non-gender conforming—others on physical traits—the disabled, the unattractive, fat people. In place of an exploitive bourgeoisie there are heterosexists, cis-gender persons, those who exploit the disabled and those who engage in "lookism," that is, those who exploit others due to their appearance.

Added to these colorful actors are the multitude of colonized people of the third world and their exploitive evil colonizers. Because this is a drama, the respective roles of colonizer and colonized are always simplified, with few benefits but much evil attributed to colonization. And even long after the departure of the colonizers from formerly colonized lands, the injustice of the original colonial sin is said to persist, as every problem of the newly independent peoples is attributed to the legacy of colonialism.

In the same way, injustices based on race and ethnicity are said to live on, in the form of the legacy of racism, even after much of the oppression is alleviated.

More recently the world has seen a northward migration of millions from impoverished and violent lands in the south. Amidst the confusion of roles—are these immigrants, migrants, or refugees?—these folks join the long line of oppressed people who are unjustly exploited and abused in their adopted countries. There is nothing more dramatic and poignant than these huddled masses, to use the words of poet Emma Lazarus.

These are new actors in an old drama around the struggle between persecutor and victim, between exploiter and exploited. Marx's focus on labor has now extended to every conceivable human difference, as if the very existence of difference is morally wrong.

**The Left Has Undergone an Unsapient Ideological Transformation**

Dr. Jonathan Haidt has observed: In the recent past, important social matters were settled though free and open discussion and debate using logic and reason. Our American civil order is predicated on this. It works well when those engaged share a conviction that universal truth exists—regardless of one's beliefs, feelings, and opinions.

For today's campus radicals, feelings have largely replaced logic and reason. A generation ago, social justice was understood as equality of treatment and opportunity. Per Haidt, "… If black people are getting discriminated against in hiring and you fight that, that's justice."

Today justice means equal outcomes. "There are two ideas now in the academic left that weren't there ten years ago," Haidt says. "One is that everyone is racist because of unconscious bias, and the other is that everything is racist because of systemic racism." That makes justice impossible to achieve: "When you cross that line into insisting if there's not equal outcomes then some people and some institutions and some systems are racist, sexist, then you're setting yourself up for eternal conflict and injustice."

Haidt is right. If the goal of this new social justice is equality of outcome, you are setting yourself up for eternal conflict, injustice, and ultimately social disintegration.

Equal outcomes can only be achieved through the tyrannical imposition of power and coercion, with a resulting loss of individual freedom. It results in human beings being objectified, manipulated, and otherwise treated unjustly.

Where it has been attempted—in places like Maoist China and the Soviet Union—the outcomes were utterly destructive. Millions were imprisoned and murdered. Millions more lost their families, livelihoods, and freedoms. These are the facts!

## Why Social Justice is Wrong to Demand Equality of Outcomes

A primary objective of the new progressive orthodoxy is to unmask or expose the many oppressive structures that are pervasive in Western civilization. Adherents do this by exposing inequalities and fighting for "social justice." There is a plethora of examples as Scott Allen shows below:

Exhibit A: Laws and regulations that excluded gays and lesbians from the institution of marriage resulted in unequal and discriminatory treatment. Social justice demands that these laws, rooted in Judeo-Christian beliefs about the exclusivity of marriage as one male and one female, be overturned. This notion of marriage was judged to be hateful, homophobic, and bigoted. It needed to be torn down—a dream realized in 2015 when the Supreme Court, by judicial fiat, made homosexual "marriage" legal in all 50 states. Family madness!

Exhibit B: Norms and civic ordinances that exclude transgendered people from using the bathrooms and locker facilities of their choice are discriminatory. Equality demands that all people, regardless of gender, be able to use the restroom facilities, locker rooms (and eventually, to play on the sports teams) of their choosing. After all, the notion of a simple gender binary male-female reality is oppressive, a legacy of Western, Judeo-Christian beliefs that were structurally imposed on everyone. Sexual madness!

Exhibit C: The percentage of black students expelled from St. Paul Minnesota public schools is greater than the number of white students expelled as a percent of their population. The superintendent cites the cause for this inequality as systemic racism. Others wonder if the actions of black students themselves might be behind their higher rates of expulsion, but the second "core doctrine" of the new religion, multiculturalism, stigmatizes anyone who would ask such a question. Crime rate madness!

To do so would be to commit the cardinal sin of blaming the victim. Blame must be attributed to larger social forces, in this case, structural or systemic racism endemic in American culture. The solution: Require teachers and administrators to bring down the numbers of black expulsions, without regard to the actions of the students themselves. The result: More violent and chaotic schools that make learning almost impossible.

## This Un-Sapient Notion of Social Justice is Relatively New

In a previous post, Os Guinness quoted New York University professor Dr. Jonathan Haidt: "A generation ago, social justice was understood as equality of treatment and opportunity... If black people are getting discriminated against in hiring and you fight that, that's justice. Today justice means equal outcomes ... an idea that wasn't there ten years ago."

Guinness summarizes this final core doctrine:

Social justice movements must each deconstruct all that oppresses its victims anywhere ... They invite an attack on all accepted truths, because unmasking the social fictions is seen as a way of liberating ourselves from the oppression of socially constructed realities that have imprisoned us without our realizing it ... It is an open invitation to an assault on tradition and on long-held ways of seeing and doing things. In other words, on Western civilization and Judeo-Christian beliefs.

First, there must be liberation from God and therefore from meaning and ethics, from solid institutions such as marriage and the family, and from all inhibiting categories such as "the binary opposites" of "male" and "female" ... There must be liberation from nature and even from what was considered our own nature.

Guinness puts his finger on an important insight when he says that the new religion is animated by a desire to be "liberated from God." The ideological roots of the new religion, whether Postmodernism, Marxist or Nietzschean, are ultimately atheistic.

The attack on Western civilization is really an indirect way of attacking Judeo-Christian beliefs, which ultimately is a kind of rage and rebellion against God and His created order. In this sense, it isn't new at all. It goes all the way back to Genesis 3 and the fallen heart's desire to overthrow God and assume ultimate authority for ourselves.

### Social Justice Warriors' Chilling Effect on Political Correctness Culture

Per Scott Allen: It has gotten to the point where people are fearful of sharing what they think about reality. In an email interview, *The Atlantic's* Conor Friedersdorf engaged a 22-year-old San Francisco resident on the stifling PC culture that has grown up around that city. He made the following observation:

Disagreement gets you labeled fascist, racist, bigoted, etc. It can provoke a reaction so intense that you're suddenly an unperson to an acquaintance or friend. There is no saying 'Hey, I disagree with you,' it's just instant shunning. Say things online, and they'll try to find out who you are and potentially even get you fired for it. Being anti-PC is not about saying 'I want you to agree with me on these issues.' It's about saying, 'Hey, I want to have a discussion and not get shouted down because I don't agree.'

We don't want to end political correctness so that we can say hateful things. We want to stop feeling silenced and condemned for having alternative viewpoints. We want to articulate thought-provoking, uncomfortable truisms, and not be told, 'you can't say that' without even a modest effort at explaining why.

When confronting people who disagree with you, the best tactic is to prove why they're wrong instead of shutting them up. Have enough faith in your own arguments to welcome dissenting opinions; if your ideas are truly superior, it will show. No need to get emotional, indignant, or defensive.

Why is this? Why has this new and expansive sense of student fragility spread so rapidly, but only among Millennials who are currently living or working on college campuses? Lukianoff and Haidt tried to explain the recent spread of trigger warnings and micro-aggression theory by examining broad historical trends, such as increases in protective parenting that began in the 1980s, and we examined more recent changes in federal laws that pressured universities to over-police language use on campus.

## How the New Religion of Progressivism Leverages Victimization

According to the tenets of the toxic new religion of progressivism—victimization accrues power. Per Scott Allen, here's how it works:

First, the religion sees reality entirely within the Marxist framework of oppressor and oppressed. Further, the principal oppressors are white, Christian, or Jewish heterosexual males. They are uniquely oppressive, "white supremacists" who have abused cultural power and privilege at the expense of every other group.

These are givens. They function as "core doctrines" of the new religion. Try arguing these points with adherents; they will be incredulous, as if you were asserting a flat earth. These are simply "self-evident" realities. If you are not white, male, Christian/Jewish, heterosexual, you are, by definition, a victim, and victimization accrues power. Ben Shapiro explains how this works:

The toxic new religion ranks the value of a view not based on the logic or merit of the view but on the level of victimization in American society experienced by the person espousing the view. An LGBT black woman is automatically considered more correct than a straight white male, before any speech exits either of their mouths. Progressivism madness!

Shapiro continues, "If a straight white male, or anyone else who ranks lower on the victimhood scale, says something contrary to the viewpoint of the higher ranking intersectionality identity, that person has engaged in a microaggression. They have engaged in hate speech or violence, and violent action is justified to silence them."

The fact that victimization accrues power helps explain the wild exaggeration and hyperbole employed by so-called victim groups. The more victimized and oppressed you paint yourself, the more your voice counts. If you say (of your experience as a black, female student at Yale University) "we are dying here!" you are setting yourself up to be taken more seriously.

But this is a dangerous delusion. Yazidis in Iraq, or Christians in North Korea, or Karin in Myanmar can truthfully claim that "we are dying here" without exaggerating. But to make the same claim as a privileged student at one of America's most prestigious universities is to mock actual violent oppression.

### Victimization Warrants Mob Tactics, Riots, and Violence

Examples of this abound in the news. In the past years we've read about mobs of students shouting down those who disagree, almost always combined with vitriol, cursing, property damage, threats of violence and actual violence: Berkeley, Evergreen, Missouri State, Yale, Middlebury, and the list goes on.

According to Deion Kathawa, the students who engage in these mobs,… fervently believe that they are the front-line troops of an infallible moral vanguard, locked in an epic struggle for the very soul of their generation—and of their nation, rotten to the core … (Given this) it is not quite so shocking that they understand themselves to have entirely legitimate grievances and are accordingly motivated to act in extreme ways.

Another (white female) Evergreen professor wrote about her own experiences of the riots.

Student activists gain license to harass and intimidate members of the Evergreen community in an effort to achieve their ends. Last Wednesday on two separate occasions I was followed by white students who yelled and cursed at me, accused me of not caring about black and brown bodies and claimed that if I did care I would follow their orders and join the protest in the library. They stood in front of me, blocking my way as I attempted to walk across campus.

Here's what jumps out at me: First, the students and faculty behind the riots "ignore (inhumane, totalitarian) tactics for the sake of the goal." Second, this mob behavior is part and parcel of the movement on many US college campuses (not only Evergreen).

This is the same totalitarianism of the Maoist Cultural Revolution or the Russian Revolution!

# 7 – Public Education Illiberalism vs. Student, Parent & Teacher Free Speech Rights

Credit: Los Angeles Times - Wrenching struggle to define
critical race theory divides an Orange County school district.

Most college students in the United States should be able to expect that freedom of expression will be upheld on their campuses. After all, public institutions are legally bound by the First Amendment, and the vast majority of private colleges and universities promise their students commensurate free speech rights.

In spite of this legal landscape, far too many colleges across the country fail to live up to their free speech obligations in policy and in practice. Often, this occurs through the implementation of speech codes: university policies that restrict expression that is protected under First Amendment standards.

University censorship regimes are teaching some students not only to live with but to embrace the conformism of thought inculcated through university speech codes, speaker dis-invitations, "safe spaces," "trigger warnings," and campus shout-downs of invited speakers.

Too many students feel afraid to speak honestly on campus for fear of offending someone, a new national survey of college students says. Furthermore, the Foundation for Individual Rights in Education (FIRE) surveyed the written policies of 466 colleges and universities, evaluating their compliance with First Amendment standards and their college rankings are disturbing.

More college students than ever claim to have reservations about free expression and this bleak view of open speech is not merely the reserve of a dismissible fringe. Forty-four percent of surveyed students told the Brookings Institution that they do not believe that the First

Amendment protects free speech, compared with the 39 percent who believe that it does. A full 20 percent of respondents maintained it acceptable to inflict physical harm on those deemed to have made "offensive and hurtful statements."

The rights that Madison worked to preserve in the name of reason and humanity now yield to the dictatorship of "culture." Professors, students, and their intellectual allies act as though our country were a tribe rather than a republic, in which any unapproved remark becomes an illicit defection from the mandated social order.

## The New Campus Illiberalism is More Than Intolerance

*Webster's Dictionary* defines illiberalism as "opposition to or lack of liberalism." In popular usage, the word is used to describe an attitude that is close-minded, intolerant, and bigoted.

The pursuit of knowledge and the maintenance of a free and democratic society require the cultivation and practice of the virtues of intellectual humility, openness of mind, and, above all, love of truth. These virtues will manifest themselves and be strengthened by one's willingness to listen attentively and respectfully to intelligent people who challenge one's beliefs and who represent causes one disagrees with and points of view one does not share.

That's why all of us should seek respectfully to engage with people who challenge our views. And we should oppose efforts to silence those with whom we disagree—especially on college and university campuses. As John Stuart Mill taught, a recognition of the possibility that we may be in error is a good reason to listen to and honestly consider—and not merely to tolerate grudgingly—points of view that we do not share, and even perspectives that we find shocking or scandalous.

None of us is infallible. Whether you are a person of the left, the right, or the center, there are reasonable people of goodwill who do not share your fundamental convictions. This does not mean that all opinions are equally valid or that all speakers are equally worth listening to. It certainly does not mean that there is no truth to be discovered. Nor does it mean that you are necessarily wrong. But they are not necessarily wrong either

All of us should be willing—even eager—to engage with anyone who is prepared to do business in the currency of truth-seeking discourse by offering reasons, marshaling evidence, and making arguments. The more important the subject under discussion, the more willing we should be to listen and engage—especially if the person with whom we are in conversation will challenge our deeply held—even our most cherished and identity-forming—beliefs.

**Intolerance as Illiberalism**

"We live in intolerant times" notes Dr. Kim R. Holmes of The Heritage Foundation from his 2014 article in *Public Discourse* "Intolerance as Illiberalism." All across America, this illiberal mindset is spreading, corrupting our culture and our politics. It is evident in the mendacity with which opposing opinions are attacked and in the way that state and federal governments conduct their business.

This mindset turns ideas like tolerance and liberalism on their heads. It weakens the checks and balances that have long protected our rights and freedoms. As a result, illiberalism threatens not only the social peace of our country, but the very future of freedom and democracy in America. We ignore this growing phenomenon at our peril.

It's all-too-common these days for people to try to immunize from criticism opinions that happen to be dominant in their particular communities. Sometimes this is done by questioning the motives and thus stigmatizing those who dissent from prevailing opinions; or by disrupting their presentations; or by demanding that they be excluded from campus or, if they have already been invited, disinvited.

Sometimes students and faculty members turn their backs on speakers whose opinions they don't like or simply walk out and refuse to listen to those whose convictions offend their values. Of course, the right to peacefully protest, including on campuses, is sacrosanct. But before exercising that right, each of us should ask: Might it not be better to listen respectfully and try to learn from a speaker with whom I disagree? Might it better serve the cause of truth-seeking to engage the speaker in frank civil discussion?

## The Culture of Illiberalism

The roots of modern American illiberalism lie in the trauma experienced by liberals in the 1960s. The rise of the New Left and its sister movement, the Counter-Culture, changed how liberals viewed not only culture but also politics. As described in *Rebound: Getting America Back to Great,* by Dr. Kim R. Holmes, rebellion for New Left liberals moved beyond mere economic class issues to ones involving gender, sex, and race.

Politics became cultural, and Marxist assumptions about the irreconcilability of class conflict were transferred to the culture wars over gender, race, and sexual identity. Channeling the ideas of philosopher Herbert Marcuse, the New Left dismissed old-fashioned liberalism that preached individualism and moral responsibility as "repressive tolerance." Liberation focused now on *groups*, not on individuals, and dissent was seen not as an individual right of conscience, but as a political weapon to overthrow traditional morality.

Since the 1960s, the radical egalitarianism of the New Left has fused with traditional progressive ideas about state and society. Feminism is no longer about giving women equal political and legal rights—it's about confronting the male power structure and the "rape" culture. Fighting racism is no longer about ensuring that African-Americans and minorities are treated equally before the law—it's about eradicating "systemic" racism and promoting affirmative action. Environmentalism is no longer about conserving natural resources—it's about "saving" the planet from overpopulation and climate change.

With such utopian causes, it seems perfectly acceptable to "break a few eggs" to make a new liberal omelet.

Over the years, the hard edges of the rebellious sixties attenuated. Many liberal Baby Boomers grew older and mellower in their views. Yet many held on to the assumptions of the Counter-Culture, particularly with respect to gender, sex, and race. Today, these people occupy the high ground of American culture, and their values are mainstream. They are university professors and trustees; intellectuals and writers; Hollywood producers and actors; lawyers litigating politically correct, high-profile cases; newsroom executives and producers; school teachers and administrators; and the pastors, deacons, priests, and bishops of some of America's mainline churches.

## Traditional American Liberalism Has Changed in Three Important Ways

The first change involves the understanding of tolerance. The old Jeffersonian notion, rooted in debates over religious freedom, holds that individual conscience is sacrosanct. This has given way to the notion that certain ideas (e.g., racism or sexism) are so heinous that no one should be allowed to hold, much less express, *any* idea about race or women or sexuality that proponents believe is socially oppressive. In other words, intolerance is now seen as a *good* thing—if it serves the purpose of a certain definition of social liberation.

The second change involves the idea of dissent. Historically, respect for dissent had its roots in debates over religious freedom and freedom of conscience. But the New Left took an entirely different view of dissent. Rather than an expression of individual conscience, dissent was now seen as a weapon to overthrow the old order. The end justified the means. It was perfectly justifiable, according to the New Left, to shut out the views of the ruling class, defined now along race, gender, and sexual orientation lines.

The third idea that has undergone a radical change is our conception of virtue. Historically, virtue has been understood as a positive habit that forms one's personal character. In this view, one acquires virtue by repeatedly choosing to treat others well and act in accord with objective standards of morality, even when it is difficult.

The Counter-Culture understood virtue very differently. The "self" was not something that had to be restrained; it was unique and had to be expressed openly, even loudly, to be fulfilled. Individual freedom was to be experienced through the liberation of one's group (i.e., one's gender, race, or sexual identity).

Traditional morality—particularly sexual morality—became a force of repression just as capitalism had been in the days of the Old Left. Virtue was politicized and defined ideologically; it was not seen as a measure of personal responsibility or as a right of individual conscience but as a measure of the collective good the government is supposed to guarantee.

As a result, it has become easy to condemn one's political opponents as utterly mendacious characters who lack decency and virtue rather than to consider them misguided people who happen to see things differently. The scarlet letter is reserved not for adulterers but for people who doubt climate change or who question calling same-sex unions "marriage."

People who see themselves as "liberal-minded" have come to justify the most illiberal of ideas—namely, curbing freedom of expression and using the power of the state to deny equal rights to Americans with whom they disagree.

Modern liberalism thus does not merely flirt with intolerance. It is now fundamentally based on it. And that is largely because it has become accepted by the culture as a good thing to employ in the service of a cause you believe in. Whatever you may call this new American culture, you cannot call it liberal, for tolerance is the acid test of true liberalism.

This is where the culture stands today. The thinkers of the New Left infect it with illiberal values consciously designed to destroy classic liberalism. It may be true that illiberalism always lurked on the edges of American progressivism in the various ideologies associated with socialism.

But for most of history, progressives had tried to keep their distance from the more blatantly illiberal values of the far Left. That resistance started breaking down in the sixties. As a result, American liberalism today has a decidedly illiberal wing eating away at its purported core values.

**Free Speech Zone Policies**

Free speech zones have repeatedly been struck down by courts or voluntarily revised by colleges as part of settlements to lawsuits brought by students. The FIRE's Stand Up For Speech Litigation Project has included successful challenges to free speech zone policies at eight colleges and universities and includes an ongoing challenge to a free speech zone policy at Pierce College in Los Angeles.

Additionally, state legislatures have continued to take action to prohibit public colleges and universities from maintaining free speech zones. Currently, twelve states have enacted laws prohibiting these restrictive policies: Virginia, Missouri, Arizona, Kentucky, Colorado, Utah, North Carolina, Tennessee, Florida, Georgia, Louisiana and Alabama.

Based on the Campus Free Expression (CAFE) Act model legislation from the FIRE, Florida's bill, which was signed into law in March 2018, states:

A person who wishes to engage in an expressive activity in outdoor areas of campus may do so freely, spontaneously, and contemporaneously as long as the person's conduct is lawful and does not materially and substantially disrupt the functioning of the public institution of higher education or infringe upon the rights of other individuals or organizations to engage in expressive activities … A public institution of higher education may not designate any area of campus as a free-speech zone or otherwise create policies restricting expressive activities to a particular area of campus …

The law also provides a right to sue a public institution of higher education in Florida if the institution violates the expressive rights guaranteed by the law.

Furthermore, the Student Press Law Center (SPLC) has worked to support, promote and defend the First Amendment and freedom of expression rights of student journalists at the high school and college level, and the advisers who support them. Working at the intersection of law, journalism and education, SPLC runs the nation's only free legal hotline for student journalists.

They also provide training, educational resources and support the grassroots non-partisan New Voices movement, seeking state-based legislative support for student press freedom. The SPLC is an independent, non-profit 501c(3) organization based in Washington, D.C. and you can learn more about them in the Appendix link.

## Clubs' Student Rights on Public School Campuses

Students form all sorts of clubs at school, including some not related to the curriculum. Sometimes school officials shut down such clubs because they believe them inappropriate or too controversial. For example, per the September 2017 "Clubs" report by David L. Hudson Jr. and Mahad Ghani of Freedom Forum Institute:

There is evidence that many school officials have prohibited student religious clubs because they fear that allowing such clubs would violate the establishment clause of the First Amendment.

In 1984, Congress passed the Equal Access Act, which forbids schools from discriminating against clubs or denying them equal access to school facilities because of their philosophical or religious viewpoints. The act was passed largely to prevent widespread discrimination against religious clubs.

Under the law if a school opens its facilities to "any noncurriculum related group," it must open its facilities to all student groups. This means that if a school allows students to form a chess club or a 4-H club, it must also allow the formation of a Bible club, gay-lesbian club or other group that some might consider controversial.

In 1990, the U.S. Supreme Court ruled in *Westside Community Board of Education v. Mergens* that the Equal Access Act was constitutional. In that case, the Court determined that a school district violated the Equal Access Act by denying use of its facilities to a religious club, while allowing a chess club, a scuba-diving club and other "noncurriculum-related" groups to use school facilities.

The Court disagreed with the officials, and found that the clubs were all noncurriculum-related. "Congress clearly sought to prohibit schools from discriminating on the basis of the content of a student group's speech, and that obligation is the price a federally funded school must pay if it opens its facilities to noncurriculum-related student groups," the Court wrote.

The Court also rejected the school board's argument that the Equal Access Act itself violated the establishment clause. The school board had argued that the primary purpose of the Equal Access Act was religious, that the primary effect of the law was to advance religion and that it caused an excessive entanglement between religion and schools.

The Court rejected all of these contentions. "Congress' avowed purpose — to prevent discrimination against religious and other types of speech — is undeniably secular," the Court wrote. "Because the Act on its face grants equal access to both secular and religious speech, we think it clear that the Act's purpose was not to endorse or disapprove of religion."

"The Mergens decision was a landmark ruling in the area of equal access involving student rights on public school campuses," said Jay Sekulow, chief counsel of the American Center for Law and Justice and the attorney who argued the case for Mergens before the high court. Mergens "upheld the constitutionality of the Equal Access Act and determined once and for all that student religious groups must be given the same access and benefits afforded to other student groups," Sekulow said."

The Mergens decision cleared the way for the tremendous growth of student Bible clubs on public school campuses across the nation. There were relatively few in place before the case began and now—some 14 years later—there are more than 15,000 student Bible clubs operating in school districts nationwide. The impact of Mergens is still felt today with the Supreme Court opinion often cited in other religious-liberties cases particularly when the rights of students are at issue."

## Curriculum and Action Civics in K–12 Schools

The dissemination of curricular content and instruction based on CRT in K–12 schools is second only in scope to the presence of CRT in post-secondary instruction, where CRT originated. The spread within college- and university-level syllabi and journal articles took place over the course of many decades throughout the 20th century, while the effects on K–12 schools in such areas as social studies, history, and civics have, by comparison, become visible more recently.

The material distracts educators and students away from rigorous learning content, while also teaching ideas that undermine the value of individual liberty and America's founding ideals and further embedding the concept of systemic racism in the public conscious. These distractions come at a time when state and school officials do not require enough civics-related instruction in school, and there are wide learning gaps in core subjects like reading and math between children from different ethnicities—all subjects that need more, not less, attention.

Academic literature produced in the past 20 years by educational theorists on K–12 curriculum argue that narrative stories and stories from personal experiences—hallmarks of CRT—should replace instruction about facts.

In a widely cited 1998 article from Qualitative Studies in Education, Gloria Ladson-Billings writes, "The use of voice or 'naming your reality' is a way that CRT links form and substance in scholarship." She further writes, "Much of reality is socially constructed." Aligned with the foundational ideals of CRT, Ladson-Billings says, "Critical race theory sees the official school curriculum as a culturally specific artifact designed to maintain a White supremacist master script."

Notably, she closes the piece by saying, "I doubt if it [CRT] will go very far into the mainstream. Rather, CRT in education is likely to become the 'darling' of the radical left, continue to generate scholarly papers and debate, and never penetrate the classrooms and daily experiences of students of color."

She was wrong.

### Districts Around the Country Have Integrated CRT Into School Curricula

Both of the nation's largest teacher unions support the Black Lives Matter organization, with the National Education Association specifically calling for the use of Black Lives Matter curricular materials in K–12 schools.

This curriculum is "committed" to ideas such as a "queer-affirming network," which have nothing to do with rigorous instructional content, and promotes racially charged essays such as "Open Secrets in First-Grade Math: Teaching about White Supremacy on American Currency."

As of 2018, officials in at least 20 large school districts, including Los Angeles and Washington, DC, were promoting Black Lives Matter curricular content and the organization's "Week of Action."

According to an Education Week survey in June 2020, 81 percent of teachers, principals, and district leaders "support the Black Lives Matter movement." However, surveys are not clear on whether the prevailing sentiment among educators is support of authentic equality among individuals or of the divisive ideas espoused within the curriculum.

State and school officials are integrating CRT material into instructional content with California leading the way. California Governor Gavin Newsom signed into law on August 17, 2020 a new 3-unit Ethnic Studies requirement for the 23-campus California State University (CSU) system. This law, AB 1460 means students in the CSU system will have to take an ethnic studies course before graduation.

The new social studies curriculum acknowledged CRT priorities such as power and white privilege, including statements such as, "Ethnic studies courses address race within the context of how white dominated culture impacts racism" and educators can "create and utilize lessons rooted in the four foundational disciplines alongside the sample key themes of (1) Identity, (2) History and Movement, (3) Systems of Power, and (4) Social Movements and Equity."

The curriculum has an entire section devoted to intersectionality, the CRT concept explained earlier that allows someone to claim victimhood based on his or her identification with more than one group (such as being from a minority ethnicity, a lower economic class, and identifying with a specific gender), accelerating a search for "power imbalances" in society.

In a review of the draft materials, Williamson Evers, former U.S. Education Department official and member of the California State Academic Standards Commission, wrote in the *Wall Street Journal*, "The revised model curriculum in California portrays capitalism as oppressive and gives considerable weight to America's socialist critics."

He further says, "The proponents of critical ethnic studies are so insulated by Marxism and identity politics that they miss insights from other fields."

**CRT Scholarship on Teaching Methods is Also Used to Advocate Activism**

CRT scholarship on teaching methods is also used to advocate activism, which is dangerous considering the movement's preference for personal narratives over knowledge and historical facts. The Obama Administration supported such activism in its 2012 report "Advancing Civic Learning and Engagement in Democracy: A Road Map and Call to Action." In the report, then-Education Secretary Arne Duncan called for a focus on "action civics" instead of "just rote memorization of names, dates, and processes."

Organizations such as the Sunrise Movement and Generation Citizen, along with the Mikva Challenge at Chicago Public Schools (CPS), to name a few, have promoted action civics in the years since the report's release.

Curricular content for action civics range from encouraging students to volunteer in their community to suggesting that teachers assign students, even elementary-age students, material that advocates for unionizing workers and protesting against "gentrification," complex subjects even for adults to consider.

While the CPS efforts endorsed anti-bullying and "School Beautification" projects, the district also advocated for student projects protesting "Police Brutality" and "LGBTQ Awareness," as well as several walk-outs and sessions to train students to speak to the media about guns and a "Keeping It Reel Film Project" that dealt with "transgender rights."

**Some School Systems Have Applied Action Civics to Teaching Disruptive Protests**

Seattle Public Schools include recommended reading material on its district website that says responses to the tragic death of George Floyd are "violent and destructive" because "police officers and the National Guard themselves are initiating violence" and "White Americans have a long, storied history of violence and destruction in this country."

The MacIver Institute in Wisconsin reports that in the 2019–2020 school year, at least five marches were endorsed by school districts across the state, taking students out of the classroom to protest climate change and immigration policies and advocate for Black Lives Matter activities and gun control, to name a few.

The action civics group Generation Citizen has sponsored student projects to advocate for "more stringent mental health and social tolerance tests for NYPD [New York Police Department] applicants"—and ban the use of plastic bags in Rhode Island retail stores, among others.

Again, if this civic instruction was a call for more volunteer work or was somehow aligned with core subjects in which minority students still lag behind their peers, such instruction would be admirable. Yet research on student achievement in civics finds that students are woefully underprepared to understand civic participation and the functions of our nation's government. Seventy-six percent of 8th graders scored at or below a basic level in civics on the most recent national comparison.

According to iCivics, "Only nine states require a full year of civic education in high school," and 10 states have no such requirement. Thirty-one states only require civics to be taught for one semester.

Just under half of all Americans cannot name all three branches of government, according to the Annenberg Public Policy Center at the University of Pennsylvania.

Teacher training steeped in critical theory (called "critical pedagogy") demands action, however, which, when paired with the denunciation of facts described above, begs the question of how students are supposed to know what kind of action is appropriate and what is not.

After the Trump Administration supported policies that drew attention to the problems with CRT in education and the so-called anti-racism training of the federal workforce, two associate professors wrote in Education Week that the U.S. Department of Education should not reject CRT but "should ensure principals and teachers learn how it can be applied to address long-standing educational inequities" and "encourage federal agencies and public schools to embrace critical race theory."

Parents, teachers, and policymakers concerned about CRT in schools are faced with significant challenges because some educators are determined to keep CRT in classrooms.

Apparently ideological "groupthink" isn't just confined to the student admissions process; it also appears to pervade the faculty hiring and tenure-granting processes as well. According to longitudinal nationwide data collected by UCLA's Higher Education Research Institute, a dramatic leftward shift in the composition of university faculty occurred between 1989 and 2014.

As far back as October 29, 2003, a special Senate report concluded after a hearing before the Committee on Health, Education, Labor, and Pensions, United States Senate, One Hundred Eighth Congress titled: *Is Intellectual Diversity an Endangered Species on America's College Campuses?* and was it becoming more scarce and beginning to lean heavily leftward.

Whereas progressives comprised roughly 40 percent of the professoriate in the late 1980s, they comprise 60 percent today. Moderates (at 28 percent) and conservatives (at twelve   percent) not only account for a smaller share of today's faculty, but conservatives have practically reached "endangered species" status (a mere five percent) in the humanities and social sciences.

There is no denying the left-leaning political bias on American college campuses. As data from UCLA's Higher Education Institute show, the professoriate has moved considerably leftward since the late 1980s, especially in the arts and humanities. In New England, liberal professors outnumber their conservative colleagues by a ratio of 28:1. This ratio is liberal madness!

## Lack of Viewpoint Diversity in the Academy

Growing skepticism about the current direction of American higher education isn't just found among those on the center-right. For example, a center-left New York University professor named Dr. Jonathan Haidt teamed with Greg Lukianoff, a former ACLU attorney who now heads the Foundation for Individual Rights in Education (FIRE), to write a 2015 article for *The Atlantic* magazine entitled, "The Coddling of the American Mind." The essay, which became the second-most-cited article in the long history of *The Atlantic*, directed heavy criticism at "microaggressions," "safe spaces," "trigger warnings," "speech codes," and other attempts to narrowly define the boundaries of acceptable discourse in higher education.

The leftward tilt of today's academic life hurts scholars—and would-be scholars—of a more conservative bent. Most all the modern arguments of progressivism, post-modernism, and the New Left fail the basic tenants of practical logic, common sense, and sapience.

Without viewpoint diversity and intellectual humility acting as the checks and balances essential to validate the academic standards, truth and logic behind new causes, issues, and programs can degrade and diminish and in turn academic and ideological orthodoxy become the norm with our academic institutions as well as the student bodies that determine the limits of free speech on campus.

Campuses that are overwhelmingly dominated by one ideological perspective are much more vulnerable to violations of free speech (and the embarrassing public relations problems that go with them) since the absence of viewpoint diversity can lead to the trampling of First Amendment rights. Put another way, free speech is more likely to be defended vigorously when more viewpoint diversity is present—the latter is perhaps the best guarantee of the former's defense.

Truth is a process, not just an end-state. *The Righteous Mind: Why Good People are Divided by Politics and Religion* is a 2012 social psychology book by Dr. Jonathan Haidt, is about the obstacles to that process, such as confirmation bias, motivated reasoning, tribalism, and the worship of sacred values. Given the many ways that our moral psychology warps our reasoning, it's a wonder we've gotten as far as we have, as a species.

That's what's so brilliant about science: it is a way of putting people together so that they challenge each other and cancel out each other's confirmation biases and tribal commitments. The truth emerges from the interaction of flawed individuals.

## Campus Administrators' Bias and the Attack on Free Speech

Almost since the start of *Power Line* in 2002, American Council of Trustees and Alumni (ACTA) has reported with dismay the descent of American colleges and universities into a leftist bastion of illiberalism. Most of their focus has been on professors, and not without reason. They are the ones who have degraded the teaching of humanities through their obsession with identify politics and disdain for Western Civilization.

However, Dr. Samuel Abrams came away from an ATHENA Roundtable Conference believing that administrators, not professors, are the primary culprits on American campuses today. The ATHENA Roundtable Conference is a program presented by the American Council of Trustees and Alumni (ACTA). ACTA is an independent, nonprofit organization committed to academic freedom, excellence, and accountability at America's colleges and universities.

The threat posed by the ever-growing ranks of college administrators was pinpointed in an address by Abrams. He's a professor of politics at Sarah Lawrence College who has not only fought courageously for academic freedom, but also studied, as an empirical matter, the threat to it.

Abrams explained that, compared to administrators, college professors exert limited influence on the lives of students. They teach relatively light course loads, have limited visiting hours, spend most of the day on research, and then head home to their family (if any).

Administrators, by contrast, are embedded in their colleges. Some live in dorms where they adjudicate disputes that, in better times, students worked out for themselves. As Abrams puts it in his American Enterprise Institute (AEI) article:

Today, many colleges and universities have moved to a model in which teaching, and learning is seen as a 24/7 endeavor. Engagement with students is occurring as much—if not more—in residence halls and student centers as it is in classrooms.

Schools have increased their hiring in areas such as residential life and student centers, offices of student life and success, and offices of inclusion and engagement. It's not surprising that many of the free-speech controversies in the past few years at places like Yale, Stanford and the

University of Delaware have concerned events that occurred not in classrooms but in student communal spaces and residence halls.

# 8 – Marxist Critical Theory and Its Two Other Illiberal Legal and Racial Derivatives

*Credit: Study.com-Marxism Lesson for Kid: Definition & Explanation Video.*

In order to understand the current paradigm of free speech suppression and expression, particularly amongst Generations X Y Z, and its driving force in America today, we must expose Critical Theory for what it is, what it's about, and how it came to be. If there is one chapter amongst the others that serves as the catalyst for an intervention, denial of truth, or a triggering event—it's this one.

We devote this highly illuminating chapter on Critical Theory (CT) and its derivatives Critical Legal Theory (CLT) and Critical Race Theory (CRT), the children and grandchildren of Critical Theory—because our generation, and every generation, must "let the proud fabric of freedom rest" upon the ideas of liberty, "a reverence for the constitution and laws," and the pursuit of a civil society that offers freedom and opportunity to all Americans, regardless of the color of their skin.

A thorough understanding of this triad of illiberal theories is very important for three critical reasons: 1) they are Marxist in origin, 2) they are the bedrock of "today's" progressivism 'regressivism' movement, and 3) collectively, they seek to fundamentally "transform" America.

To one degree to another, all of the illiberal groups, unsapient ideologies, and unjust causes covered in the first seven chapters of *Free Speech Madness*, are manifestations of CT, CLT and CRT—and until you read this chapter—you cannot begin to fathom how these three theories share a common goal of free speech suppression, Marxist indoctrination, and anti-Americanism.

The importance of this "critical" topic cannot be understated and as we continue on with the rest of the chapters—we begin exposing the influence these theories place on the heart and soul, the social fabric, the essence of America—in a most profound and negative way.

With an open mind and heightened awareness—you'll begin to see in sharp focus what our esteemed team of Mike Gonzalez and Jonathan Butcher at the Heritage Foundation have researched and presented throughout the rest of this chapter.

## Critical Race Theory, the New Intolerance, and Its Grip on America

Critical Race Theory began as an academic concept, but we can find the ideas all around us today, from schoolhouses to the corporate world to Hollywood. Racism and intolerance should have no place in America, but CRT is more than just a philosophical objection to discrimination. When followed to its logical conclusion, CRT is destructive and rejects the fundamental ideas on which our constitutional republic is based.

From the in depth December 2020 report by Jonathan Butcher and Mike Gonzalez at The Heritage Foundation "Critical Race Theory, the New Intolerance, and Its Grip on America" with Allison Hayman contributing to this report:

Most readers and scholars after reviewing this section will be surprised how CRT underpins identity politics, an ongoing effort to reimagine the United States as a nation riven by groups, each with specific claims on victimization. In entertainment, as well as the education and workforce sectors of society, CRT is well-established, driving decision-making according to skin color—not individual value and talent.

As Critical Theory ideas become more familiar to the viewing public in everyday life, CRT's intolerance becomes "normalized," along with the idea of systemic racism for Americans, weakening public and private bonds that create trust and allow for civic engagement.

As its name should make abundantly clear, **Critical Race Theory (CRT)** is the child of **Critical Theory (CT)**, or, to be more precise, its grandchild. Critical Theory is the immediate forebearer of **Critical Legal Theory (CLT)**, and CLT begat CRT and there are strong thematic components linking CT, CLT, and CRT. Among these are:

- The Marxist analysis of society made up of categories of oppressors and oppressed;

- An unhealthy dollop of Nietzschean relativism, which means that language does not accord to an objective reality, but is the mere instrument of power dynamics;

- The idea that the oppressed impede revolution when they adhere to the cultural beliefs of their oppressors—and must be put through re-education sessions;

- The concomitant need to dismantle all societal norms through relentless criticism; and

- The replacement of all systems of power and even the descriptions of those systems with a worldview that describes only oppressors and the oppressed.

Far from being merely esoteric academic exercises, these philosophies have real-life consequences as this report will explore in greater detail.

This section then provides sapient policy recommendations that are aimed at restoring the concepts of judging people not by the color of their skin (as is the foundation of CRT) but by their conduct (as in content of character empowered MLK) and the need to protect liberty so that everyone, regardless of ethnicity or background, has the opportunity to pursue the American Dream.

## Critical Theory (CT) Exposed

The origins of Critical Theory can be traced to the 1937 manifesto of the Institute for Social Research in Frankfurt, colloquially known as the Frankfurt School. One of the first examples of what has come to be called the Western Marxist schools of thought, the Institute modeled itself on the Moscow-based Marx-Engels Institute.

Critical Theory was, from the start, an unremitting attack on Western institutions and norms in order to tear them down. This attack was aimed only at the West. Even though the manifesto, titled Traditional and Critical Theory, was written at the height of Joseph Stalin's purges, show trials, and famines, the school "maintained an almost complete official silence about events in the USSR."

The manifesto, written by the school's second director, Max Horkheimer, claimed that traditional theory fetishized knowledge, seeing truth as empirical and universal. Critical theory, on the other hand, "held that man could not be objective and that there are no universal truths."

This relativism was inherited from Friedrich Nietzsche and filtered through the dialectics of Georg Friedrich Hegel and his best-known disciple, Karl Marx. The Frankfurt School philosophers believed that "a true epistemology must end the fetish of knowledge as such, which as Nietzsche demonstrated, leads to abstract systematizing."

As for their Marxism, three years earlier, Horkheimer had let his true feelings for the Soviet state be known in a collection of short essays known as Dammerung (in German, both "dawn" and "twilight"). "He who has eyes for the meaningless injustice of the imperialist world, which in no way is to be explained by technical impotence, will regard the events in Russia as the progressive, painful attempt to overcome this injustice."

## Critical Theory (CT) and Its Early Applications

In the context of the era, Critical Theory's demolition of Western traditions and norms was nothing less than a tool to implement the counter-hegemony called for in the Theory of Cultural Hegemony enunciated in the first decades of the 20th Century by Antonio Gramsci. Marx and Friedrich Engels had promised constant revolution by the workers of the world, but by the early 1930s, few had succeeded.

The founder of the Italian Communist Party, Gramsci had come to believe that the workers were not revolting and overthrowing the bourgeoisie because they had bought into the belief system of the ruling class—family, nation-state, the capitalist system, and God. What was needed was struggle sessions in which the revolutionary vanguard would teach the workers how to think. But first the norms needed to be torn down.

That is where Critical Theory—and, as we will see, all its offshoots—come in.

Horkheimer and the other Frankfurt scholars left Germany to escape the Third Reich, fleeing first to Geneva, then to New York, where Columbia University allowed them to set up camp in 1935 at Teachers' College. In the United States they developed the same disdain for the American worker that Gramsci had felt for his Italian counterpart. "They insist unwaveringly on the ideology by which they are enslaved," Horkheimer wrote with another Frankfurt School scholar, Theodor Adorno, about the American worker.

After the defeat of the Nazi regime, Horkheimer, Adorno, and the others were able to return to Germany. But they left behind Horkheimer's assistant, Herbert Marcuse, who became one of the leading spokesmen of the New Left.

A witness to the upheavals caused by the riots and violence associated with the Civil Rights era and the anti–Vietnam War Movement, Marcuse discovered in them a new agent of change: minorities, of which more categories would need to be created. "Underneath the conservative popular base is the substratum of the outcasts and outsiders, the exploited and persecuted of other races and other colors," Marcuse wrote. They would still need to be led ideologically— "their opposition is revolutionary even if their consciousness is not"—but the potential to stoke grievances among them was there in a way that did not exist with workers as a category.

## Critical Legal Theory (CLT)

It is at this point that Critical Legal Theory takes over. Its scholars self-consciously acknowledge their debt to Critical Theory and other Marxist movements that came before the Frankfurt School. "Although CLS has been largely contained within the United States, it was influenced to a great extent by European philosophers, such as Karl Marx, Max Weber, Max Horkheimer, Antonio Gramsci, and Michel Foucault," reads the entry for CLT in the Cornell Law School's Legal Information Institute.

The Cornell entry for Critical Legal Studies explains:

Critical legal studies (CLS) is a theory which states that the law is necessarily intertwined with social issues, particularly stating that the law has inherent social biases. Proponents of CLS believe that the law supports the interests of those who create the law. As such, CLS states that the law supports a power dynamic which favors the historically privileged and disadvantages the historically underprivileged. CLS finds that the wealthy and the powerful use the law as an instrument for oppression in order to maintain their place in hierarchy.

Then comes the kicker: "Many in the CLS movement want to overturn the hierarchical structures of modern society, and they focus on the law as a tool in achieving this goal."

Just as with Critical Theory, Critical Legal Theory is, then, an instrument to overturn society for those who follow its tenets, this time from a legal perspective. The law, they argue, is simply the cultural hegemony codified in statutes and defended by a jurisprudence that aims to support the powerful against the claims of the marginalized. CLT proponents trace their founding to the first Conference on Critical Legal Studies, held at the University of Wisconsin at Madison in 1977.

Among its main theorists figure Duncan Kennedy, Roberto Mangabeira Unger, and Robert W. Gordon.

In a 2002 essay, Kennedy acknowledges the debt Critical Legal Theory owes to both Marxism and post-modernism (championed by a mostly Parisian set of intellectuals who preached that texts could be "deconstructed" by the reader, a complicated philosophical concept that involves reinterpreting words to replace ideas based on objective physical existence), two separate critiques of bourgeois reality that nevertheless can rub uneasily against each other. "Critical legal studies," he writes, "operates [sic] at the uneasy juncture of two distinct, sometimes complementary and sometimes conflicting enterprises, which we will call the left and the modernist/postmodernist projects."

"Leftism aims to transform existing social structures on the basis of a critique of their injustice, and, specifically, at the injustices of racist, capitalist patriarchy. The goal is to replace the system, piece by piece or in medium- or large-sized blocs, with a better system," writes Kennedy.

## Post-Modernism Borrows Heavily From the Nietzschean Attack on Objectivity

Post-modernism is a much more complex phenomenon, but it aims at the same destruction of society as the Marxist project, starting with the use of reason itself. We can gain a sense of such complexity in Kennedy's own abstruse writing on Modernism/Postmodernism (or MPM). He explains:

[MPM] is a critique of the characteristic forms of rightness of this same culture and aims at liberation from inner and outer experiences of constraint by reason, in the name, not of justice and a new system, but of the dialectic of system and anti-system, mediated by transgressive artifacts that paradoxically reaffirm the "higher" forms of the values they seem to traduce.

Just as with Critical Theory, post-modernism borrows heavily from the Nietzschean attack on objectivity. Writes Kennedy:

For the [MPM] project, the demand for agreement and commitment on the basis of representation with the pretension to objectivity is an enemy. The specific enemies have been the central ethical/theoretical concepts of bourgeois culture, including God, the autonomous individual choosing self, conventional morality, the family, manhood and womanhood, the nation state, humanity.

CLT scholars also display an awareness of the rising identity groups that Marcuse identified as the new revolutionary base. Kennedy quotes approvingly his fellow university professor Cornell West as asserting the existence of an inchoate, scattered yet gathering progressive movement that is emerging across the American landscape. This gathering now lacks both the vital moral vocabulary and the focused leadership that can constitute and sustain it. Yet it will be rooted ultimately in current activities by people of color, by labor and ecological groups, by women, by gay people.

Kennedy adds that "in the United States, by the end of the 1970s, with the rise of identity politics, left discourse merged with liberal discourse, and the two ideas of the rights of the oppressed and the constitutional validity of their legal claims superseded all earlier versions of rightness."

Harvard's Berkman Klein Center's entry on Critical Legal Theory neatly teases out the link between the legal analysis of power relations with the emerging identity-based politics. It writes that CLT scholars:

focused from the start on the ways that law contributed to illegitimate social hierarchies, producing domination of women by men, nonwhites by whites, and the poor by the wealthy. They claim that apparently neutral language and institutions, operated through law, mask relationships of power and control. The emphasis on individualism within the law similarly hides patterns of power relationships while making it more difficult to summon up a sense of community and human interconnection."

## Critical Race Theory (CRT)

From there it is a short step to Critical Race Theory. Unsurprisingly, given its name, CRT makes everything about race the prism through which its proponents analyze all aspects of American life—and do so with a degree of persistence that has helped CRT impact all aspects of American life.

Derrick Bell, referenced above, the widely-acknowledged "godfather" of CRT, explains in the essay cited earlier that the work of CRT authors "is often disruptive because its commitment to anti-racism goes well beyond civil rights, integration, affirmative action, and other liberal measures."

Bell quotes Angela P. Harris as explaining that CRT inherits from its Critical Legal Theory ancestor the commitment to dismantle all aspects of society through unremitting criticism—and at the same time eschews the wooly deconstructionist excesses of the postmodernists and adopts the practicality of the Civil Rights movement. Bell points to theorist and professor Charles Lawrence and says he "speaks for many critical race theory adherents when he disagrees with the notion that laws are or can be written from a neutral perspective."

Because the law "systematically privileges subjects who are white," CRT calls for a "transformative resistance strategy."

### CRT's Theoretical Applications

Because CRT is so intent on real-life transformation, some aspects of post-modernism and its deconstructionism had to be jettisoned, or at least sidelined. Kimberle Crenshaw, the CRT scholar who first came up with the CRT term "intersectionality," put the need to abandon the Parisian post-modernism best when she wrote:

While the descriptive project of postmodernism of questioning the ways in which meaning is socially constructed is generally sound, this critique sometimes misreads the meaning of social construction and distorts its political relevance…. But to say that a category such as race or gender is socially constructed is not to say that that category has no significance in our world. On the contrary, a large and continuing project for subordinated people—and indeed, one of the projects for which postmodern theories have been very helpful in thinking about—is the way power has clustered around certain categories and is exercised against others.

In the end, the identity politics that CRT exists to implement was more important than salon revelries. Adherents can apply intersectionality, for example: Someone can claim to be oppressed in more than one way by citing association with more than one social group, or "axis."

CRT writers Patricia Hill Collins and Sirma Bilge explain that with intersectionality, "people's lives and the organization of power in a given society are better understood as being shaped not by a single axis of social division, be it race or gender or class, but by many axes that work together and influence each other."

In this way, write Helen Pluckrose and James Lindsay, CRT results in people looking for "power imbalances, bigotry, and biases that it assumes must be present," which reduces everything to prejudice, "as understood under the power dynamics asserted by Theory."

Of the three critical schools of thought analyzed here, CRT is the least intellectually ethereal and the most explicitly political. Its use of story-telling—easy to understand fictional vignettes that seek to portray in every-day life terms the "systemic racism" that CRT scholars insist exists in America—is but one of the ways that CRT scholars seek to effect change.

CRT's ceaseless assault on all American institutions and norms is pure Critical Theory, however. This assault includes the liberal order—in the classical sense, referring to Enlightenment ideas and political arrangements in which law protects individuals pursuing their own interests— something CRT scholars openly admit.

## CRT Clashes With Classical Liberal Ideas

CRT's proponents, writes Bell, "are highly suspicious of the liberal agenda, distrust its method, and want to retain what they see as a valuable strain of egalitarianism which may exist despite, and not because of, liberalism."

This is an important departure from the original goals of the Civil Rights movement, which sought to redeem America's promise by calling for color-blind equality. "Unlike traditional civil rights discourse, which stresses incrementalism and step-by-step progress, critical race theory questions the very foundations of the liberal order, including equality theory, legal reasoning, Enlightenment rationalism, and neutral principles of constitutional law," acknowledges Delgado.

The radical egalitarianism obviously clashes with strong protections of property rights and any notion of equal protection under the law. These are not the only liberal rights to be thrown overboard. Freedom of speech is also in CRT's sights. "Being committed to 'free speech' may seem like a neutral principle, but it is not. Thus, proclaiming that 'I am committed equally to allowing free speech for the KKK and 2LiveCrew' is a non-neutral value judgment, one that asserts that the freedom to say hateful things is more important than the freedom to be free from the victimization, stigma, and humiliation that free speech entails."

Even the idea of rights itself—the very concept upon which this country was founded—is a target of CRT. "Crits are suspicious of another liberal mainstay, namely, rights," observes

Delgado, using the informal abbreviation CRT writers sometimes employ to describe themselves. The "more radical CRT scholars with roots in racial realism and an economic view of history believe that moral and legal rights are apt to do the right holder much less good than we like to think … Think how that system applauds affording everyone equality of opportunity but resists programs that assure equality of results." Rights are "alienating. They separate people from each other—'stay away, I've got my rights'—rather than encouraging to form close, respectful communities."

The liberal principle that we universally derive these rights from a common humanity and human faculties we all share equally comes under the gun. Classical liberalism is "overly caught up in the search for universals," writes Delgado. What CRT proponents want is "individualized treatment—'context'—that pays attention to minorities' lives."

"The concepts of rights is indeterminate, vague and disutile," in Bell's words.

Legal and administrative neutrality, too, is an enemy because it gets in the way of uplifting such minority voices. Also—and this is a recurring theme with all critical schools, starting with Horkheimer, if not Nietzsche—neutrality is impossible to attain. On this point, Bell cites Lawrence again:

Charles Lawrence [a law professor] speaks for many critical race theory adherents when he disagrees with the notion that laws are or can be written from a neutral perspective. Lawrence asserts that such a neutral perspective does not, and cannot, exist—that we all speak from a particular point of view, from what he calls a 'positioned perspective.' The problem is that not all positioned perspectives are equally valued, equally heard, or equally included. From the perspective of critical race theory, some positions have historically been oppressed, distorted, ignored, silenced, destroyed, appropriated, commodified, and marginalized—and all of this, not accidentally.

## CRT is Purposely Political and Dispenses With the Idea of Rights

CRT is purposely political and dispenses with the idea of rights because it blames all inequalities of outcome on what its adherents say is pervasive racism in the United States. "White supremacy," a term that comes up repeatedly in CRT discourse and continues to be heavily used today by leaders of the Black Lives Matter organizations, must be smashed. White supremacy does not mean an actual belief in the superiority of white people, however. It can mean anything from classical philosophers to Enlightenment thinkers to the Industrial Revolution.

One of the most famous practitioners of CRT today, Robin DiAngelo, writes in her book, White Fragility:

White supremacy is a descriptive and useful term to capture the all-encompassing centrality and assumed superiority of people defined and perceived as white and the practices based on this assumption. White supremacy in this context does not refer to individual white people and their individual intentions or actions but to an overarching political, economic, and social system of domination. Again, racism is a structure, not an event. While hate groups that openly proclaim white superiority do exist and this term refers to them also, the popular consciousness solely associates white supremacy with these radical groups. This reductive definition obscures the reality of the larger system at work and prevents us from addressing this system.

"I hope to have made clear that white supremacy is something much more pervasive and subtle than the actions of explicit white nationalists. White supremacy describes the culture we live in," DiAngelo writes.

Its use is a very successful example of the Left's use of strategic ambiguity in the pursuit of a rather large and ambitious goal. The target is a free-market system that rewards hard work, ability, and other virtuous traits. Other CRT terms that have specific and unique meanings when used by its practitioners are "equity," "diversity," "inclusion," and "people of color."

CRT speakers have also developed peculiar turns of phrase that are specific to the group; supporters are said to be "in allyship" or "in relationship." The U.S. is said to be a "carceral state."

## How Does Critical Race Theory Affect You?

Because of their strong political commitment to transforming the United States, CRT writers make clear that they do not intend for what happens on college campuses to stay on campus. "It is our hope that scholarly resistance will lay the groundwork for wide-scale resistance. We believe that standards and institutions created by and fortifying white power ought to be resisted," writes Bell.

On that score, we must pronounce CRT to have been a resounding success. CRT has broken out of the classroom and become the philosophy of wide-scale resistance. It is useful to identify a few of the ways with which it impacts the daily lives of Americans.

**Identity Politics Care of Marcuse**

CRT has become the academic body of work that underpins identity politics, an ongoing effort to reimagine the United States as a nation not of individuals and local communities united under common purposes, but as one riven by groups based on sex, race, national origin, or gender—each with specific claims on victimization. These identity categories correspond to Marcuse's new revolutionary base ("the substratum of the outcasts and outsiders, the exploited and persecuted of other races and other colors").

The identities are often artificial ones manufactured by government itself, examples being the Hispanic and Asian-American pan-ethnicities contrived in 1977 by the Office of Management and Budget (OMB), or the 31 genders approved by the New York City Commission on Human Rights.

Under identity politics, America is no longer a country where the individual is the central agent in society, who, because of his very existence possesses individual rights. Instead, membership in the official categories becomes the identity that matters when it comes to rights (mostly positive rights, not natural ones), responsibilities, and everything else. Identity politics has become the new paradigm under which many Americans now operate. Victimhood is what commands attention, respect, and entitlements, seen as compensatory justice.

CRT emerged contemporaneously with the proliferation of these identity categories in America and became the philosophical tool to implement identity politics and the attempt to transform the United States. *Race, Racism and American Law* by Derrick Bell includes toward the end a chapter for "Racism and Other Nonwhites," among whom he names for the United States the Chinese, the Japanese, and the Mexicans.

It was published in 1972, two years before the Census Bureau bureaucrats, under pressure from leftist activists, opened the first national racial and ethnic advisory committee.

### Trump Takes Aim at Critical Race Theory, Signs Executive Order on 'Patriotic Education'

President Donald Trump said in September 2020 that the left's "cancel culture," including critical race theory and the New York Times' "1619 Project," is "toxic propaganda" that must be eliminated from schools and workplaces. Later, he signed an executive order on Sept. 22, 2020 that bans federal agencies, contractors, subcontractors, and grantees from instructing their

Per the *Epoch Times* September 2020 article titled "Trump Takes Aim at Critical Race Theory, Signs Executive Order on 'Patriotic Education'" by Jack Phillips:

The theories are based on the Marxist concept of "struggle," pitting races and sexes against each other by labeling them "oppressors" and the "oppressed." It then reinterprets society and history as being rooted in this "struggle." The theories have become the preferred creed of progressive intellectuals and have spread throughout academia, government institutions, public education, and the corporate world.

"American parents are not going to accept indoctrination in our schools, cancel culture at work, or the repression of traditional faith, culture, and values in the public square. Not anymore," the president said at the National Archives in Washington. "Critical Race Theory, the 1619 Project, and the crusade against American history is toxic propaganda—an ideological poison that, if not removed, will dissolve the civic bonds that tie us together."

During the event, Trump instead proposed "patriotic education," applauding a grant awarded by the National Endowment for the Humanities to come up with a "pro-American curriculum that celebrates the truth about our nation's great history." He also signed an executive order establishing a commission to "promote patriotic education," which is called the "1776 Commission."

However, after Trump lost the presidency, on Jan. 20, 2021, during his first day in office, President Biden issued a new executive order, "Advancing Racial Equity and Support for Underserved Communities Through the Federal Government," that immediately revoked the curtailed trainings for federal agencies and contractors that Trump's executive order had enacted.

The order not only rescinded the diversity training restrictions but also required all agencies to prioritize and create opportunities for communities that have been historically underserved: "By advancing equity across the federal government, we can create opportunities for the improvement of communities that have been historically underserved, which benefits everyone."

**Republicans Are Right to Push Back Against CRT in the Classrooms**

A bevy of Republican-backed bills in various states would place limits on CRT-inspired instruction as reported in the editors' "Republicans Are Right to Push Back Against CRT in the Classrooms" article in the National Review in July 2021: Much of the criticism of these bills has been inaccurate and dishonest—for example, claiming that these bills would prevent teaching about slavery or Jim Crow.

The truth is something closer to the opposite: The Texas bill, for example, mandates that students be taught "the history of white supremacy, including but not limited to the institution of slavery, the eugenics movement, and the Ku Klux Klan, and the ways in which it is morally wrong."

It forbids the questionable practice of giving students academic credit for participating in political protests, forbids teachers from being subjected to certain kinds of compelled speech and demands that in discussions of current events they "strive to explore such issues from diverse and contending perspectives without giving deference to any one perspective," and mandates that students read certain historical documents (the Federalist Papers, Tocqueville, the Civil Rights Act of 1964), etc.

What many of the bills attempt to address is using the class to inculcate students in a crude theory of collective racial guilt—the idea that contemporary whites bear some kind of effectively hereditary guilt for the actions of slavers and segregationists. Some take a similar attitude toward the rhetoric of "white privilege."

These bills do not represent unprovoked Republican cultural aggression ex nihilo. The left-wing indoctrination and politicization that Americans associate with higher education has long worked its way down into K–12 teaching. The goal of the bills is not political indoctrination but its opposite: classrooms that equip children with the facts to form their own ideas without an authority figure preaching leftist ideology.

## Policy Recommendations

Critical Race Theory began as an academic concept, but we can find the ideas all around us today, from schoolhouses to the corporate world to Hollywood. Racism and intolerance should have no place in America, but CRT is more than just a philosophical objection to discrimination. When followed to its logical conclusion, CRT is destructive and rejects the fundamental ideas on which our constitutional republic is based.

**Critical Race Theory and identity politics should not drive the government's creation of categories through the Census and other surveys.** The government at all levels should get out of the business of creating official identity categories, without which identity politics would wither away. It should go back to asking citizens for national origin, language spoken in the home, etc.—actual facts, not synthetic concoctions. It could also introduce questions on family structure (i.e., whether there is both a mother and a father in house, how many children were born in non-intact families, etc.).

**The federal government should not support so-called diversity trainings that claim the presence of Critical ideas such as "unconscious bias."** Federal officials should keep in place President Trump's Executive Order eliminating CRT trainings in the federal workforce and among federal contractors and use its bully pulpit to encourage the private sector to similarly discontinue these counter- productive "trainings."

**Parents should know what is being taught in their children's K–12 schools.** State policymakers should require that public schools make their curricular resources available to the public. Parents and taxpayers should have access to the material that teachers are using in the class-room. Some charter schools provide models to follow and already make these resources available.148 Such transparency will help families as they make decisions about how and where their children learn by evaluating the offerings of different schools and education institutions.

**Federal directives should not micromanage local schools' student discipline policies.** Federal officials should not allow for the reinstatement of the Obama Administration's 2014 "Dear Colleague" Letter on disparate impact, and policymakers should review other sections of federal law to remove the concept of disparate impact.149 For example, disparate impact theory is included in the Individuals with Disabilities Education Act (IDEA), the federal law governing services and spending for children with special needs in public schools.150 The Obama Administration further embedded this idea in IDEA's regulations at the end of his Administration.

Federal, state, and local officials should allow educators and parents to work together to evaluate disciplinary incidents according to the circumstances and actions involved. School districts should not be required to maintain certain quotas of students who do or do not face exclusionary discipline.

**State policymakers must protect free speech on public college campuses—especially when college administrators do not.** State lawmakers should consider proposals that require public university systems to provide student orientation sessions discussing free speech on campus. Policymakers in Alabama, Arizona, Georgia, North Carolina, and Wisconsin have models that other state officials should follow.

State officials should also require public university governing boards to create policies that require university administrators to sanction anyone in a university community, including students, that violate someone else's expressive rights, up to and including suspension and expulsion. Administrators should refer violations of the law to law enforcement, but university officials should protect expressive rights through the enforcement of school codes of conduct.

# 9 – Free Speech Degradation Within America's Academic, Justice, Scientific & Corporate Communities

*Credit: American Federation of Teachers.*

Increasingly since 2014, the Heterodox Academy reports that students and professors are heavily self-censoring, learning to "walk on eggshells." Is this going on in your classroom, or at your university or high school? If so, then it is vital to know which students are feeling intimidated, about what topics, and why? Are students primarily afraid of the professors, or of other students? Is it happening in all departments, or only in a few?

Protests on college campuses that shut down events hosting conservative speakers has prompted universities around the country to pledge more tolerance for diverse opinions, "I think there's a lot of embarrassment on campuses, so some kind of statement from the top might have good-sounding words but actions speak louder than words," said Jack Citrin, a professor of political science at Berkeley and a member of the Heterodox Academy. "I'd like to see what happens the next time (conservative intellectuals) Charles Murray or Ayaan Hirsi Ali try to speak on a campus."

The Heterodox ranking lists Berkeley as 105 out of 106 schools, citing the protests that stopped Yiannopoulos and Coulter from speaking as well as a missive from the University of California system urging faculty "not to criticize affirmative action or to refer to America as a melting pot."

A protestor recently turned to violence against a young man named Hayden Williams as he recruited students for a conservative group at the University of California Berkeley. President Trump said Williams "took a hard punch in the face for all of us... and we can never allow that to happen."

Neither Williams nor his attacker Zachary Greenberg attends UC Berkeley – but his story is emblematic of an education system that critics say shuns conservative voices. At CPAC, Williams stated, "there's so many conservative students across the country who are facing discrimination, harassment, and worse, if they dare to speak up on campus."

**Berkeley's Intolerance for Conservative Viewpoints is Obvious**

A Senate Judiciary Committee, Senator Chuck Grassley (R., Iowa) criticized Berkeley for failing to adequately punish violent protesters. "Higher education rests on the free flow of ideas," he said.

A Berkeley spokesman said a misperception has taken root about the school's tolerance for conservative viewpoints is lacking. "We would resist the notion that this campus has been anything other than welcoming to speakers from across the political spectrum," spokesman Dan Mogulof said. For any sapient being, this is clearly a contradictory statement of the facts and education madness!

The top-ranked school for freedom of speech is the University of Chicago. Provost Dr. Daniel Diermeier said the ideal of viewpoint diversity is central to the university's mission. "We believe that the best education we can provide students to prepare them for the world is to hear diverse points of view even if they feel uncomfortable," Diermeier said. "We want to provide them with the tools to find counterarguments.

But these students need and deserve every encouragement from outside their closed and claustrophobic environs. As one of them put it to me, "There's more faculty interest in climate control than in the Western canon." Multiculturalism guarantees that courses on Islam highlight all the good that can be said of Muhammad and the Quran, but there is no comparable academic commitment to reinvigorating the foundational teachings of American liberal democracy or to strengthening the legacy bequeathed to us by "dead white males."

## Let's Embrace Constructive Disagreement

Constructive Disagreement occurs when people who don't see eye-to-eye are committed to exploring an issue together, alive to their own fallibility and the limits of their knowledge—and open to learning something from others who see things differently than they do.

When people lack the skill or the will to disagree constructively, disputes about theories, methods, data, analysis, or solutions can take on the character of zero-sum power struggles rather than opportunities for mutual growth and discovery. People become more polarized and closed-minded. They grow less likely to share and cooperate, and more likely to withhold key information, or engage in bad-faith for competitive advantage.

Mistakes and failures are more likely to be weaponized against scholars rather than being understood as an unavoidable part of the iterative process of exploration, trial, error, discovery, and revision that lies at the core of the scientific method. People grow less likely to take risks or tolerate uncertainty. Under these circumstances, increased diversity can become a liability—a source of additional paranoia and strife—rather than an asset.

Many students, faculty and staff have insufficient training in how to constructively engage across difference—especially as it relates to fundamental ideological commitments. To help resolve this campus wide problem, the Heterodox Academy that partners with professors, administrators, and others to create an academy eager to welcome people who approach problems and questions from different points of view, has a set of tools and ten steps professors can take to promote open inquiry and constructive disagreement in their classrooms.

## Engaging With Underrepresented Perspectives Meaningfully and Charitably in the Curriculum

However, constructive disagreement cannot simply be taught from the armchair—it's a skill people refine through real-world engagement. In many contexts this is difficult due to the aforementioned demographic and ideological distortions within institutions of higher education.

Many students lack opportunities to engage with underrepresented perspectives meaningfully and charitably in the curriculum. Many professors who are concerned about this problem don't know where or how to begin introducing missing perspectives, as they often do not have a solid foundation in them either.

In many academic contexts, from class discussions to academic research, there are apparent incentives towards competition which can be counterproductive to learning and growth. It often seems easier to build a reputation by attacking others—to elevate oneself at the expense of others—than to seek opportunities for mutual growth and collaborative discovery among people who seem to be on opposite sides of an issue.

The background political culture in the contemporary United States is highly polarized and increasingly toxic. In such an environment, differences of opinion are more likely to be attributed to moral or intellectual defects in one's interlocutors. People are easily branded as sellouts or traitors for collaborating with "the enemy"—or providing ammunition for the "enemy" by defying the consensus of their tribe known as identify politics.

## We All Suffer From Confirmation Bias

Per Dr. Jonathan Haidt, "We all suffer from confirmation bias—the tendency to use all of our powers of reasoning to seek out proof of why we are right. The only known cure for confirmation bias is engaging with other people who see things differently. Only they can find reasons why you might be wrong. Only they can help you improve your thinking. Therefore, an orthodox university cannot make you smarter, it can only confirm the prejudices you brought with you."

A heterodox university, in contrast, elevates everyone's ability to reason and sets students up with more realistic expectations about the world they will enter after commencement. In an interview with ACTA's *The Forum* he continues:

*The Forum*: What are the effects on individuals who live, work, and study in an environment that tolerates only one viewpoint—or orthodoxy?

Haidt: In such an environment, individuals with contrasting views are silenced either by peers or—more often—through self-censorship, walking on eggshells. What we want to break is the echo chamber in which people who have the same perspective endlessly reinforce each other, deepening orthodoxy and lessening the potential for cross-partisan conversations and empathy.

The future of liberal democracy depends in no small measure on empathy—the ability to humanize and understand others. Students need to see those with whom they disagree politically as people—or else they risk alienating and demonizing

## Various Justice Departments Are Being Weaponized Against Conservatives

As noted during the Republican National Committee on June 25, 2021, President Joe Biden and the Democrats are weaponizing the Department of Justice to attack commonsense election integrity laws recently enacted in Georgia.

Why? Because the Democrats failed to pass their federal power grab, HR1 – appropriately renamed by the GOP as "the Corrupt Politicians Act"—so now, they're looking to the Department of Justice to attack Georgia's commonsense voter integrity law based on their false narratives, flying in the face of the will of the American people, who believe states, not the federal government, should decide voting rules and regulations, and the will of the people of Georgia.

As a reminder of recent 2021 polling Georgia related to fair elections and voter integrity:

- 65% of individuals surveyed support requiring a driver's license number to verify absentee ballots.

- 74% support additional absentee ID requirements.

- 52% said voting laws should prioritize establishing safeguards against fraud.

- 52% support shortening the runoff period to 4 weeks instead of 9 weeks.

- 55% believe that ballot drop boxes should only be allowed "inside early voting sites."

- 60% endorse an "earlier deadline to request absentee ballots," with a cutoff of 11 days instead of four days before election day.

- 54% support prohibiting election officials from mailing unsolicited absentee ballot applications to registered voters.

A majority say the law increased their confidence in the state's election system and not only did Georgia's law establish commonsense, widely supported voter integrity measures, it "expanded" opportunities to vote, making it easier to vote than in many Democrat-run states contrary to statements made by Stacey Abrams and other Democratic Party pundits.

### Democrats' Weaponization of the DOJ is Back Under the Biden Administration

Furthermore, from the October 2021 EMBO Reports story by Katie Pavlich titled "Democrats' Weaponization of the DOJ is Back Under the Biden Administration," in 2009, a national, grassroots movement known as the Tea Party emerged in cities across the country to combat then-President Obama's radical spending agenda and government takeover of American health care. Bureaucrats at the IRS and Department of Justice quickly took notice and got to work to stop it. After all, with midterm elections right around the corner, Obama's political agenda was at stake.

"This was not an accident. This is a willful act of intimidation to discourage a point of view. What the government did to our little group in Wetumpka, Alabama is un-American," Wetumpka Tea Party President Becky Gerritson testified at a June 2013 congressional hearing. "The demands for information in the questionnaire shocked me as someone who loves liberty and the First Amendment. I was asked to hand over my donor list including the amounts that they gave and the dates in which they gave them."

**The IRS Was Targeting Tea Party Members**

"We knew we were being targeted because fellow Tea Party organizers across this nation were getting the same types of letters and questionnaires," she continued.

While IRS officials in Washington, D.C., claimed the targeting was an isolated, rogue operation in an Ohio office, documents showed the IRS was asked by Sen. Sheldon Whitehouse (D-R.I.) and Rep. Elijah Cummings (D-Md.) to "look into" the groups.

Right on cue, IRS official Lois Lerner had a series of meetings with DOJ officials about how to criminally prosecute conservative groups with a goal of making them an example. Groups applying for tax-exempt status with the words "tea party" or "patriot" in their titles were singled out for extra scrutiny.

"One IRS prosecution would make an impact and they wouldn't feel so comfortable doing the stuff," Lerner said in a 2013 email. In another email, Lerner said the "Tea Party Matter [is] very dangerous." It was obvious the IRS was attempting to quash political dissent. Lerner eventually admitted the targeting was wrong, retired and then the IRS "lost" thousands of her emails.

**The FBI Was Weaponized Against Trump As Well**

Fast-forward to 2016, and politically motivated FBI agents, who regularly exchanged text messages about their disdain for former President Trump, used a fake dossier commissioned and paid for by the Clinton campaign to go after Hillary Clinton's presidential political opponent.

While the FBI maintains the fake document wasn't used to obtain FISA warrants against Trump campaign adviser Carter Page, bad information was. Years later and after significant damage, a FISA judge berated the bureau and ruled two warrants were illegal. Former FBI lawyer Kevin Clinesmith falsified information on FISA applications in order to get them approved.

"This manufactured scandal and associated lies caused me to adopt the lifestyle of an international fugitive for years," Page said during a court hearing about the illegal surveillance. "I often have felt as if I had been left with no life at all. Each member of my family was severely impacted."

**The DOJ is Being Re-Weaponized Against Conservatives**

Now that Democrats are back in charge at DOJ, the political weaponization of the agency has returned and concerned parents are the target.

After President Biden received a letter from the National School Boards Association (NSBA) requesting DOJ treat parents as domestic terrorists, with an assist from the Patriot Act, Attorney General Merrick Garland coincidently released an official memo warning the FBI would be monitoring school board meetings. During recent congressional testimony, Garland admitted the letter from NSBA, not an independent investigation or evidence of "threats," was used for the DOJ memo.

**The NSBA and Garland's "Domestic Terrorists" Letter**

After heavy criticism and outrage, with many school boards disavowing the letter, the NSBA backtracked and issued an apology.

"There was no justification for some of the language included in the letter. We should have had a better process in place to allow for consultation on a communication of this significance," the NSBA wrote in a follow up letter. "The voices of parents should and must continue to be heard when it comes to decisions about their children's education, health and safety."

As of this writing, Garland hasn't withdrawn the DOJ memo issuing federal law enforcement scrutiny to local meetings. NSBA President Viola Garcia has been appointed by Education Secretary Miguel Cardona to the National Assessment Governing Board, where she will give guidance on education policy. She is the author of the original letter calling for DOJ to go after parents.

Given the left's history of using powerful government agencies to target political opponents, Americans opposed to Biden's agenda should understand Garland's memo about parents was simply a test run.

## Challenges and Threats to Free Speech From Science of Social Psychology

What does the science of social psychology have to tell us about the current challenges and threats to free speech? A great deal, according to Dr. Jonathan Haidt, Thomas Cooley Professor of Ethical Leadership at New York University's Stern School of Business.

Haidt is one of three co-founders of Heterodox Academy (HxA) in 2015, an exciting new alliance of academics seeking to expand support for political diversity and highlight the challenges of ideological orthodoxy in higher education. ACTA's *The Forum* sat down with Haidt and his team at Heterodox Academy to discuss this innovative organization's approach to changing the culture in higher education and expanding viewpoint diversity:

The Heterodox Academy's membership has grown to 5,000 plus "In the wake of the Middlebury protests and violence, we're seeing a lot of liberal-left professors standing up against illiberal-left professors and students," Haidt says. Less than a fifth of the organization's members identify as "right or conservative;" most are centrists, liberals, or progressives.

By giving more academic jobs and tenure to outspoken libertarians and conservatives seems like the most effective way to change the campus culture, if only by signaling to self-censoring students that dissent is acceptable.

## The Problem: Orthodoxy in the Academy

Per Haidt: In September 2015, a few weeks before the wave of student protests began, Heterodox Academy was founded to address a very specific problem: the loss of viewpoint diversity, especially political diversity, among the faculty in colleges and universities across America.

But as campus debate heated up in the fall of 2015, political passions rose and students who dissented from the prevailing orthodoxy found themselves increasingly under attack. Why should students feel like they cannot express themselves? Why should any subgroup of students be able to deem what is appropriate speech and which speaker is worthy of being heard? Are we engineering a climate where students will graduate without any exposure to contrasting viewpoints? What does that mean for businesses who hire grads unable to deal with those with whom they disagree politically?

A culture that will not tolerate divergence of opinion harms students, but academic research is also at risk when dominant theories and opinions no longer encounter counterclaims that test their validity.

The Heterodox Academy's goal is to create a network of academic stakeholders united in their intent to see the university live up to its ideals of truth, civil disagreement, and intellectual discovery. We want administrators and professors to stand up for free speech and free inquiry. We envision a campus where ideas can be expressed, beliefs challenged and theories critically analyzed so as to help students develop a more comprehensive and valid understanding of varied social and political perspectives, freed from the fear of intimidation by peers.

## The Case for Intellectual Humility

The Templeton Foundation is leading research in intellectual humility and its many benefits. Psychologists and philosophers are working to tease apart the ways we respond to new ideas and information—and the possible benefits of a humble approach. Over the last decade, psychologists, philosophers, and other researchers have begun to explore intellectual humility, using analytical and empirical tools aimed at understanding its nature and implications.

At once theoretically fascinating and practically weighty, the study of intellectual humility calls for collaboration among researchers from fields of inquiry including psychology, epistemology, neuroscience, and educational research. In recent reviews of research commissioned by the John Templeton Foundation, Fordham University philosopher Nathan Ballantyne and Duke University psychologist Mark Leary synthesized findings from dozens of recently published articles on the topic, highlighting both the answers, and the questions, they raise.

From the 2018 paper by Leor Zmigrod, et. al., titled, "The psychological roots of intellectual humility: The role of intelligence and cognitive flexibility," intellectual humility has been identified as a character virtue that allows individuals to recognize their own potential fallibility when forming and revising attitudes. Intellectual humility is therefore essential for avoiding confirmation biases when reasoning about evidence and evaluating beliefs.

The present study investigated the cognitive correlates of intellectual humility. The results indicate that cognitive flexibility, measured with objective behavioral assessments, predicted intellectual humility. Intelligence was also predictive of intellectual humility.

## COVID-19 and Misinformation: Is Censorship of Social Media a Remedy?

In February this year, when the new coronavirus began to spread outside China, the Director General of the World Health Organization (WHO), Tedros Adhanom Ghebreyesus, announced: "we're not just fighting an epidemic; we're fighting an "infodemic." The term, coined in 2003 in the context of the first SARS epidemic, refers to a rapid proliferation of information that is often false or uncertain.

Academic researchers, international organizations such as the United Nations and the European Union, individual governments and the media have acknowledged and discussed the prevalence of the alleged COVID-19 infodemic and the importance of fighting it. Information campaigns have been launched to provide wider audiences with reliable information about COVID-19. Main social media platforms have also actively fought against false information by filtering out or flagging content considered as misinformation.

Per the October 2020 report by Emilia Niemiec of EMBO Reports, she explains the censorship on social media platforms related to COVID-19 and the problems it raises along with an alternative approach to counteract the spread of perceived medical and scientific misinformation.

### Censorship on Social Media Platforms

Censorship on major social media platforms, such as Facebook, Twitter and YouTube, is not a new phenomenon. These companies regularly remove content that they consider as objectionable based on continually updated categories outlined in their policies.

Examples of "objectionable content" include "hate speech," "glorification of violence" or "harmful and dangerous content." These categories are not only often broader than the exceptions to the freedom of speech entrenched in legislations of democratic countries, but also implicitly vague and leave plenty of room to interpretation.

Indeed, an analysis of content banned on social networks suggests that the moderation is often politically biased (Stjernfelt & Lauritzen, 2020). Some very recent examples of moderation with apparent political ramifications include Twitter's labelling of US President Donald J. Trump's tweets as violating Twitter's policy about glorifying violence or abusive behavior, or adding a warning suggesting that a post was factually inaccurate.

Social media platforms are private companies and as such, one could argue, they should be able to decide what content they tolerate or not. However, such a view overlooks salient aspects of the issue. First, censorship on Facebook, Twitter or YouTube appears to contradict the very idea of these communication networks, that is, of spaces where everyone can express their opinion.

YouTube, for example, declares on its website that its "mission is to give everyone a voice." Twitter's manager once described his company as "the free speech wing of the free speech party." Mark Zuckerberg, the CEO of Facebook, has similarly been vocal about Facebook's commitment to the freedom of speech.

Many users of social media might have believed in these ideals when joining the online communities—or, at least, they did not expect biased censorship on the platforms. From this point of view, appeals to the freedom of speech made by the social networks seem unfair or deceptive.

Another important point to consider is the fact that a few big tech companies currently dominate social media services, which also serve as a source of news to many users. According to a 2020 survey by the Reuters Institute for the Study of Journalism, 36% of 24,000 respondents from 12 countries use Facebook for news weekly, while 21% of the surveyed use YouTube for the same purpose. If we add to this the fact that Google is the most popular search engine, it becomes clear that a few tech companies have huge power over what information Internet users can see and how their views are shaped.

Referring among others to the role of the "modern public square" ascribed to online platforms, then President Trump issued an executive order in 2020 which aims to limit the current legal protections of the big tech companies and prevent the censorship on their platforms, which can counteract the tech giants' role in shaping public discourse which has become so apparent.

While it is difficult to overlook the politically motivated censorship on online platforms and its implications, the removal of misinformation related to medical topics such as COVID-19 may seem to belong to a different category—not political, but rather one of science, where information can be objectively judged based on scientific evidence. At a closer look, however, this does not seem to be the case.

## Censorship of information About COVID-19

In response to calls to combat misinformation about COVID-19, a group of companies, including among others Facebook, Twitter and YouTube, issued a joint statement in March 2020 essentially stating they are "jointly combating fraud and misinformation about the virus, elevating authoritative content on [their] platforms".

Their actions include the introduction of "educational pop-ups connecting people to information from the WHO" (Facebook), adding warning labels to content considered as false or misleading (Facebook, Twitter), removing content contradicting health authorities or the WHO (YouTube) and content that could directly contribute or lead to (physical) harm (Facebook and Twitter).

One example is a video removed by YouTube, in which a researcher, John Ioannidis, discussed data related to COVID-19, questioned the need to continue the ongoing lockdown and raised concerns about the negative impact of the restrictions. Other cases of censorship on major social media platforms have been reported, for example removal of information about anti-quarantine protests on Facebook.

A major question regarding the policies of the communication platforms is who exactly defines and how which information is deemed to be false or harmful? And can we rely on these judgements?

One of the authoritative sources that all three major social media platforms mention in their policies on COVID-19 is the WHO. YouTube and Twitter also refer to guidelines from local health authorities. Although these are usually developed by experts and may be legally binding, this does not imply that they are unerring.

There has been disagreement among researchers in medical sciences about the necessity for lockdown measures (Melnick & Ioannidis, 2020). Furthermore, researchers and many healthcare professionals have indicated numerous and serious negative impacts of the policies introduced to combat the spread of COVID-19, and expressed doubts about the evidence supporting these measures (Ioannidis, 2020).

## The COVID-19 Pandemic Science is 'Not' Settled

This variety of opinions on how to handle the COVID-19 pandemic is related, among others, to the fact that it is a new disease and the knowledge about it is relatively limited and unsettled. Moreover, the implications of the pandemic and measures taken to counteract it exceed the remit of epidemiology or public health experts and fall into areas of economy, education, psychology and sociology. Meanwhile, experts who develop policies or express opinions about COVID-19 may not have a complete overview of the implications of pandemic-related policies.

Processes of reviewing research results, drawing conclusions, and preparing guidelines may be complex, prone to mistakes and not immune to political or commercial interests.

Additionally, there are the "usual" problems related to evaluation and translation of evidence into medical or public health practice. They include questions about the validity of a given study, limitations of methods, reproducibility of results and so on. Processes of reviewing research results, drawing conclusions and preparing guidelines may be complex, prone to mistakes and not immune to political or commercial interests.

Retracted articles on COVID-19, including publications in The Lancet, the New England Journal of Medicine, and 200 plus more as tracked by Retraction Watch (for a complete list see the Appendix) which suggest that research on COVID-19 is not an exception to problems related to the ethics of research.

Constructive critique, questioning of evidence and opinions of scientists and policy-makers are thus necessary to identify and correct potential errors and to prevent them from being propagated. By following their policies on COVID-19, social media platforms filter out content which contradicts specific views that are not necessarily correct or unanimously accepted, with respect to the underlying scientific evidence or represented values and political views.

If critique of these views is eliminated or restricted, the possibility to correct errors, contribute to the understanding of the topic and inform public debate is limited. Additionally, since the censorship is not based solely on science—as scientific evidence is an iterative process and medical experts still disagree on various topics—other factors influence decisions to remove content.

Questions about the commitment to the freedom of speech of the social media providers and risk of manipulation of public opinion are therefore relevant also in case of information about COVID-19.

**The Remedy to Medical Misinformation and Unfounded Censorship**

If censorship of scientific information does not seem to be an adequate solution to the problem of false medical news on social media, what then is a fitting remedy to the "infodemic"? In order to adequately address this question, a general understanding of how social media function may help users make informed decisions about the use of Facebook, YouTube, Twitter and similar services, in accordance with one's goals and values is needed.

In particular, the fact that social media platforms are provided and operated by private companies, which are interested primarily in making profit, and the implications of this fact may be worth to consider. The business model of social media companies is based on revenue from ads tailored to the users: the more users and the more time they spend on their websites, the higher the profit.

Consequently, these companies use knowledge from psychology and huge amounts of personal data to design ever more efficient mechanisms to motivate users to spend more time on their websites.

Sean Parker, a former president of Facebook, put it this way: "…we need to sort of give you a little dopamine hit every once in a while, because someone liked or commented on a photo or a post or whatever. And that's going to get you to contribute more content, and that's going to get you … more likes and comments. It's a social-validation feedback loop … exactly the kind of thing that a hacker like myself would come up with, because you're exploiting a vulnerability in human psychology."

Although the censorship on social media may seem an efficient and immediate solution to the problem of medical and scientific misinformation, it paradoxically introduces a risk of propagation of errors and manipulation. This is related to the fact that the exclusive authority to define what is "scientifically proven" or "medically substantiated" is attributed to either the social media providers or certain institutions, despite the possibility of mistakes on their side or potential abuse of their position to foster political, commercial or other interests.

## The Corporate Workplace and CRT Trainings

The CRT-influenced trainings that are often seen in America's workplaces and schools are little more than modern-day versions of the struggle sessions that Gramsci recommended for European workers in 1920s, in the sense that they seek to replace what its practitioners see as a "cultural hegemony" with a "counter-hegemony."

A well-known example of this indoctrination came in 2020 from the National Museum for African American History and Culture, a Smithsonian Institution. Until President Trump and others criticized it, forcing administrators to take it down, the museum ran an "anti-racist" chart that disparaged "hard work" and "cause and effect relationships" and criticized ideas such as "hard work is the key to success," "work before play," and "objective, rational linear thinking," saying these are attributes of "white dominant culture, or whiteness."

But even after taking down the racist chart, the museum continued to host this web portal on "whiteness." It says, among other things, that "whiteness and the normalization of white racial identity throughout America's history have created a culture where nonwhite persons are seen as inferior or abnormal."

Other examples of CRT training in the federal workforce include the Treasury Department holding a session telling employees that "virtually all White people contribute to racism" and the Department of Homeland Security hosting a training on "microaggressions, microinequities, and micro assaults," in which white employees were told that they had been "socialized into oppressor roles."

Nor are the efforts to subvert society limited to the federal workforce. The Society for Human Resources Management (SHRM), the lobbying arm of human resource (HR) professionals, uses empathetic language in its descriptions of diversity training sessions, such as making work "a place where we, our members, and our business community can bring our unique professional talents to stand together against all forms of social injustice."

### SHRM's Training Materials Follow Design of Other Modern-Day Applications of CRT

The Society for Human Resources Management (SHRM) is influential, noting in its promotional material that the organization has over 300,000 human resource and business executive members in 165 countries—and impacts some 115 million workers. So employers and employees alike should be concerned when its "Conversation Starters" initiative contains verbiage found in CRT scholarship, such as "unconscious bias."

Examples of this text include the organization's survey finding that "52 percent of organizations have provided or plan to provide new training on implicit/unconscious bias, equity, inclusion, or other diversity-related topics," followed by guided questions such as: What types of new training has your organization provided on implicit/unconscious bias, equity, inclusion, or other diversity-related topics? Have you sought out guidance or education on how to address your own implicit/unconscious bias?

The SHRM's survey reports that "60 percent of HR professionals believe organizations have a responsibility to take a stance on important social/societal issues and to communicate that position," which can put those who are not comfortable having such work conversations in compromising positions. While SHRM's encouragement to "listen and ask thoughtful questions" and "invite a colleague to coffee" are reasonable, organizations should not pressure employees to become activists or look for examples of unconscious bias.

The SHRM reports that 68 percent of black HR professionals "would decrease or have decreased the amount of goods or services purchased from a company that remained silent on the topic of racial injustice," again, pushing the singular view of systemic oppression from the perspective of CRT into the business sector.

# 10 – American Censorship Inspired by the CCP's Totalitarian Social Credit System

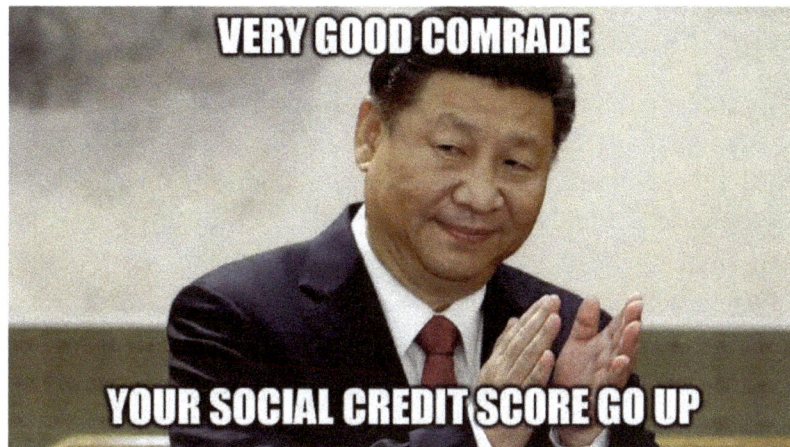

*Credit: Pinterest-idlememe.com*

It's common to hear anecdotes about friends or family who just don't feel comfortable discussing politics anymore. It's not that most of these people are bomb-throwing radicals, but many seem to think the country is so polarized that nothing good can come from voicing their own opinion.

From A Zaid Jilani's July 2020 Forward report "Most Americans are now self-censoring. We're regressing" a new poll from the Cato Institute and YouGov suggests that this fear is widespread. It found that 62 percent of Americans say they have political views they are afraid to share as noted Forward journalist Zaid Jilani.

This sentiment is most common among Republicans, with 77 percent agreeing that they are fearful of sharing some of their political views, but majorities of Democrats (52 percent) and independents (59 percent) share the same view.

In fact, nearly every ideological grouping believes they have to self-censor, with 52 percent of liberals, 64 percent of moderates and 77 percent of conservatives agreeing that the current political climate prevents them from saying things they believe.

Interestingly, the only group where a majority of people do not hold that view is among strong liberals – the most left-wing segment of the public. And still, 42 percent of them say that they self-censor in the same fashion.

## Self-Censorship is Now the Norm For Much of the American Public

This suggests that self-censorship is now the norm for much of the American public, across ideological lines, with perhaps the most liberal American citizens having a little less fear of speaking their minds than the rest of us.

That last bit of information may be no surprise if you're familiar with some statistics about how liberal-leaning some American institutions have become. One survey found that by 2014, for instance, the ratio of liberals to conservatives at American colleges and universities was six to one; among New England's institutions of higher education, it's 28 to one.

It's hardly a surprise that when corners of American society become dominated by one ideological group, they start to see dissenters from orthodoxy with deep suspicion. We can, for instance, witness hundreds of professors and graduate students signing a letter denouncing the liberal psychologist Steven Pinker for some mild dissents from some of the assertions common in the Black Lives Matter movement (namely that race is the variable most strongly correlated with police shootings).

Pinker is a rich and famous man who will likely escape any attempt at censorship thrown at him, but what should worry us more is the lowly graduate assistant or professor without tenure who worries that publishing an objective research finding will get them in hot water with their university if its results don't confirm the ideological priors of whatever group happens to be hegemonic in the culture.

Even more worrying than the general climate of fear are the lengths with which some Americans are willing to go to punish their political opponents. The survey found that 50 percent of strong liberals support firing a business executive who, in their personal capacity, donated to Donald Trump's re-election campaign. 36 percent of strong conservatives, on the other hand, supported firing executives who donated to former vice president Joe Biden's current presidential campaign.

Meanwhile, 32 percent of Americans, about a third of the country, worries that their political views could harm their employment. That would be a reasonable enough worry if you're part of the tiny sliver of Americans who works in explicitly political organizations, like a think tank or a campaign, but the number suggests that people who work jobs unrelated to politics still fear that their views could cost them their employment. This includes a quarter of Democrats and a whopping 60 percent of Republicans.

Taken together, the implication of these results is that America is a place where most people are deeply worried about honestly engaging in the political process, something that could over time do real damage to our democracy.

We could, for example, see widespread "pluralistic ignorance." Pluralistic ignorance is a situation where members of a group may privately reject an idea, but they believe most of the other members of the group believe that idea, so they decide to accept it. This phenomenon is quite common on social media channels, where you're rewarded for conforming to group trends and punished for stepping outside the bounds of you cohort.

Running an entire country on pluralistic ignorance would prevent us from addressing the actual concerns members of the public have. If our ancestors were paralyzed from speaking in favor of causes that were unpopular, we wouldn't have all kinds of advances from women's suffrage to civil rights.

In order to address this climate of fear, we have to stop being afraid. Yes, sometimes people will say things that upset or outrage us, and sometimes we will upset or outrage others. But that's the price of living in a messy but beautiful society with all kinds of people who disagree. In order to make things a little easier, it would be wise to heed the counsel of psychologist Jonathan Haidt, who says we should "give less offense" by being more polite and "take less offense" by charitably interpreting other's statements and offering forgiveness when we screw up.

## The Second Great Age of Political Correctness

From the January 2022 issue of Reason and the article by Dr. Greg Lukianoff "The Second Great Age of Political Correctness:" The 1994 movie PCU, about a rebellious fraternity resisting its politically correct university, was a milestone. Not because the movie was especially good—it wasn't. It was a milestone because it showed that political correctness had officially become a joke.

The derisive term "P.C." (political correctness) had referred to a genuine and powerful force on campus for the previous decade. But by the mid-1990s, it had become the butt of jokes from across the political spectrum. The production of a mainstream movie mocking political correctness showed that its cultural moment had passed.

At the same time, punitive campus speech codes were being struck down. Among the most prominent cases was Stanford Law School, which boasted a notorious speech code banning "speech or other expression…intended to insult or stigmatize" an individual on the basis of membership in a protected class arguably including every living human. You don't have to be a lawyer to see how a ban on anything that "insults" would be abused: Even showing PCU itself, which makes fun of campus activists, feminists, and vegetarians, could potentially get you in trouble under such a broad and vague rule. The 1995 court defeat of the Stanford speech code marked the end of the First Great Age of Political Correctness.

Some assumed this meant political correctness was a fad that was gone forever. On the contrary, it gathered strength over the next two decades, rooting itself in university hiring practices and speech policing, until it became what people now refer to as "wokeness" or the much-abused term "cancel culture."

Political correctness didn't decline and fall. It went underground and then rose again. If anything, it's stronger than ever today. Yet some influential figures on the left still downplay the problem, going so far as to pretend that the increase in even tenured professors being fired for off-limits speech is a sign of a healthy campus. And this unwillingness to recognize a serious problem in academia has helped embolden culture warriors on the right, who have launched their own attacks on free speech and viewpoint diversity in the American education system.

The P.C. culture of the '80s and '90s didn't decline and fall. It just went underground. Now it's back and we've fully entered the Second Great Age of Political Correctness. Not surprisingly, it's

Big Tech, so heavily invested in China, that is leading the way in implementing an American version of China's Orwellian social credit system—a free speech suppression system that has found widespread praise in academic, progressive, and Democratic Party circles.

## When College Students Self-Censor, Society Loses

Colleges—the intended training ground for the sort of creative and integrative thinking such problem-solving requires—have become increasingly characterized by orthodoxy in what types of questions can be asked and what sort of comments can be shared in the classroom and around campus.

As a result, many students and even some faculty elect to self-censor. As citizens who are counting on students' future contributions to our shared social and civic endeavors, we all suffer when students elect to sit on the sidelines of their own learning or opt-out of scholarship because they feel they do not "belong" at institutions of higher learning.

Indeed, it is vital for America's future to encourage a diversity of opinions on college campuses. But what will it take to achieve that goal? Academic stakeholders must create campuses eager to welcome professors, students and speakers who approach problems and questions from different points of view, explicitly valuing the role such diversity plays in advancing the pursuit of knowledge, discovery, and innovation.

Rather than merely tolerating fellow learners whose views are wildly different from one's own, all should seek out and cherish that difference. Because we see things differently, we will be better able to explore the nuances of the topics we study, deepening our understanding and thus equipping us to be better able to move the needle on those issues we care about most.

### This is Not a Left-Right Issue

This is about creating intellectual institutions where learners can come together, humbled by their incomplete knowledge, curious what they can learn from others, able to share their own ideas and perspectives and eager to think together with nuance, open minds, respect and goodwill—all in service to understanding the complexities of our world more deeply.

The concept of constructive disagreement centers around creating a dynamic where key stakeholders in an organization can and are compelled to disagree. The word constructive alludes to the need to raise issues, debate, and resolve them. In the academy, this no longer or rarely happens--but it does in the corporate world.

To achieve that goal in academia where it's sorely lacking, academic stakeholders must enact policies and practices that support heterodox classrooms and campuses. This requires three ingredients:

First, stakeholders must value open inquiry and constructive disagreement. The good news is the available data suggest students, faculty and administrators overwhelmingly do value these things (in principle).

Second, stakeholders must have access to, or be willing to create, effective strategies for enacting these values. For students, this could mean forming or participating in freedom of speech organizations or related initiatives.

For professors, it could be about strategies they deploy in the classroom to create an environment conducive to open inquiry and constructive disagreement or signaling a desire for viewpoint diversity in job ads during faculty searches.

In other cases, it's as simple as the chief academic officer being a vocal and visible cheerleader for the role constructive disagreement across lines of difference plays in realizing the very mission of the institution.

Other interventions are a heavier lift, like actually following through on the consequences stated in an existing policy even when there's tremendous social pressure to do otherwise. Organizations like Heterodox Academy, OpenMind and Village Square continue to design and distribute tools and resources to support these efforts of administrators and faculty.

Third, stakeholders must perceive social permission to act on these values. This is a tougher nut to crack. For instance, even if professors set a good tone, students could be concerned about social sanction from peers.

Many of America's colleges and universities have fallen into a narrow orthodoxy in what is acceptable to say and to think on campus. Now is the time for all of us who value the pursuit of knowledge to support a new heterodoxy that welcomes, supports, and encourages a diversity of viewpoints.

The concept of constructive disagreement centers around creating a dynamic where key stakeholders in the faculty and student body are compelled to disagree. The word constructive alludes to the need to raise issues, debate, and resolve them reasonably. In the academy, this no longer or rarely happens--but it does so in the corporate world.

Our future as the world's leader in higher-education innovation depends on it.

## Censorship Used to Come Primarily From the Top Down But Now Coming From Students

Samantha Harris, director of policy research at the Foundation for Individual Rights in Education (FIRE), said censorship used to come primarily from the top down but now is coming from students. "Students increasingly seem to be arriving on campus believing that there is a generalized right not to be offended beyond the actual right to be free from harassment and threats, this amorphous right to emotional safety. It's a troubling trend," she said.

At Amherst College, in November, hundreds of students crammed into Robert Frost Library and demanded that students who had posted "Free Speech" and "All Lives Matter" posters go through "extensive training for racial and cultural competency" and possibly discipline. They wanted the administration to apologize for "our institutional agency of white supremacy," among many other forms of discrimination like "heterosexist, cis-sexism, xenophobia, ableism, mental health stigma and classism."

The University of Wisconsin at Milwaukee declared that the phrase "politically correct" is a "microaggression." The master of Yale's Pierson College said that his title reminds students of slavery.

A Washington State University professor said she would lower the grade of any student who uses the term "illegal immigrants" when referring to immigrants who are in the country illegally.

Another Washington State professor, in her syllabus for "Women and Popular Culture," noted that students risk "failure for the semester" if they use "derogatory/oppressive language" such as "referring to women/men as females or males."

The University of California system stipulated that "hostile" and "derogatory" thoughts include "I believe the most qualified person should get the job" and "America is the land of opportunity."

## Who Is in Control? The Need to Rein in Big Tech

The following is adapted from a speech delivered at Hillsdale College on November 8, 2020, during a Center for Constructive Alternatives conference on Big Tech that is covered in the "Who Is in Control? The Need to Rein in Big Tech" article in the January 2021 issue of *Imprimis* by Allum Bokhari:

In January 2021, when every major Silicon Valley tech company permanently banned the President of the United States from its platform, there was a backlash around the world. One after another, government and party leaders—many of them ideologically opposed to the policies of President Trump—raised their voices against the power and arrogance of the American tech giants.

These included the President of Mexico, the Chancellor of Germany, the government of Poland, ministers in the French and Australian governments, the neoliberal center-right bloc in the European Parliament, the national populist bloc in the European Parliament, the leader of the Russian opposition (who recently survived an assassination attempt), and the Russian government (which may well have been behind that attempt).

Common threats create strange bedfellows. Socialists, conservatives, nationalists, neoliberals, autocrats, and anti-autocrats may not agree on much, but they all recognize that the tech giants have accumulated far too much power. None like the idea that a pack of American hipsters in Silicon Valley can, at any moment, cut off their digital lines of communication.

Bokhari published a book on this topic prior to the November election, *Who Is in Control? The Need to Rein in Big Tech* and many who called him alarmist then are not so sure of that now. He built the book on interviews with Silicon Valley insiders and five years of reporting as a Breitbart News tech correspondent. Breitbart created a dedicated tech reporting team in 2015—a time when few recognized the danger that the rising tide of left-wing hostility to free speech would pose to the vision of the World Wide Web as a free and open platform for all viewpoints.

## Moving From the Freedom of Information to the Control of Information

This inversion of that early libertarian ideal—the movement from the freedom of information to the control of information on the Web—has been the story of the past five years.

When the Web was created in the 1990s, the goal was that everyone who wanted a voice could have one. All a person had to do to access the global marketplace of ideas was to go online and set up a website. Once created, the website belonged to that person. Especially if the person owned his own server, no one could deplatform him. That was by design, because the Web, when it was invented, was competing with other types of online services that were not so free and open.

It is important to remember that the Web, as we know it today—a network of websites accessed through browsers—was not the first online service ever created. In the 1990s, Sir Timothy Berners-Lee invented the technology that underpins websites and web browsers, creating the Web as we know it today. But there were other online services, some of which predated Berners-Lee's invention. Corporations like CompuServe and Prodigy ran their own online networks in the 1990s—networks that were separate from the Web and had access points that were different from web browsers. These privately-owned networks were open to the public, but CompuServe and Prodigy owned every bit of information on them and could kick people off their networks for any reason.

In these ways the Web was different. No one owned it, owned the information on it, or could kick anyone off. That was the idea, at least, before the Web was captured by a handful of corporations.

We all know their names: Google, Facebook, Twitter, YouTube, Amazon. Like Prodigy and CompuServe back in the '90s, they own everything on their platforms, and they have the police power over what can be said and who can participate. But it matters a lot more today than it did in the '90s. Back then, very few people used online services. Today everyone uses them—it is practically impossible not to use them. Businesses depend on them. News publishers depend on them. Politicians and political activists depend on them. And crucially, citizens depend on them for information.

Today, Big Tech doesn't just mean control over online information. It means control over news. It means control over commerce. It means control over politics. And how are the corporate tech giants using their control? Judging by the three biggest moves they have made since I wrote my book—the censoring of the New York Post in October when it published its blockbuster stories on Biden family corruption, the censorship and eventual banning from the Web of President Trump, and the coordinated takedown of the upstart social media site Parler—it is obvious that Big Tech's priority today is to support the political Left and the Washington establishment.

## Big Tech Is Now the Most Powerful Election-Influencing Machine in America

It is not an exaggeration to say that if the technologies of Silicon Valley are allowed to develop to their fullest extent, without any oversight or checks and balances, then we will never have another free and fair election. But the power of Big Tech goes beyond the manipulation of political behavior. As one of my Facebook sources told me in an interview for my book: "We have thousands of people on the platform who have gone from far right to center in the past year, so we can build a model from those people and try to make everyone else on the right follow the same path." Let that sink in. They don't just want to control information or even voting behavior—they want to manipulate people's worldview.

Is it too much to say that Big Tech has prioritized this kind of manipulation? Consider that Twitter is currently facing a lawsuit from a victim of child sexual abuse who says that the company repeatedly failed to take down a video depicting his assault, and that it eventually agreed to do so only after the intervention of an agent from the Department of Homeland Security. So Twitter will take it upon itself to ban the President of the United States, but is alleged to have taken down child pornography only after being prodded by federal law enforcement.

How does Big Tech go about manipulating our thoughts and behavior? It begins with the fact that these tech companies strive to know everything about us—our likes and dislikes, the issues we're interested in, the websites we visit, the videos we watch, who we voted for, and our party affiliation. If you search for a Hannukah recipe, they'll know you're likely Jewish. If you're running down the Yankees, they'll figure out if you're a Red Sox fan. Even if your smart phone is turned off, they'll track your location. They know who you work for, who your friends are, when you're walking your dog, whether you go to church, when you're standing in line to vote, and on and on.

As I already mentioned, Big Tech also monitors how our beliefs and behaviors change over time. They identify the types of content that can change our beliefs and behavior, and they put that knowledge to use. They've done this openly for a long time to manipulate consumer behavior—to get us to click on certain ads or buy certain products. Anyone who has used these platforms for an extended period of time has no doubt encountered the creepy phenomenon where you're searching for information about a product or a service—say, a microwave—and then minutes later advertisements for microwaves start appearing on your screen. These same techniques can be used to manipulate political opinions.

I mentioned that Big Tech has recently demonstrated ideological bias. But it is equally true that these companies have huge economic interests at stake in politics. The party that holds power will determine whether they are going to get government contracts, whether they're going to get tax breaks, and whether and how their industry will be regulated. Clearly, they have a commercial interest in political control—and currently no one is preventing them from exerting it.

To understand how effective Big Tech's manipulation could become, consider the feedback loop. As Big Tech constantly collects data about us, they run tests to see what information has an impact on us. Let's say they put a negative news story about someone or something in front of us, and we don't click on it or read it. They keep at it until they find content that has the desired effect. The feedback loop constantly improves, and it does so in a way that's undetectable.

What determines what appears at the top of a person's Facebook feed, Twitter feed, or Google search results? Does it appear there because it's popular or because it's gone viral? Is it there because it's what you're interested in? Or is there another reason Big Tech wants it to be there? Is it there because Big Tech has gathered data that suggests it's likely to nudge your thinking or your behavior in a certain direction? How can we know?

## Partisans differ over whether calling out others on social media for potentially offensive content represents accountability or punishment

*% of U.S. adults who say in general, when people publicly call out others on social media for posting content that might be considered offensive, they are more likely to …*

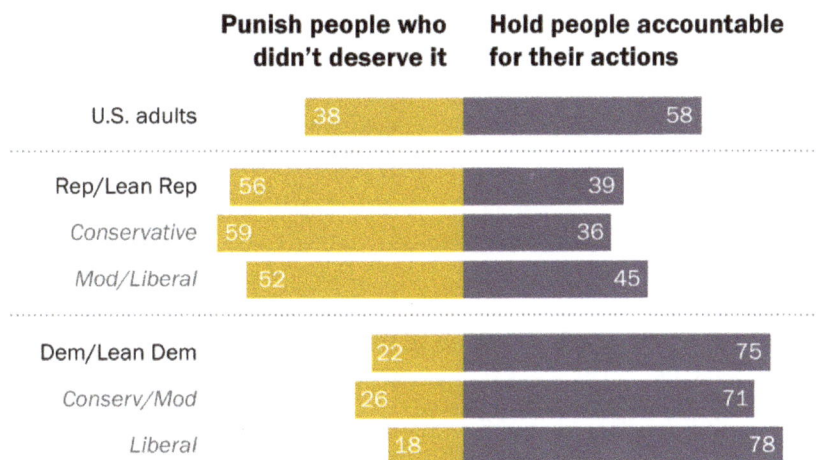

| | Punish people who didn't deserve it | Hold people accountable for their actions |
|---|---|---|
| U.S. adults | 38 | 58 |
| Rep/Lean Rep | 56 | 39 |
| Conservative | 59 | 36 |
| Mod/Liberal | 52 | 45 |
| Dem/Lean Dem | 22 | 75 |
| Conserv/Mod | 26 | 71 |
| Liberal | 18 | 78 |

Note: Those who did not give an answer are not shown.
Source: Survey of U.S. adults conducted Sept. 8-13, 2020.
"Americans and 'Cancel Culture': Where Some See Calls for Accountability, Others See Censorship, Punishment"

**PEW RESEARCH CENTER**

## Big Tech Openly Manipulates the Content People See

We know, for example, that Google reduced the visibility of Breitbart News links in search results by 99 percent in 2020 compared to the same period in 2016. We know that after Google introduced an update last summer, clicks on Breitbart News stories from Google searches for "Joe Biden" went to zero and stayed at zero through the election. This didn't happen gradually, but in one fell swoop—as if Google flipped a switch. And this was discoverable through the use of Google's own traffic analysis tools, so it isn't as if Google cared that we knew about it.

Speaking of flipping switches, I have noted that President Trump was collectively banned by Twitter, Facebook, Twitch, YouTube, TikTok, Snapchat, and every other social media platform you can think of. But even before that, there was manipulation going on. Twitter, for instance, reduced engagement on the President's tweets by over eighty percent. Facebook deleted posts by the President for spreading so-called disinformation.

But even more troubling, I think, are the invisible things these companies do. Consider "quality ratings." Every Big Tech platform has some version of this, though some of them use different names. The quality rating is what determines what appears at the top of your search results, or your Twitter or Facebook feed, etc. It's a numerical value based on what Big Tech's algorithms determine in terms of "quality." In the past, this score was determined by criteria that were somewhat objective: if a website or post contained viruses, malware, spam, or copyrighted material, that would negatively impact its quality score. If a video or post was gaining in popularity, the quality score would increase. Fair enough.

Over the past several years, however—and one can trace the beginning of the change to Donald Trump's victory in 2016—Big Tech has introduced all sorts of new criteria into the mix that determines quality scores. Today, the algorithms on Google and Facebook have been trained to detect "hate speech," "misinformation," and "authoritative" (as opposed to "non-authoritative") sources. Algorithms analyze a user's network, so that whatever users follow on social media—e.g., "non-authoritative" news outlets—affects the user's quality score. Algorithms also detect the use of language frowned on by Big Tech—e.g., "illegal immigrant" (bad) in place of "undocumented immigrant" (good)—and adjust quality scores accordingly. And so on.

This is not to say that you are informed of this or that you can look up your quality score. All of this happens invisibly. It is Silicon Valley's version of the social credit system overseen by the Chinese Communist Party. As in China, if you defy the values of the ruling elite or challenge narratives that the elite labels "authoritative," your score will be reduced, and your voice suppressed. And it will happen silently, without your knowledge.

This technology is even scarier when combined with Big Tech's ability to detect and monitor entire networks of people. A field of computer science called "network analysis" is dedicated to identifying groups of people with shared interests, who read similar websites, who talk about similar things, who have similar habits, who follow similar people on social media, and who share similar political viewpoints. Big Tech companies are able to detect when particular information is flowing through a particular network—if there's a news story, a post, or a video, for instance, that's going viral among conservatives or among voters as a whole. This gives them the ability to shut down a story they don't like before it gets out of hand. And these systems are growing more sophisticated all the time.

If Big Tech's capabilities are allowed to develop unchecked and unregulated, these companies will eventually have the power not only to suppress existing political movements, but to anticipate and prevent the emergence of new ones. This would mean the end of democracy as we know it, because it would place us forever under the thumb of an unaccountable oligarchy.

### Protecting Freedom of Speech by Reining in the Tyrannical Tech Giants

And the way is simple: take away their power to filter information and filter data on our behalf.

All of Big Tech's power comes from their content filters—the filters on "hate speech," the filters on "misinformation," the filters that distinguish "authoritative" from "non-authoritative" sources, etc. Right now these filters are switched on by default. We as individuals can't turn them off. But it doesn't have to be that way.

The most important demand we can make of lawmakers and regulators is that Big Tech be forbidden from activating these filters without our knowledge and consent. They should be prohibited from doing this—and even from nudging us to turn on a filter—under penalty of losing their Section 230 immunity as publishers of third party content. This policy should be strictly enforced, and it should extend even to seemingly non-political filters like relevance and popularity. Anything less opens the door to manipulation.

Our ultimate goal should be a marketplace in which third party companies would be free to design filters that could be plugged into services like Twitter, Facebook, Google, and YouTube. In other words, we would have two separate categories of companies: those that host content and those that create filters to sort through that content. In a marketplace like that, users would have the maximum level of choice in determining their online experiences. At the same time, Big Tech would lose its power to manipulate our thoughts and behavior and to ban legal content—which is just a more extreme form of filtering—from the Web.

This should be the standard we demand, and it should be industry-wide. The alternative is a kind of digital serfdom. We don't allow old-fashioned serfdom anymore—individuals and businesses have due process and can't be evicted because their landlord doesn't like their politics. Why shouldn't we also have these rights if our business or livelihood depends on a Facebook page or a Twitter or YouTube account?

This is an issue that goes beyond partisanship. What the tech giants are doing is so transparently unjust that all Americans should start caring about it—because under the current arrangement, we are all at their mercy. The World Wide Web was meant to liberate us. It is now doing the opposite. Big Tech is increasingly in control. The most pressing question today is: how are we going to take control back?

## Orwell's 1984 and Today

Larry P. Arnn is the twelfth president of Hillsdale College and below are excerpts from his "Orwell's 1984 and Today" *Imprimis* article in December 2020:

In George Orwell's *1984*, there are telescreens everywhere, as well as hidden cameras and microphones. Nearly everything you do is watched and heard. It even emerges that the watchers have become expert at reading people's faces. The organization that oversees all this is called the Thought Police.

If it sounds far-fetched, look at China today: there are cameras everywhere watching the people, and everything they do on the Internet is monitored. Algorithms are run and experiments are underway to assign each individual a social score. If you don't act or think in the politically correct way, things happen to you—you lose the ability to travel, for instance, or you lose your job. It's a very comprehensive system.

And by the way, you can also look at how big tech companies here in the U.S. are tracking people's movements and activities to the extent that they are often able to know in advance what people will be doing. Even more alarming, these companies are increasingly able and willing to use the information they compile to manipulate people's thoughts and decisions.

The protagonist of 1984 is a man named Winston Smith. He works for the state, and his job is to rewrite history. He sits at a table with a telescreen in front of him that watches everything he does. To one side is something called a memory hole—when Winston puts things in it, he assumes they are burned and lost forever.

Winston's job is to fix every book, periodical, newspaper, etc. that reveals or refers to what used to be the truth, in order that it conform to the new truth.

Winston's awareness of this endless, mighty effort to alter reality makes him cynical and disaffected. He comes to see that he knows nothing of the past, of real history: "Every record has been destroyed or falsified," he says at one point, "every book has been rewritten, every picture has been repainted, every statue and street and building has been renamed, every date has been altered. And that process is continuing day by day and minute by minute. Nothing exists except an endless present in which the Party is always right."

## Does Any of This Sound Familiar?

In his disaffection, Winston commits two unlawful acts: he begins writing in a diary and he begins meeting a woman in secret, outside the sanction of the state. The family is important to the state because the state needs babies. But the women are raised by the state in a way that they are not to enjoy relations with their husbands. And the children—as in China today, and as it was in the Soviet Union—are indoctrinated and taught to spy and inform on their parents.

Parents love their children but live in terror of them all the time. Think of the control that comes from that—and the misery.

There are three stratums in the society of 1984. There is the Inner Party, whose members hold all the power. There is the Outer Party, to which Winston belongs, whose members work for—and are watched and controlled by—the Inner Party. And there are the proles, who live and do the blue collar work in a relatively unregulated area.

Winston ventures out into that area from time to time. He finds a little shop there where he buys things. And it is in a room upstairs from this shop where he and Julia, the woman he falls in love with, set up a kind of household as if they are married. They create something like a private world in that room, although it is a world with limitations—they can't even think about having children, for instance, because if they did, they would be discovered and killed.

In the end, it turns out that the shopkeeper, who had seemed to be a kindly old man, is in fact a member of the Thought Police. Winston and Julia's room contained a hidden telescreen all along, so everything they have said and done has been observed. In fact, it emerges that the Thought Police have known that Winston has been having deviant thoughts for twelve years and have been watching him carefully.

When the couple are arrested, they have made pledges that they will never betray each other. They know the authorities will be able to make them say whatever they want them to say—but in their hearts, they pledge, they will be true to their love. It is a promise that neither is finally able to keep.

After months of torture, Winston thinks that what awaits him is a bullet in the back of the head, the preferred method of execution of both the Nazis and the Soviet Communists. In Koestler's Darkness at Noon, the protagonist walks down a basement hallway after confessing to crimes that he didn't commit, and without any ceremony he is shot in the back of the head—eradicated as if he were vermin. Winston doesn't get off so easy. He will instead undergo an education, or more accurately a re-education. His final stages of torture are depicted as a kind of totalitarian seminar. The seminar is conducted by a man named O'Brien, who is portrayed marvelously in the film by Richard Burton. As he alternately raises and lowers the level of Winston's pain, O'Brien leads him to knowledge regarding the full meaning of the totalitarian regime.

As the first essential step of his education, Winston has to learn doublethink—a way of thinking that defies the law of contradiction. In Aristotle, the law of contradiction is the basis of all reasoning, the means of making sense of the world. It is the law that says that X and Y cannot be true at the same time if they're mutually exclusive. For instance, if A is taller than B and B is taller than C, C cannot be taller than A. The law of contradiction means things like that.

## The Law of Contradiction

In our time, the law of contradiction would mean that a governor, say, could not simultaneously hold that the COVID pandemic renders church services too dangerous to allow, and also that massive protest marches are fine. It would preclude a man from declaring himself a woman, or a woman declaring herself a man, as if one's sex is simply a matter of what one wills it to be—and it would preclude others from viewing such claims as anything other than preposterous.

The Law of Contradiction also means that we can't change the past. What we can know of the truth all resides in the past, because the present is fleeting and confusing and tomorrow has yet to come. The past, on the other hand, is complete. Aristotle and Thomas Aquinas go so far as to say that changing the past—making what has been not to have been—is denied even to God. Because if something both happened and didn't happen, no human understanding is possible. And God created us with the capacity for understanding.

That's the law of contradiction, which the art of doublethink denies and violates. Doublethink is manifest in the fact that the state ministry in which Winston is tortured is called the Ministry of Love. It is manifest in the three slogans displayed on the state's Ministry of Truth: "War is peace. Freedom is slavery. Ignorance is strength." And as we have seen, the regime in 1984 exists precisely to repeal the past. If the past can be changed, anything can be changed—man can surpass even the power of God. But still, to what end?

Why do you think you are being tortured? O'Brien asks Winston. The Party is not trying to improve you, he says—the Party cares nothing about you. Winston is brought to see that he is where he is simply as the subject of the state's power. Understanding having been rendered meaningless, the only competence that has meaning is power.

"Already we are breaking down the habits of thought which have survived from before the Revolution," O'Brien says.

We have cut the links between child and parent, and between man and man, and between man and woman. No one dares trust a wife, a child, or a friend any longer. But in the future there will be no wives and no friends. Children will be taken from their mothers at birth, as one takes eggs from a hen. The sex instinct will be eradicated. Procreation will be an annual formality like the renewal of a ration card.

There will be no loyalty, except loyalty toward the Party. There will be no love, except the love of Big Brother. There will be no laughter, except the laugh of triumph over a defeated enemy.

All competing pleasures will be destroyed. But always—do not forget this Winston—always there will be the intoxication of power, constantly increasing and constantly growing subtler. Always, at every moment, there will be the thrill of victory, the sensation of trampling on an enemy who is helpless. If you want a picture of the future, imagine a boot stamping on a human face—forever.

Nature is ultimately unchangeable, of course, and humans are not God. Totalitarianism will never win in the end—but it can win long enough to destroy a civilization. That is what is ultimately at stake in the fight we are in. Today we can see the totalitarian impulse among powerful forces in our politics and culture. We can see it in the rise and imposition of doublethink, and we can see it in the increasing attempt to rewrite our history.

# 11 – How Big Tech's Anti-Conservative Bias & Censorship Affect American Elections

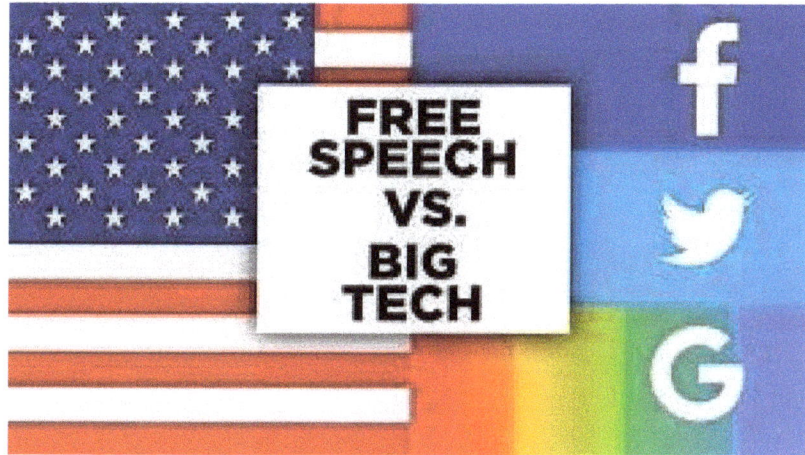

*Credit: Change.org.*

If questioning the results of a presidential election were a crime, as many have asserted in the wake of the controversial 2020 election and its aftermath, then much of the Democratic Party and media establishment should have been indicted for their behavior following the 2016 election.

As revealed by Mollie Hemingway in her 2021 book *Rigged: How the Media, Big Tech, and the Democrats Seized Our Elections*: In fact, the last time Democrats fully accepted the legitimacy of a presidential election they lost was in 1988.

Rather than accept that Trump won, and Clinton lost fair and square in 2016, the political and media establishments desperately sought to explain away Trump's victory. They settled on a destructive conspiracy theory that crippled the government, empowered America's adversaries, and illegally targeted innocent private citizens whose only crime was not supporting Hillary Clinton.

The Russia collusion hoax had all the elements of an election conspiracy theory, including baseless claims of hacked voting totals, illegal voter suppression, and treasonous collaboration with a foreign power. Pundits and officials speculated openly that President Trump was a foreign asset and that members of his circle were under the thumb of the Kremlin.

But despite the patent absurdity of these claims, the belief that Trump stole the 2016 election had the support of the most powerful institutions, individuals, and even government agencies of the country. To question the legitimacy of the 2016 election wasn't to undermine our democracy; it was considered by some our most elevated public figures a patriotic duty.

## It's Okay to Question the 2016 Election Results—But Now It's Not in 2020

"I know he's an illegitimate president," Clinton claimed of Trump a few months later? She even said during an interview with CBS Sunday Morning that "voter suppression and voter purging and hacking" were the reasons for her defeat.

Former president Jimmy Carter agreed. " [Trump] lost the election and was put into office because the Russians interfered on his behalf," be told NPR in 2019. "Trump didn't actually win the election in 2016."

Their view was shared by most prominent Democrats in Congress. Representative John Lewis of Georgia, for example, said he was skipping Trump's inauguration in 2016 because he believed Trump was illegitimate:" [T)he Russians participated in helping this man get elected. That's not right. That's not fair. That's not an open democratic process."! Lewis had also skipped the inauguration of President George W. Bush, claiming Bush, too, was an illegitimate president.

A few members of Congress joined him in 2001. By 2017, one out of three Democrats in the U.S. House of Representatives boycotted Trump's inauguration as an "illegitimate" president.

The corporate media didn't condemn leading Democrats' refusal to accept the results of the 2016 election. In fact, the media amplified the most speculative claims of how Trump and Russia had colluded to steal the election from Clinton. They dutifully regurgitated inaccurate leaks from corrupt intelligence officials suggesting Trump and his staff had committed treason. They ran stories arguing that Republicans who didn't support their conspiracy theory were insufficiently loyal to the country or somehow compromised themselves.

It was all nonsense. Even Robert Mueller, who ran a multi-year and multi-million-dollar government investigation into claims that Trump personally colluded with Russian president Vladimir Putin to steal the election from Hillary Clinton, found no evidence to support the fevered accusations.

The reporters who pushed this conspiracy theory were never held accountable by their peers and fact checkers for peddling leaks and lies. They received raises and promotions, honors and awards, and the applause of their colleagues. Some were given Pulitzer Prizes for "reporting" that was closer to fan fiction than an accurate description of events!

Stunned by the turbulence of the 2020 election, millions of Americans are asking the forbidden question: what really happened?

It was a devastating triple punch. Capping their four-year campaign to destroy the Trump presidency, the media portrayed a Democratic victory as necessary and inevitable. Big Tech, wielding unprecedented powers, vaporized dissent and erased damning reports about the Biden family's corruption. And Democratic operatives, exploiting a public health crisis, shamelessly manipulated the voting process itself. Silenced and subjected, the American people lost their faith in the system.

For years, there have been whispers about Big Tech's tendency to muffle those who dare to challenge mainstream liberal orthodoxy. In 2018, the Pew Research Center found, "72% of the public thinks it likely that social media platforms actively censor political views that those companies find objectionable." By a four-to-one margin, respondents were more likely to say Big Tech supports the views of liberals over conservatives than vice versa.

## How Big Tech Bias Threatens Free and Fair Elections

Microsoft's social media researcher Danah Boyd said, "No amount of 'fixing' Facebook or Google will address the underlying factors shaping the culture and information wars in which America is currently enmeshed." She continues, "The short version of it all is that we have a cultural problem, one that is shaped by disconnects in values, relationships, and social fabric. Our media, our tools, and our politics are being leveraged to help breed polarization by countless actors who can leverage these systems for personal, economic, and ideological gain."

Big Tech companies have drawn intense scrutiny for perceived political bias and alleged unbalanced moderation of users' content. Critics say much of the companies' moderation in the 2020 election and during all of President Trump's term, unfairly targeted conservative speech and free speech from individuals deemed to be supporters of former President Donald Trump.

Meanwhile, groups on the other side of the aisle have been taking issue with how social media companies are operating, claiming that the Silicon Valley companies have failed to adequately address misinformation that is being proliferated online by conservatives and far right groups, particular those in connection with the Capitol Riot.

Google announced it has awarded its first round of grants to media outlets throughout North America from a pool of $300 million the internet giant has set aside to bolster largely left-leaning mainstream and legacy media organizations per the October 2019 "Google Awards Grants to Left-Wing Media Outlets, Critics Say" by *Epoch Times* writer Matthew Vadum:

Google LLC says it wishes only to index objective facts and link to media outlets without putting its thumb on the scale, but conservative critics say the company is trying to shape the news. Left-of-center media receive prime placement in search results, while right-of-center media receive less favorable placement or are banned outright, critics say.

Google, Facebook, and Twitter in particular has been put under the microscope in recent years as critics accuse the private companies of playing political favorites, engaging in censorship, and manipulating search users through algorithm abuse, cancel culture, and censorship. All three companies strenuously deny the claims.

Conservatives have long decried what they described as unfair treatment from major technology companies. "Shadowbanning"—the surreptitious suppression of a user's content by social media platforms, is also often pointed to per the October 2019 "Robert Epstein: How Big Tech Bias Threatens Free and Fair Elections" article by Irene Luo and Jan Jekielek for the *Epoch Times*.

**Majorities across parties say social media sites likely censor political views, but conservative Republicans stand out for thinking this is *very* likely**

*% of U.S. adults who say it is ___ that social media sites intentionally censor political viewpoints they find objectionable*

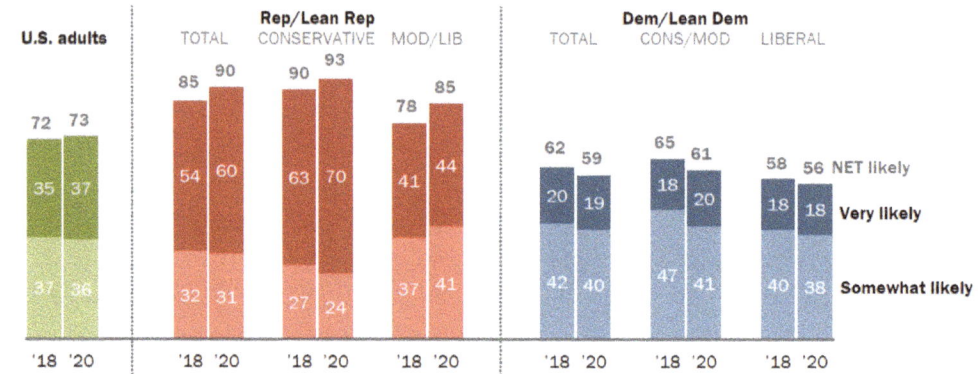

Note: Those who did not give an answer or who gave other responses are not shown.
Source: Survey of U.S. adults conducted June 16-22, 2020.
"Most Americans Think Social Media Sites Censor Political Viewpoints"

PEW RESEARCH CENTER

Then President Donald Trump tweeted that "Google & others are suppressing voices of Conservatives and hiding information and news that is good. They are controlling what we can & cannot see. This is a very serious situation-will be addressed!"

## Big Tech's Assault on Free Speech

Per the August 2020 *The Hill* article "Big Tech's Assault on Free Speech" by Chris Talgo: As the 2020 elections approach, Big Tech has upped the ante in its limiting of free speech. This is a dangerous development that undermines the fundamental principles upon which the United States was founded. If left unchecked, it could lead to an Orwellian nightmare and, ultimately, to the end of the republic as we know it.

In the past few years, there have been countless cases of social media giants — Facebook, Instagram, Twitter and YouTube — muzzling conservatives and libertarians, for apparent political motives. For example, it is well documented that Twitter uses "shadow bans" to prevent users from sharing their posts to the hundreds of millions of Twitter users.

Somehow, shadow bans overwhelmingly have been applied to those on the right end of the political spectrum. Coincidence? I think not.

Although those on the left claim this is exaggerated, it happens all the time. And it seems that Twitter and others are clamping down more and more on prominent users who have the audacity to question the so-called consensus on a variety of issues.

Recently, Twitter has come under increased scrutiny because it has targeted conservatives such as Donald Trump Jr. who have posted material that question mainstream narrative about protests, coronavirus treatments, the wisdom of lockdowns and several other pressing issues.

The Trump Jr. case is particularly spine-chilling because all the president's son did was post a video from a group of doctors who presented a case for using hydroxychloroquine as a treatment for COVID-19. According to Twitter, "Tweets with the video are in violation of our Covid-19 misinformation policy. We are taking action in line with our policy here."

Shortly after, Facebook and YouTube also scrubbed the video. Although this may seem like no big deal, it certainly is.

## In 2020, Most Americans Receive Their News Via Social Media

The sheer power held by these companies concerning the flow of information is overwhelming. And they can use their power to shift public opinion, as demonstrated in the 2010 election when Facebook launched a get-out-the-vote campaign that it claims resulted in 343,000 more voters going to the polls.

If Facebook and other social media giants can nudge Americans to vote, how long before they also shift public opinion in the direction they desire? It seems as if this Rubicon may have already been crossed.

In some ways, Google has more power over information than the social media companies because Google completely dominates internet searches. Over the past year, Google's market share of worldwide internet searches has hovered around 92 percent.

According to a recent study titled "An analysis of political bias in search engine results," Google's "top search results were almost 40% more likely to contain pages with a 'Left' or 'Far Left' slant than they were pages from the right. Moreover, 16% of political keywords contained no right-leaning pages at all within the first page of results."

In other words, according to that study, Google's algorithm is politically biased to favor the left over the right. Maybe that explains why Google and other Big Tech companies contribute so much money to the Democratic Party compared to the Republican Party.

According to the Center for Responsive Politics, 70 percent of donations by Facebook and its employees in the 2020 campaign cycle have gone to Democrats. Eighty-one percent of Google's political contributions have gone to Democrats. The same trend applies to Amazon (74 percent) and Apple (91 percent).

Fortunately, Big Tech's bias is becoming more and more apparent. Most Americans are well aware that in general, Big Tech favors leftwing causes, politicians and opinions.

Since it seems that Congress is unwilling to do anything about this in the near future, the question is, what can and should "we the people" do about it?

## Did Google 'Actively Interfere' in the 2020 Elections?

Robert Epstein, a senior research psychologist at the American Institute for Behavioral Research and Technology and former editor-in-chief of *Psychology Today*, has devoted the past 6 1/2 years to researching tech giant bias, especially with Google, which dominates the search engine market. He told *The Epoch Times* that Google has access to a number of powerful manipulation methods mostly through "ephemeral experiences" that can shift votes.

As exposed in the August 2019 "Google Will 'Actively Interfere' in 2020 Elections, Researcher Says" by *Epoch Times* writer Bowen Xiao, the researcher is Robert Epstein, and he warns: "Google will actively interfere in the 2020 elections. They'll actively interfere in their lobbying efforts, they'll actively interfere with their political donations, and they'll actively interfere using the online methods of manipulation that I've studied and probably other methods that I haven't yet discovered."

Per Epstein: Online ephemeral experiences are brief moments where information is generated instantaneously, such as search suggestions. They are not stored anywhere and can't be tracked. Leaked internal emails from Google in 2018 found employees specifically discussing launching "ephemeral experiences" to counter Trump's then-travel ban, the *Wall Street Journal* reported.

In his congressional testimony in July 2019, Epstein noted that if all major technology companies came together to support the same candidate in 2020—which he said was likely—they could shift 15 million votes without leaving a paper trail. Epstein has discovered a dozen methods Google uses to manipulate public opinion or votes, including search engine manipulation effect and search suggestion effects.

In 2016, Epstein conducted a secret monitoring project that showed Google hid negative auto-complete search results for Hillary Clinton months before the election. His peer-reviewed research found Google's algorithms can easily shift 20 percent or more of votes among voters and up to 80 percent in some demographic groups, the latter being Zillennials, Millennial and Generation X.

In a more recent study, Epstein analyzed Google's "Go Vote" reminder on Election Day 2018 and found it gave the Democratic party between 800,000 and 4.6 million more votes than it gave Republicans. He used the same calculations Google's data analysts performed before they added the prompt. Epstein characterized it as "vote manipulation," not a public service.

"These two processes put in the hands of a very small number of business executives are extremely dangerous to humanity," he said. "They are a danger to democracy, they undermine a fair and free election." Google's manipulation tactics, Epstein said, are legal and save the company money when compared to using other methods of influence, such as donations.

"Google can do whatever they want," he said. "In the U.S., there are no regulations, no laws restricting their ability to manipulate opinions or votes. By favoring one candidate or cause in search results or search suggestions, it costs Google—nothing."

Google can still be fined. In March 2019, the company was hit with its third antitrust penalty, a $1.7 billion fine by the European Union. In 2017, it was fined $2.7 billion for giving its own shopping service a more prominent placement than others.

What Google does with these methods is new and not like billboards or television advertisements, Epstein said. "There's no way to fight them, there's no way to counteract them. They are not competitive. That's a kind of power that has never existed before in human history. It's perfectly legal for these companies to use these techniques," he said. "It costs them little to nothing to use them, so of course they will."

To prevent Google from interfering in the 2020 elections, Epstein said one solution would be to set up a large-scale monitoring system utilizing artificial intelligence to "catch these companies in the act." He described Google as a "mind-control machine."

U.S. authorities are considering the idea that the company has an antitrust issue. Google controls about 92 percent of the internet search market.

A Google spokesman, in response to reports of election interference, told *The Epoch Times* in a previous email that they "go to great lengths to build our products and enforce our policies in ways that don't take political leanings into account."

**Shifting Opinions, Thinking, Attitudes, Beliefs, Purchases, and Votes Without People Knowing**

"Americans see Google search results about 500 million times a day. Google controls roughly 90 percent of search. The next largest search engine, Bing, controls about 2 percent of search," Epstein said.

Robert Epstein's peer-reviewed research found that research participants were remarkably susceptible to bias: search engine bias could easily shift 20 percent or more of the votes of undecided voters in an election. He also found that while results on Google leaned left substantially, results on Bing and Yahoo did not.

On Sept. 9, 2019, it was announced that 48 U.S. states, the District of Columbia, and Puerto Rico have opened a bipartisan antitrust probe into Google. The new investigation follows existing investigations by the Justice Department and the Federal Trade Commission into Facebook, Google, Apple, and Amazon.

One major form of bias featured in Epstein's research is the search engine manipulation effect, something he began exploring after finding research in 2012 on how search result rankings affected purchases and clicks. It said that users tended to trust the highest-ranked search results the most, so much so that 50 percent of clicks went to the top two items.

To study how search engine rankings could shift voting preferences, he conducted a series of experiments in which he showed groups of randomly assigned people biased search results. They used a Google-like search engine, Kadoodle, that featured real search results and web pages taken from Google. The only difference was the ranking of the results.

One group was shown results biased to one candidate, one saw results biased to the other candidate, and the control group was shown mixed results, with bias in both directions. Before and after looking at the search results, participants were asked about their thoughts on the candidates, and who they'd vote for if they had to decide at that moment.

"I thought I could produce a shift in voting preferences and opinions of maybe 2 or 3 percent," Epstein said. "The first experiment I ran, the shift I got was 48 percent."

Epstein conducted more than a dozen different experiments, in which he found substantial shifts every time. In one large-scale national study across all 50 states with more than 2,000 participants, Epstein found that among different demographic groups, some were especially susceptible to manipulation (such as Generations X Y Z), with shifts in preferences as high as 80 percent.

These shifts are reflective of actual behavior in the ballot box, Epstein said. Survey research has shown that "if you ask people who they're going to vote for, it turns out that's a very good predictor of who they actually vote for," he said. "Generally speaking, we're talking about 90, 95 percent accuracy in predictions."

And according to Epstein, what they found in their experiments likely underestimated the real impact that Google has since most of his experiments had participants conducting only one online search.

"In real life, people are conducting many searches over a period of weeks or months that are election-related. If they're undecided, that means they're being hit over and over and over again with biased search results, taking them to web pages that favor one candidate," he said.

So far, Epstein has identified 12 major techniques of tech giants that can shift perceptions and opinions.

**No Paper Trail**

"Most of these types of influence have never existed before in human history. They're made possible by the Internet. They're made possible by these huge tech monopolies, and they're entirely in the hands of these tech monopolies.

"In elections, we're influenced by billboards, by radio shows, and TV shows, and advertisements, and so on. All of that is competitive. And in that sense, it's probably a good thing. It's a good thing for democracy that there is so much competition out there vying for your attention and trying to convince you of this or that. But if there's bias in search results, that's controlled by the platform, in this case, Google. That's not competitive."

Even if you found and could measure such bias, "you cannot counteract it," he said.

**What About the 2016 Election?**

In 2016, Robert Epstein set up a secret monitoring system that showed that Google results were significantly skewed toward Clinton in the months leading up to the presidential election. Epstein had 95 field agents in 24 states conduct election-related searches with neutral search terms on Google, Bing, and Yahoo. The results from all these searches were then saved.

"We were able to preserve 13,207 election-related searches as well as the 98,044 webpages to which the search results linked," Epstein said. In effect, they were able to permanently preserve snapshots of what are normally "ephemeral" experiences.

Epstein decided only to collect the data, but not to analyze it prior to the 2016 election, because if he found bias, he would face an impossible dilemma. "What would I do? I mean, if I announced it, there would have been absolute chaos, especially, I think, if there was bias against Donald Trump. And if I didn't announce it, then I would be complicit in the rigging of an election," he said.

In the analysis, "we found substantial bias favoring Hillary Clinton in all 10 search positions on the first page of search results on Google (but not Bing or Yahoo)," he said, adding that the probability that the bias was solely due to chance was less than 1 in 1000.

Through a series of calculations, Epstein concluded that if this level of bias was present nationwide, it would've shifted somewhere between 2.6 million and 10.4 million votes to Clinton.

Epstein describes himself as a moderate who leans liberal. And he had been a longtime supporter of the Clintons. "But I felt very strongly that since our results were so clear that I had a responsibility to report the findings," he said.

Clinton won the popular vote by more than 2.8 million votes, but the popular vote "might have been very different," Epstein said, if there had been no bias in Google's search results.

"It was uncomfortable for me to have to acknowledge that, to have to announce that. But that's what I concluded from the research."

People trust in Google's search rankings, he said, because they believe it's generated by a computer algorithm, and thus must be impartial. What was especially disturbing was the subliminal manipulation; in most cases, "people can't see the bias in search results."

For the 2018 midterm elections, Epstein set up a larger monitoring system focusing on three Republican districts in Orange County, California, which all ended up flipping Democrat. He found that on Google (but not Bing or Yahoo), search results were strongly biased in favor of Democratic candidates.

Based on Epstein's worst case scenario calculations, if that same level of bias was present nationwide in 2018, it would have shifted more than 78.2 million votes across the different elections at the state, regional, and local levels.

**Is Tech Giant Bias Intentional?**

Google has insisted that their algorithms for search ranking evolve according to the "organic" activity of users interacting with the algorithm.

Per Robert Epstein, "In my mind, that's complete nonsense. I've been a programmer since I was a teenager," Epstein said. "The fact is Google has total control over what happens. "So what I realized was it's very possible that a lot of important events right now in human history are being determined not by plans and goals and strategies of human beings at a company like

Google, but by computer programs that are just being left to do their own thing. To me, that's far more frightening than thinking that a Google executive is out to rule the world.

"The fact is, we have let loose upon humanity powerful computer algorithms, which are impacting humanity."

**Combating Bias in 2020**

For the 2020 elections, Epstein plans to launch a much more ambitious monitoring system to track tech-giant bias. It will be interesting to see those results once published.

"I think that the tech companies are going to go all out" in 2020, he said. "I think they were very cautious and underconfident in 2016. I think there's a lot of crazy things they could have done to shift votes that they just didn't do."

He believes that Google could easily remove political bias in its search results using techniques it's already developed to deal with what they describe as "algorithmic unfairness."

Such techniques were thrust into the spotlight by the massive trove of documents recently leaked by former senior Google software engineer Zachary Vorhies. A simple example is the search term "American inventors." Whereas the original results might have shown a majority of white males, more black Americans can be boosted to the top of search results to make the results more "fair."

If machine learning fairness techniques can correct for what Google engineers see as racial unfairness, the same could easily be done for political bias, in Epstein's view.

"And I think we have to think beyond the United States because a company like Google is impacting more than 2 billion people around the world. Within three years, that number will swell to over 4 billion people," he said.

"They can literally impact thinking behavior, attitudes, beliefs, elections in almost every country in the world.

"In my mind, that means building larger, better-monitoring systems to keep an eye on companies like Google. I think that's necessary, not only to protect democracy around the world but to protect human autonomy."

## Google Engineer Leaks Nearly 1,000 Internal Documents, Proving Conservative Bias & Censorship

In August 2019, whistleblower Zachary Vorhies, a former computer scientist at Google, shared nearly 1,000 documents with Project Veritas internal documents that purportedly evidenced Google's left-wing political bias. Among the documents was a list of popular conservative media outlets blacklisted by Google, including NewsBusters, American Thinker, Legal Insurrection, Twitchy, FrontPageMag, and GlennBeck.com.

The software engineer, Zach Vorhies, first provided the documents to Project Veritas, a right-leaning investigative journalism nonprofit, as well as the Justice Department's antitrust division, which has been investigating Google for potentially anti-competitive behavior as reported in the

August 2019 "Google Engineer Leaks Nearly 1,000 Internal Documents, Alleging Bias, Censorship" from *Epoch Times* writer Petr Svab.

"The reason why I collected these documents was because I saw something dark and nefarious going on with the company, and I realized that they were going to not only tamper with the elections but use that tampering with the elections to essentially overthrow the United States," Vorhies said at the time.

**Going Public**

Vorhies said he worked for Google for eight years, making $260,000 a year, when counting in the gains from the Google stock he owns. Changes at the company that worried him started in 2016, he said.

"I had every incentive in the world to stay at the company and just collect the paycheck," he said, noting that most others would do that. "But I could never live with myself knowing that, if Google was able to implement the plans that they were planning, that I, at the moment of choice, backed out because I was selfish."

After Vorhies first came to Project Veritas more than a month ago, disclosing some documents and answering questions with his face hidden and his voice disguised. When he returned to work, however, Google sent him a letter demanding, among other things, that he turn over his employee badge and work laptop, which he did, and "cease and desist" from disclosing "any non-public Google files." Afraid for his safety, he posted on Twitter that if something would happen to him, all the documents he took would be released to the public.

Google then did a "wellness check" on him, he said. The San Francisco police received a call that Vorhies may be mentally ill. A group of officers waited for him outside his house and put him in handcuffs. "This is a large way in which they intimidate their employees that go rogue on the company," he said.

Vorhies then decided that it would be safer for him to go public.

Vorhies called Google a "political machine" bent on preventing anybody like President Donald Trump from getting elected again. He said there are other Google employees who "see what's going on and they are really scared."

**Conservative, Republican and Trump Bias**

The documents Vorhies provided previously, together with his explanations and hidden camera recordings by Project Veritas of other Google employees, indicate that the company has created a concept of "fairness" through which it infuses the political preferences of its mostly left-leaning workforce into its products.

Several studies have shown that Google News, in particular, is biased to the left.

Google has repeatedly denied political bias in its products. Vorhies suggested, though, that Google tries to present itself as a neutral platform to preserve legal protection under Section 230, which shields internet services from liability for user-generated content.

## Parler Files New Lawsuit Against Amazon, Says Tech Giant Tried to 'Destroy' App

Social media company Parler filed a new lawsuit against Amazon Web Services on March 2, 2021 and accused the Seattle-based tech giant of attempting to destroy its business after the breach of the Capitol on Jan. 6, 2021. Parler accused Amazon of a breach of contract, defamation, and anticompetitive behavior per the "Parler Files New Lawsuit Against Amazon, Says Tech Giant Tried to 'Destroy' App" March 2021 article by Jack Phillips of the *Epoch Times*:

Amazon Web Services (AWS) terminated Parler's hosting contract and alleged that violent threats were made on the app, claiming Parler didn't act to remove them. It came after the breach of the Capitol on Jan. 6. Parler's suit stated that Amazon defamed the app by making it a scapegoat of the Jan. 6 breach, noting that Twitter and Facebook also hosted content in connection with the incident.

"Because of AWS's malicious defamatory statements, Parler's public reputation suffered severe damage and Parler has had many potential service providers refuse to work with it, hampering and delaying its ability to get back online," the company's lawyers wrote. The lawsuit (pdf) was filed this week in a Washington state court. The firm didn't give an explanation for why it dropped its previous lawsuit this week.

Parler's new lawsuit alleged that Amazon engaged in deceptive and unfair trade practices and defamation while saying Parler was victimized by "Amazon's efforts to destroy an up-and-coming technology company through deceptive, defamatory, anticompetitive, and bad faith conduct."

When Amazon suspended Parler's service, it effectively removed the firm from the internet—with the company only coming back online in mid-February with a new hosting service. Google's Play Store and Apple's App Store also removed the app. The Henderson, Nevada-based firm got its services back online with the help of SkySilk, a Los Angeles-based cloud-computing company.

"Parler has been unable to regain the reputation and success it enjoyed before AWS terminated its services," Parler stated in its new complaint, adding that in the weeks it was offline, Parler lost "tens of millions of" users. "Not surprisingly, when an internet-based company cannot get on the internet, the damage is extraordinary."

In the dropped lawsuit, Parler—citing messages between former CEO John Matze and an Amazon representative—also claimed that Amazon didn't care about the content posted on the social media app but was more concerned with whether former President Donald Trump would join the social media app after he was suspended from Twitter, Facebook, and other Big Tech websites.

An Amazon Web Services spokesperson told news outlets on March 3, 2021, that Parler's newest legal challenge has "no merit."

"AWS provides technology and services to customers across the political spectrum, and we respect Parler's right to determine for itself what content it will allow. However, as shown by the evidence in Parler's federal lawsuit, it was clear that there was significant content on Parler that encouraged and incited violence against others, which is a violation of our terms of service," the spokesperson said.

"Further, Parler was unable or unwilling to promptly identify and remove this content, which coupled with an increase in this type of dangerous violent content, led to our suspension of their services."

## PragerU Censored by Google/YouTube

The often-censored Prager University has been dropped from service by yet another technology company, apparently because of its conservative, pro-American educational videos that it says have attracted more than 5 billion views over 10 years per the June 2020 "PragerU Censored by Video Platform" article by the *Epoch Times'* Matthew Vadum

New York-based JW Player, which claims to "have a global footprint of over 1 billion unique users," kicked the nonprofit off its video hosting platform, while it continues to serve left-wing media outlets The Young Turks and Vice, which generate videos that, according to PragerU, divide the country and teach young people to resent America.

The move came after JW Player blindsided PragerU, claiming to have updated its "community guidelines," after which it decided not to renew the annual service contract, claiming without providing any evidence that "Prager U's content is misleading."

"In true cowardly fashion, JW Player has refused to give us specifics and opted to hide behind third-party 'fact-checkers' to get rid of us," Marissa Streit, CEO of PragerU, said in a statement. Craig Strazzeri, Prager U's chief marketing officer, elaborated in an interview. In 2016, "YouTube really started censoring our videos and restricting hundreds of our videos," he told The Epoch Times. "We decided we needed to gain some independence on our website."

PragerU sued YouTube, and its parent company, Google, in U.S. District Court for the Northern District of California in October 2017, but lost the suit. The lawsuit cited more than 50 PragerU videos that have either been restricted or demonetized by YouTube on various subjects presenting a conservative point of view, along with a video by Harvard Law professor emeritus Alan Dershowitz on the founding of Israel.

PragerU previously compiled a complete list of its restricted videos here, including "Why America Must Lead," "The Ten Commandments: Do Not Murder," "Why Did America Fight the Korean War," and "The World's Most Persecuted Minority: Christians."

"This is speech discrimination plain and simple, censorship based entirely on unspecified ideological objection to the message or on the perceived identity and political viewpoint of the speaker," PragerU lawyer Pete Wilson, a former governor of California, said at the time.

Strazzeri said the nonprofit found JW Player three years ago, which allowed PragerU to host videos natively on its own site and not have to rely on big tech companies. "And we never had any issues until just a few months ago when they contacted us," advising that as a result of a change in content guidelines PragerU was in violation of the company's policies and would no longer be working with the nonprofit, he said.

"We have over 1,000 videos on our library and to be forced to transition … to an alternative in a very short timeframe was incredibly disruptive. And financially, it was expensive to do that … so it's very disruptive, and it's something the other side [i.e., the left] doesn't have to deal with." It's "really scary" that "these smaller independent companies" are now getting into the content moderation business, "restricting speech and opinions on issues," he said.

**Google/YouTube's Main Goal is to Suppress, Conceal or Cancel Conservative Ideas**

"And their main goal is they don't want conservative ideas to get out there." The tech company declined to be specific about what prompted the decision to drop PragerU as a client. "JW Player has decided not to comment at this time," company spokesperson Fatimah Nouilati told The Epoch Times via email.

Strazzeri said JW Player did tell PragerU that its decision was influenced by its "independent, fact-checking news companies, and one in particular named News Guard," which gave the nonprofit a low credibility score.

The break with JW Player has led to users clicking on PragerU links on social media and being greeted with "a disclaimer saying News Guard says, 'This is not a very credible source,' PragerU, so be careful and go at-your-own-risk type of messaging," Strazzeri said.

Twitter allows PragerU to post but has banned it from running advertising without explaining why, he said.

At the same time, Facebook has been threatening for a year "to unpublish our page entirely," claiming multiple community violations, based solely on "third-party left-wing fact-checkers who are targeting our content and flagging them as misleading or false despite us having facts and sources to back up every claim that we've ever made."

Facebook ignores Prager U's complaints, Strazzeri said. "We appeal every single one, and then nothing happens," he said. "So the fact-checkers are now the arbiters of truth of the internet. And that's a really dangerous and scary thought." Something has to be done about the social media censorship problem, he said.

"We think we need to fight from every angle, we need to fight legally, we need to fight in the court of public opinion, most importantly, because, unfortunately, because of the censorship, so many Americans don't even know this is going on.

"We just want to see the censorship end. We want to see these platforms, stop silencing speech. "We'd like to see go back to where it was 10 years ago, when all these big tech platforms started, they basically had very simple guidelines that prohibited violent content, and pornographic content. But anything else that was opinion-based, education-based, it would be unheard of 10 years ago, that that type of stuff would be blocked or censored."

# 12 – Facts, Truths & Wisdom Censored by Big Tech, Government, School Boards & Academia

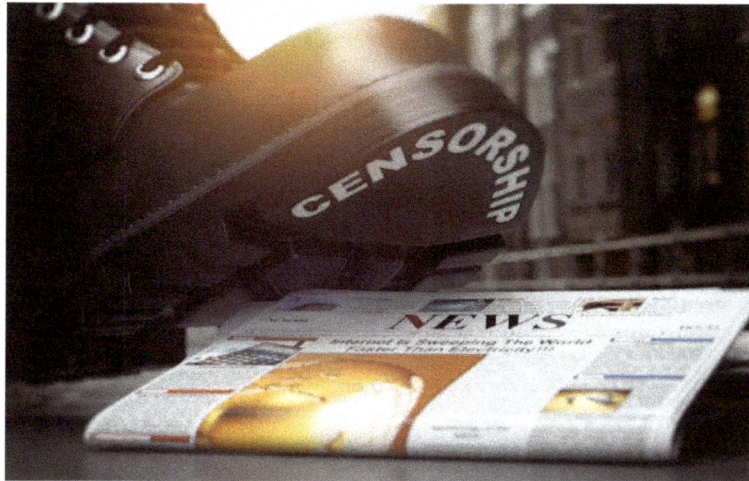

*Credit: The Tack Online.*

In *The Case Against the New Censorship: Protecting Free Speech from Big Tech, Progressives, and Universities* 2021 book by Alan Dershowitz—*New York Times* bestselling author and one of America's most respected legal scholars—he analyzes the current regressive war against freedom of speech being waged by well-meaning but dangerous censors and proposes steps that can be taken to defend, reclaim, and strengthen freedom of speech and other basic liberties that are under attack.

Alan Dershowitz has been called "one of the most prominent and consistent defenders of civil liberties in America" by Politico and "the nation's most peripatetic civil liberties lawyer and one of its most distinguished defenders of individual rights" by Newsweek. He is also a fair-minded and even-handed expert on the Constitution and our civil liberties, and in this book offers his knowledge and insight to help readers understand the war being waged against free speech by the ostensibly well-meaning forces seeking to constrain this basic right.

The Case Against the New Censorship is an analysis of every aspect of the current fight against freedom of speech, from the cancellations and deplatformings practiced by so-called progressives, to the powerful, seemingly arbitrary control exerted by Big Tech and social media companies, to the stifling of debate and controversial thinking at public and private universities. It assesses the role of the Trump presidency in energizing this backlash against basic liberties and puts it into a broader historical context as it examines how anti-Trump zealots weaponized, distorted, and weakened constitutional protections in an effort to "get" Trump by any means.

In the end, *The Case Against the New Censorship* represents an icon in American law and politics exploring the current rapidly changing attitudes toward the value of free speech and assessing potential ways to preserve our civil liberties. It is essential reading for anyone interested in or concerned about freedom of speech and the efforts to constrain it, the possible effects this could have on our society, and the significance of both freedom of speech and the battle against it in a greater historical and political context.

## The Many Issues With Big Tech: Media Research Center

From the Media Research Center's guidebook, *CENSORED! How Online Media Companies Are Suppressing Conservative Speech*, like it or not, social media is the communication form of the future—not just in the U.S., but worldwide. Just Facebook and Twitter combined reach 1.8 billion people. More than two-thirds of all Americans (68 percent) use Facebook. YouTube is pushing out TV as the most popular place to watch video. Google is the No. 1 search engine in both the U.S. and the world.

The Media Research Center has undertaken an extensive study of the problem at major tech companies—Twitter, Facebook, Google and YouTube—and the results are far more troubling than most conservatives realize. Here are some of the key findings:

**Twitter Leads in Censorship:**

Project Veritas recently caught Twitter staffers admitting on hidden camera that they had been censoring conservatives through a technique known as shadow banning, where users think their content is getting seen widely, but it's not. The staffers had justified it by claiming the accounts had been automated if they had words such as "America" and "God." In 2016, Twitter had attempted to manipulate election-related tweets using the hashtags "PodestaEmails" and "#DNCLeak." The site also restricts pro-life ads from Live Action and even Rep. Marsha Blackburn (R-Tenn.), but allows Planned Parenthood advertisements.

**Facebook's Trending Feed Has Been Hiding Conservative Topics:**

A 2016 Gizmodo story had warned of Facebook's bias. It had detailed claims by former employees that Facebook's news curators had been instructed to hide conservative content from the "trending" section, which supposedly only features news users find compelling. Topics that had been blacklisted included Mitt Romney, the Conservative Political Action Conference (CPAC) and Rand Paul. On the other hand, the term "Black Lives Matter" had also been placed into the trending section even though it was not actually trending. Facebook had also banned at least one far-right European organization but had not released information on any specific statements made by the group that warranted the ban.

**Google Search Aids Democrats:**

Google and YouTube's corporate chairman Eric Schmidt had assisted Hillary Clinton's presidential campaign. The company's search engine had deployed a similar bias in favor of Democrats. One study had found 2016 campaign searches were biased in favor of Hillary

Clinton. Even the liberal website Slate had revealed the search engine's results had favored both Clinton and Democratic candidates. Google also had fired engineer James Damore for criticizing the company's "Ideological Echo Chamber." The company had claimed he had been fired for "advancing harmful gender stereotypes in our workplace." Damore is suing Google, saying it mistreats whites, males and conservatives.

**YouTube Is Shutting Down Conservative Videos:**

Google's YouTube site had created its own problems with conservative content. YouTube moderators must take their cues from the rest of Google—from shutting down entire conservative channels "by mistake" to removing videos that promote right-wing political views. YouTube's special Creators for Change section is devoted to people using their "voices for social change" and even highlights the work of a 9/11 truther. The site's very own YouTube page and Twitter account celebrate progressive attitudes, including uploading videos about "inspiring" gay and trans people and sharing the platform's support for DACA.

**Tech Firms Are Relying on Groups That Hate Conservatives:**

Top tech firms like Google, YouTube and Twitter partner with leftist groups attempting to censor conservatives. These include the Southern Poverty Law Center (SPLC) and the Anti-Defamation League (ADL). Both groups claim to combat "hate," but treat standard conservative beliefs in faith and family as examples of that hatred. George Soros funded ProPublica is using information from both radical leftist organizations to attack conservative groups such as Jihad Watch and ACT for America, bullying PayPal and other services to shut down their funding sources. The SPLC's "anti-LGBT" list had also been used to prevent organizations from partnering with AmazonSmile to raise funds.

**Liberal Twitter Advisors Outnumber Conservatives 12-to-1:**

Twelve of the 25 U.S. members of Twitter's Trust and Safety Council—which helps guide its policies—are liberal, and only one is conservative. Anti-conservative groups like GLAAD and the ADL are part of the board. There is no well-known conservative group represented.

**Tech Companies Rely on Anti-Conservative Fact-Checkers:**

Facebook and Google both had partnered with fact-checking organizations in order to combat "fake news." Facebook's short-lived disputed flagger program had allowed Snopes, PolitiFact and ABC News to discern what is and is not real news. Google's fact-checkers had accused conservative sources of making claims that did not appear in their articles and disproportionately "fact-checked" conservative sources. On Facebook, a satire site, the Babylon Bee, had been flagged by Snopes for its article clearly mocking CNN for its bias. YouTube also had announced a partnership with Wikipedia in order to debunk videos deemed to be conspiracy theories, even though Wikipedia has been criticized for its liberal bias.

**Shadow Banning**

A report by Vice Media, which can hardly be considered right of center, found that Twitter appeared to suppress certain accounts of conservative groups, individuals, and politicians. As previously mentioned, it's called "shadow banning," in which Twitter engages in subtle blocking of conservative accounts on the site's search function. It amounts to making one side of the political debate—mainly, conservatives and libertarians—far less visible in searches than the liberal and progressive side.

The report said: "The Republican Party chair Ronna McDaniel, several conservative Republican congressmen, and Donald Trump Jr.'s spokesman no longer appear in the auto-populated drop-down search box on Twitter, Vice News has learned. It's a shift that diminishes their reach on the platform—and it's the same one being deployed against prominent racists to limit their visibility."

None of the above are racists and for those who state otherwise—sapient beings challenge you to *prove* it.

Meanwhile, "Democrats are not being 'shadow banned' in the same way," the report said. "Not a single member of the 78-person Progressive Caucus faces the same situation in Twitter's search." In other words, once again a progressive-dominated tech-site biases its service towards the left-side of the political spectrum to the detriment of the conservative-libertarian right. It's not just Twitter, of course. Facebook is having problems now for the same reason: It treats Republicans and conservatives differently than Democrats and leftists on its site.

Of course, conservatives don't have to have Facebook or Twitter accounts. But then, if those two social media define themselves as politically oriented sites, the rules change somewhat. That may be what Florida Republican Rep. Matt Gaetz was getting at as he was one of a number of well-known mainstream Republicans, including several other members of Congress and even the chair of the Republican National Committee, who had their accounts obscured by Twitter.

## Section 230 of the Communications Decency Act of 1996

From the day he announced his presidential ambitions, through his four tenuous years as president, to the post Trump era—Donald Trump is right that social media companies have been targeting conservatives—himself particularly—by restricting their freedom of speech and expression.

Twitter, in particular, has been engaging in a relentless attack on the American political process by censoring conservatives and banning Trump from their platform along with Facebook and others following their lead.

The social media giants have been shielded from such liability by Section 230 of the Communications Decency Act of 1996, legislation enacted in the salad days of the internet, when few anticipated how these companies would evolve into global monopolies and concerns were different.

Most recently, in May 2020, Twitter escalated its battle with President Trump by starting to fact check Trump's tweets nearly five months from a presidential election. Trump responded to Twitter's rulings by signing an executive order on May 28, 2020 that targets a law at the heart of the internet industry: Section 230 of the Communications Decency Act.

In the order, Trump asks government agencies to reinterpret the law in a way that would allow them to penalize companies for content decisions they deem politically biased. He has also threatened to push Congress to pass legislation to amend or revoke Section 230, a potentially existential threat to the companies' business models.

Per Trump, "I'm signing an Executive Order to protect and uphold the free speech and rights of the American people. Currently, social media giants like Twitter receive an unprecedented liability shield based on the theory that they are a neutral platform, which they are not."

This obvious anti-conservative bias is not healthy, not for our democracy or for the companies involved. America's traditions of free speech, open debate and the marketplace of ideas deserve respect. Rank political bias against conservatives, libertarians and the Republican Party is not acceptable.

### David vs. Goliath: Prager U Fights Google/YouTube Censorship

War is being declared on the conservative movement in this space and conservatives are losing—badly. If the right is silenced, billions of people will be cut off from conservative ideas and conservative media. It's the new battleground of media bias. But it's worse. That bias is not a war of ideas. It's a war against ideas. It's a clear effort to censor the conservative worldview from the public conversation.

Google and YouTube advertise YouTube to the public as a forum intended to defend and protect free speech where members of the general public may express and exchange their ideas. They have represented that their platforms and services are intended to effectuate the exercise of free speech among the public. According to Google and YouTube: "voices matter." YouTube states that it is "committed to fostering a community where everyone's voice can be heard."

"However," said Eric George of Browne George Ross, the firm representing Prager U, "Google and YouTube use restricted mode filtering not to protect younger or sensitive viewers from 'inappropriate' video content, but as a political gag mechanism to silence Prager U. Google and YouTube do this not because they have identified video content that violates their guidelines or is otherwise inappropriate for younger viewers, but because Prager U is a conservative nonprofit organization that is associated with and espouses the views of leading conservative speakers and scholars."

"This is speech discrimination plain and simple, censorship based entirely on unspecified ideological objection to the message or on the perceived identity and political viewpoint of the speaker," said former California Governor Pete Wilson of Browne George Ross. "Google and YouTube's use of restricted mode filtering to silence Prager U violates its fundamental First Amendment rights under both the California and United States Constitutions. It constitutes unlawful discrimination under California law, is a misleading and unfair business practice, and breaches the warranty of good faith and fair dealing implied in Google and YouTube's own Terms of Use and 'Community Guidelines.'"

"There is absolutely nothing 'inappropriate' about the content of the Prager U videos censored by Google and YouTube; the videos do not contain any profanity, nudity or otherwise inappropriate 'mature' content and they fully comply with the letter of YouTube's Terms of Use and Community Guidelines," said Marissa Streit, Prager U's chief executive officer who has engaged in a year-long-effort to try and persuade Google to stop censoring Prager U content. Streit continues, "It's clear that someone doesn't like what we teach and so they intend on stopping us from teaching it. Can you imagine what the world would look like if Google is allowed to continue to arbitrarily censor ideas they simply don't agree with?"

"This is not a left/right issue. It is a free speech issue, which is why prominent liberals, such as Harvard law professor Alan Dershowitz, are supporting our lawsuit," Prager concluded. Nonetheless, under the protection of Section 230 of the Communications Decency Act of 1996, Google/YouTube prevailed because as private companies they are not restricted from free speech suppression rules and guidelines as would be most public agencies.

Unfortunately for on-line free speech and expression, this is the currently reality that must be changed.

## The Dangerous Liberal Ideas for Censorship in the United States

Almost everywhere you turn today, politicians are telling the public to "get used to the new normal" after the pandemic as covered in Jonathan Turley's May 2020 article in *The Hill* titled "The Dangerous Liberal Ideas For Censorship in the United States."

Turley explains: The most chilling suggestion comes from the politicians and academics who have called for the censorship of social media and the internet. The only thing spreading faster than the coronavirus has been censorship and the loud calls for more restrictions on free speech. The *Atlantic* recently published an article by Harvard Law School professor Jack Goldsmith and University of Arizona law professor Andrew Keane Woods calling for Chinese style censorship of the internet.

They declared that "in the great debate of the past two decades about freedom versus control of the network, China was largely right and the United States was largely wrong" as "significant monitoring and speech control are inevitable components of a mature and flourishing internet, and governments must play a large role in such practices to ensure that the internet is compatible with society norms and values."

The justification for that is the danger of "fake news" about coronavirus risks and cures. Yet this is only the latest rationalization for rolling back free speech rights. For years, Democratic leaders in Congress called for censorship of "fake news" on social media sites. Twitter, Facebook, and YouTube have all engaged in increasing levels of censorship and have a well-known reputation for targeting conservative speech.

Hillary Clinton has demanded that political speech be regulated to avoid the "manipulation of information" and stated that Facebook founder Mark Zuckerberg "should pay a price for what he is doing to our democracy" by refusing to remove any opposition postings. In Europe, free speech rights are in a free fall, and countries such as France and Germany are imposing legal penalties designed to censor speech across the world.

Many of us in the free speech community have warned about the growing insatiable appetite for censorship in the West. Yet we have been losing the fight, and free speech opponents are now capitalizing on the opportunity presented by the pandemic. Representative Adam Schiff sent a message to the executives of Google, Twitter, and YouTube demanding censorship of anything deemed "misinformation" and "false information."

Yet YouTube did exactly that a few days earlier by removing two videos of California doctors who called for the easing of state lockdown orders. The doctors argued that the coronavirus is not as dangerous as suggested and that some deaths associated with the pandemic are not accurate. There is ample reason to contest their views but, instead, YouTube banned the two videos to keep others from reaching their own conclusions.

Facebook will not only remove posts it considers misinformation about the coronavirus but will issue warnings to those who "like" such postings. Facebook said that it wants to protect people from dangerous remedies and false data. Ironically, the World Health Organization praised Sweden for its rejection of the very restrictions criticized by the two doctors. The group declared that Sweden is a "model" country despite its rejection of lockdown measures being protested in the United States.

Moreover, many mainstream media sources have reported information that is now known to be false from the lack of any benefits of wearing masks to the failure in trials of drugs like Remdesivir to the shortage of thousands of ventilators. Despite those being wrong, related opposing views were often treated as either fringe or false positions. Fake news madness!

This subjectivity of censorship is why the cure is worse than the illness. The best cure for bad speech is more speech rather than regulation. The fact is that the pandemic, as Clinton reminded voters, is a "terrible crisis to waste." Yet the waste for some would be to emerge from the pandemic with free speech still alive.

## Democrats Propose a Federal Speech Czar

Tucked inside a supposedly 'moderate' voting bill is a provision that would empower a lone bureaucrat to wield outsized control over elections as exposed in Bradley A. Smith's October 2021 "Democrats Propose a Federal Speech Czar" article in *The Hill*:

Deep inside the Democrats' latest "compromise" proposal on elections and campaign finance is a new cup of poison for free speech and fair campaigns. Of course, the sponsors bragged that they dropped some controversial provisions. One such provision altered the Federal Election Commission (FEC), which polices campaign-finance laws, from a bipartisan agency to one with a partisan majority appointed by the president.

The bill, now dubbed the Freedom to Vote Act, abandons that direct attempt to give the president a partisan majority at the FEC. But it still abolishes the principle of bipartisan approval of enforcement actions. Even worse, it rigs court review of FEC decisions against defendants.

In a sign of the bill's hostility to free speech, the measure also proposes doubling the statute of limitations for most violations of federal campaign-finance laws to 10 years. That's longer than the statute of limitations for the crime of attempted assassination of a member of Congress.

The FEC was created nearly 50 years ago, in the wake of Watergate, to prevent the president from weaponizing campaign-finance laws against political opponents. The most important feature is the Commission's bipartisan makeup — six commissioners, with no more than three from any one party. At least four commissioners must approve initiating investigations or finding violations, thus assuring some measure of bipartisan agreement that a law may have been violated.

## A Less Democratic But More Bureaucratic Approach

Under the Democrats' proposal, the Federal Election Commission (FEC) would keep the same structure, but scrap the bipartisan requirement for enforcement action. Instead, the Commission's general counsel would take control of actions such as starting an investigation and declaring a violation. The council's decision would prevail unless, within 30 days, four commissioners voted to overrule it.

In other words, it would take a bipartisan coalition of four commissioners to stop an investigation rather than launch one. It would also take four votes to declare that no violation occurred. The bipartisan requirement for finding a violation is removed, just as it was in the earlier bill.

The FEC general counsel is a career civil servant, but we should not assume that he is without political preferences or bias. What kind of person aspires to regulate speech about campaigns and elections?

Few free-speech advocates probably would think to apply for such a job. Nor are counsels without partisan preferences. One former FEC general counsel later served as general counsel to Senate Democratic leaders Tom Daschle (S.D.) and Harry Reid (Nev.), and to one of Joe Biden's presidential campaigns. Another later worked for former Massachusetts Republican governor William Weld.

Even assuming the integrity of a Democratic Party ruled counsel, partisan views can influence how one sees cases in partisan elections. That is a major reason current law requires a bipartisan vote to launch an investigation or find a violation. Under the proposed act, it would no longer be necessary to convince anyone from the opposing party to declare a violation.

If a vacancy in the general-counsel position occurs, the most senior attorney at the FEC would become the acting general counsel until replaced. This means the commissioners could have no say in picking the acting general counsel. If this person turns out to be a hard-core partisan, he or she can stay in the position indefinitely, provided there is support by three partisan commissioners.

The bill further stacks the deck against free speech by rigging the judicial-review process against defendants. Under current law, if the FEC rules that there is no violation, the complainant can appeal to the federal courts. Conversely, if the agency finds a violation, the defendant can demand a day in court.

The bill would keep this system intact, but with new rules for the court. Under what is known as Chevron deference, if a law is subject to more than one interpretation, federal courts give deference to an agency's interpretation of the law. Under the proposed Freedom to Vote Act, however, if the FEC dismisses a complaint, courts give no deference to the Commission's interpretation of the law. But if the Commission finds a violation, the courts will defer to the FEC's interpretation of the law, pursuant to Chevron deference. In other words, the bill would put a thumb on the scale of justice, tilting it toward finding that speakers violate the law.

It's hard to think of the measure that would do more to undermine confidence in the fairness of our campaign-finance laws.

## Marxist Historian Howard Zinn's Views on Teaching Social Studies

It's hard to know what's worse—brainwashing kids or lying about it.

Parents worried their kids are being indoctrinated with critical race theory can't get straight answers. Local school boards and principals lie to them, claiming children are merely being taught to be "critical thinkers."

On Saturday June 12, 2021, the truth came out. Teachers unions and activists held rallies in 22 cities to support critical race theory. What they said was eye-popping. They unabashedly declared that their goal is indoctrinating students in far-left causes.

The Zinn Education Project, which organized Saturday's events, produces race-centric material for junior high and high schools across the country. Lesson plans are offered free for teachers to download. Parents wondering where the critical race theory their children are getting comes from can go to the website. They'll be shocked.

Zinn was founded by the late Howard Zinn, a Marxist historian who said that teaching social studies wasn't about dates and events. It was to make students want to change the world, overthrowing the status quo.

A Zinn lesson called "Students Design a Reparations Bill" explains that students will be asked to improve on the "flimsy" reparations bills currently in Congress. Critical thinking isn't encouraged. This isn't a debate about whether there should be reparations. This is one-sided indoctrination. "As racial justice activists, student are all on the 'same side,' in this role play," says the Zinn website.

Other extreme left groups supplying social studies materials for schools include the Southern Poverty Law Center and Black Lives Matter at School. SPLC tells educators to stand their ground against parents "and vigorously resist efforts to maintain the status quo." No wonder parents are getting the run around.

**It's Not Just White Families Protesting**

Keisha King, a black mother from Duval County, Florida, warned the Florida Board of Education that telling a child he's the victim of oppression is "the essence of holding a child back."

Michael Rivera, a Virginian, explains that he "married a wonderful woman who happens to be white. My son is white." He objects that "according to critical race theory, my son should have white guilt and white privilege."

More than 500 people have signed a petition demanding a curriculum that allows students to learn "without the titles of racist and victim" in Guilford, Connecticut, a small town outside of New Haven. Yet the Guilford school superintendent insists schools aren't teaching critical race theory. Does he think parents are lying about the homework in their kids' backpacks?

In Greenwich, Connecticut, parents went to the microphone at a May 20 school board meeting, parents to quote materials their children had brought home, including a "white bias" survey for seventh graders. The school board members and school superintendent sat silently. Last week, the superintendent sent out an email to parents explaining that Greenwich wants students to be "critical thinkers" but deftly denying that critical race theory is part of the curriculum.

That may be technically true. Critical race theory originated in law schools. But what's being taught in elementary and secondary schools across the country is a simplified version. For the sake of protecting America's social cohesion from identity politics—as well as the other sapient points covered in *Free Speech Madness*--it must be fought on all fronts.

## Replacing School Board Officials Promoting CRT & Canceling Free Speech

Since school administrators will lie and obfuscate to push ahead with critical race theory, parents have only one choice. They have to organize and run candidates to replace the local school boards. School board elections are usually quiet because unions and other insiders like it that way. Now's the time for parents to grab control.

Twenty states with Republican legislative majorities are trying to ban critical race theory (CRT). They're not calling for whitewashing American history, as some activists claim, but they require diversity of viewpoints and prohibit lessons that would shame students for their "privilege."

Even so, state bans are not ideal. They may run afoul of the First Amendment. And it's hard to know what's going on in each school. That's what local school boards are for.

Even in blue states, Republican candidates who challenge local school boards will make inroads and gain converts to the GOP. This is a winning issue.

Parents—whether independents, Democrats, Republicans or black, white, Hispanic, and Asian—want their children to be educated—not indoctrinated.

This section's content courtesy of the *Epoch Times* "Opinion: The Leftists Writing Your Child's Social Studies Lessons" by Betsy McCaughey, former lieutenant governor of New York.

### Marshall v. Amuso: Pennsbury's School Board Aggressive Censorship

Per the details in the October 2021 article "Marshall v. Amuso" from the Institute For Free Speech: After being repeatedly censored, badgered, and shouted down by school board officials, a group of parents and community members filed a federal lawsuit against the leaders of the Pennsbury School Board. The Board's policies and actions restricting speech at public meetings violate the First Amendment.

"Pennsbury officials are trampling on the First Amendment rights of parents and residents to speak their mind about their schools. They have cut off parents in the middle of sentences, yelled over critics to prevent them from being heard, edited remarks out of recordings of public meetings, and intimidated speakers by forcing them to publicly announce their home address," said Institute for Free Speech Vice President for Litigation Alan Gura.

Video of Pennsbury's aggressive censorship (see the Appendix for the link), which went viral this summer, shows community members being silenced simply for raising arguments Board officials disagreed with. While school boards may terminate comments that are obscene, exceed the allotted time limit, or lack decorum, they may not censor speech based on its viewpoint.

During one public meeting held on May 20, Pennsbury Assistant Solicitor Peter Amuso repeatedly interrupted residents who raised concerns about a new district policy, shouting "You're done!" until they left the microphone. When a resident criticized the same policy at an earlier March 18 meeting, the School Board removed the remarks from its video recording of the meeting. Internal district emails confirmed that Board leaders removed the comment due to the views expressed by the speaker.

The Board has also recently adopted a new policy to expand the grounds on which it can silence dissenting views. In addition to targeting critics of school policies, the Board has sought to prevent residents from criticizing individual members of the Board or the procedures for speaking at public meetings. Yet all of this speech is relevant to board meetings and protected by the First Amendment, the lawsuit explains.

"It is axiomatic that criticism of school officials, school employees, school rules and regulations, school budgets, and school curricula are germane to the business of school boards—regardless of whether school board members want to hear such criticism or believe that it is fair," reads the complaint. "The First Amendment prohibits the exclusion of these viewpoints from public speech at school board meetings."

The plaintiffs in the lawsuit are four local parents and residents whose First Amendment rights have been violated by the Pennsbury School Board: Douglas Marshall, Simon Campbell, Robert Abrams, and Tim Daly. They are represented by Institute for Free Speech attorneys Alan Gura, Del Kolde, and Martha Astor; and by Michael Gottlieb of Vangrossi & Recchuiti. The defendants in the case include Amuso, the members of the Pennsbury School Board, Board President Christine Toy-Dragoni, and other current and former district officials.

"This lawsuit serves as a valuable civics lesson for America's public school students. Pennsbury's censorship-promoting School Board is not above the law. When government officials strive to silence the First Amendment rights of American citizens, those officials can be held liable in federal court," said Simon Campbell, who served on the Pennsbury School Board between 2009 and 2013.

"For years, the Board's attorneys have attempted to deny that residents have a right to speak during public comment periods. With this lawsuit, we hope to end their illegal censorship and force the Board to respect our God-given and constitutional rights," said Robert Abrams.

"In May, Assistant Solicitor Amuso told me, 'You're done,' and I told him, I'll see you in court. The filing of this lawsuit fulfills the promise I made to ensure that the School Board members that violated my rights are held accountable," Tim Daly explained.

Americans have the right to express their views about local schools and their leaders at public meetings. Elected officials, including school board members, must be able to tolerate criticism and dissent. Most of all, they must respect the First Amendment rights of the communities they serve.

The lawsuit, *Marshall v. Amuso*, asks the United States District Court for the Eastern District of Pennsylvania, located in Philadelphia, to declare the Pennsbury School Board's speech policies unconstitutional and award damages to the plaintiffs.

## Majority of Republicans say major technology companies support the views of liberals over conservatives

*% of U.S. adults who say major technology companies support the views of ...*

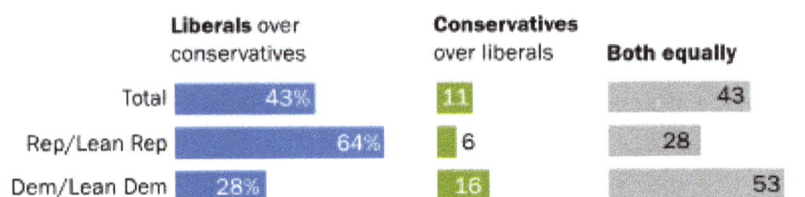

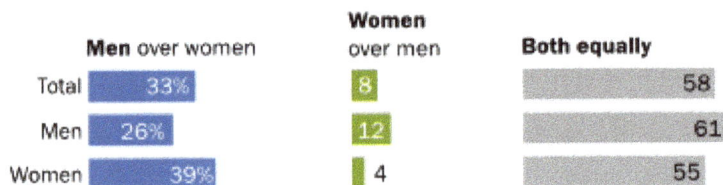

| | Liberals over conservatives | Conservatives over liberals | Both equally |
|---|---|---|---|
| Total | 43% | 11 | 43 |
| Rep/Lean Rep | 64% | 6 | 28 |
| Dem/Lean Dem | 28% | 16 | 53 |

| | Men over women | Women over men | Both equally |
|---|---|---|---|
| Total | 33% | 8 | 58 |
| Men | 26% | 12 | 61 |
| Women | 39% | 4 | 55 |

Note: Respondents who did not give an answer are not shown.
Source: Survey conducted May 29-June 11, 2018.
"Public Attitudes Toward Technology Companies"

**PEW RESEARCH CENTER**

## A New Wave of Censorship Culminating in US Government Agencies

The removal of Lt. Col. Matthew Lohmeier from the U.S. Space Force this month after he publicly stated his opposition to Marxism and critical race theory is part of a broader, more dangerous new wave of censorship that is culminating in the United States, says constitutional expert Alan Dershowitz.

In an interview with Epoch TV's "Crossroads," Dershowitz, a former Harvard Law School professor, expressed concern over Lohmeier's dismissal, as well as other incidents such as the removal of former President Donald Trump from Twitter, Facebook, and other Big Tech platforms in January following the Jan. 6 Capitol breach.

As reported in the March 2021 article "'Dangerous' New Wave of Censorship Culminating in the US: Dershowitz" by Isabel van Brugen and Joshua Philipp of the *Epoch Times:* The Space Force on May 19 relieved Lohmeier from the 11th Space Warning Squadron over allegations that he was "politically partisan" when he denounced the spread of Marxism in the military during an interview.

In explaining his dismissal, the department said Lohmeier made "public comments" deemed to be "partisan political activity." Lohmeier in a podcast warned about the spread of Marxist ideology within the military and the detrimental consequences of Defense Secretary Lloyd Austin's agenda to push critical race theory.

Critical race theory, which is rooted in Marxism, has been heavily promulgated throughout academia, entertainment, government, schools, and the workplace in recent years, coming to new prominence following the rise of far-left groups such as Antifa and Black Lives Matter. Some employers have included concepts from the doctrine—which some claim teaches that the United States is a fundamentally racist country, and that one race is inherently superior to another—in their "racial and cultural sensitivity" training.

Like Marxism, it advocates for the destruction of institutions, such as the Western justice system, free-market economy, and orthodox religions, while demanding that they be replaced with institutions compliant with the theory's ideology.

"We're in a very, very dangerous situation now where the left, which has enormous influence on American universities, has enormous influence on social media, has enormous influence on certain kinds of politics in the media, are trying to suppress free speech, and they're succeeding, and we have to fight back," Dershowitz said.

Big Tech companies such as Facebook, Twitter, and Google are today engaging in "massive censorship" that endangers the freedom of speech itself, Dershowitz said.

"That's not good for the country, it's not good for the Constitution, it's not good for freedom of speech. It's not good by any standards, and it has to stop. And we the consumers have to demand that Facebook and YouTube and Twitter stop this censorship," he continued.

**NIH: Check Out Wikipedia to See Why Great Barrington Declaration is 'Dangerous'**

In 2021, the National Institutes of Health (NIH) and its top officials are doubling down on criticism of the Great Barrington Declaration after emails showed they quickly moved in 2020 to oppose it per the December 2021 *Epoch Times'* article "NIH: Check Out Wikipedia to See Why Great Barrington Declaration is 'Dangerous'" by Zachary Stieber.

The declaration, penned in 2020, said lockdowns were producing negative short- and long-term effects on public health, such as lower childhood vaccination rates, fewer cancer screenings, and worsening mental health. The experts who signed on called for focusing COVID-19 prevention efforts on the most vulnerable, particularly the elderly, while loosening restrictions on the young and healthy, who are at little risk of developing severe COVID-19.

Dr. Martin Kulldorff, at the time a professor of medicine at Harvard University, Dr. Sunetra Gupta, an epidemiologist at Oxford University, and Dr. Jay Bhattacharya, an epidemiologist at Stanford University Medical School, signed the declaration, as did hundreds of other medical experts.

But top officials in the United States government were displeased with the declaration, which they felt wasn't based on sound science. New emails obtained and published by the American Institute for Economic Research (AIER) and a congressional panel (pdf) show Dr. Francis Collins, who just stepped down as head of the NIH, directed a top subordinate, Dr. Anthony Fauci, to publish "a quick and devastating published takedown" of the declaration's premises.

Fauci ended up going on television to criticize the declaration while Collins spoke publicly about his opposition to the *Washington Post*. Fauci also sent links to two op-eds he said "debunked" and served as a "refutation" of the approach promoted by the declaration, the 2020 emails show.

Some experts have said the messages from top health officials amount to unnecessary censorship. At the time Collins called for a takedown, no COVID-19 vaccines were available, and harsh restrictions had led to soaring unemployment, school closures, and businesses being forced to shut down.

"When it comes to lockdowns or school closures, the answer to the question of whether the benefits exceed the harms and, if so, under what conditions, is far from certain, and scientists will continue to study this for decades. As a good scientist, Collins should have recognized the massive uncertainty around these policies," Dr. Vinay Prasad, an associate professor of epidemiology at the University of California, San Francisco, wrote in an op-ed.

"In public, Anthony Fauci and Francis Collins urge Americans to 'follow the science.' In private, the two sainted public-health officials schemed to quash dissenting views from top scientists," added the *Wall Street Journal* editorial board.

The NIH and Collins are standing by the opposition to the Great Barrington Declaration.

# 13 – The Return of Freedom of Speech, Viewpoint Diversity, Intellectual Humility & Sapience

*Credit: Talksub.*

Leftist indoctrination is spreading well beyond academia, big tech, government, corporations, and educations organizations and we don't act now, it's only a matter of time before its oppressive and dysfunctional policies overtake all of America. Our treasured and God-given liberties, freedoms and way of life are at risk of being lost forever and an Orwellian wave of progressivism madness will overtake America from sea to shining sea.

Sapient individuals and organizations who understand the many blessings to humankind that are the direct result of American exceptionalism, Western European culture, and Judeo-Christian values—will not stand idly for this. As Dennis Prager so eloquently states, "I refuse to be forever labeled as 'the generation that lost America'—and I know you agree!"

To avoid that catastrophe, we must not merely double our efforts, but triple them and commit to educating our youth for the long haul. Humility, openness, engagement, a strong and maturing self that is always a work in progress; these are the necessary ingredients for a free society, and for shared progress, according to John Stuart Mill.

For far too long, sapient beings have failed to pass on their values to the next generation and to fight for them within the discourse of the marketplace of ideas. Clearly, we need to better market our successful, freedom-boosting values and ideas that will protect and nourish our republic—and deny those the opportunity who are intent on destroying it.

As strange as it may sound at first-- that destruction starts with the addition and reinterpretation of words in the American lexicon.

**The Pronoun Wars**

Once upon a time and in a place very near America in a Canadian province called Ontario and its oh-so-proudly tolerant and diverse city called Toronto, on the campus of its celebrated and eponymous University, there was a professor, a clinical psychologist. And his name was Jordan Peterson as reported in the December 2021 Epoch Times' article "How the 'Cancel Culture' Mob's Attempt to Silence Jordan Peterson Backfired" by Rex Murphy.

It was at the beginning of what history now calls the Pronoun Wars, denoted by one sage observer, and the greatest nightmare grammarians have ever endured, and sparked by the emergence of the "trans" movement. A concentrated account must suffice. Dr. Jordon Peterson, a near anonymous figure in those days, objected to the idea that he could be mandated to use any of the glittering array of new-fangled (and frankly ridiculous) bedspread of invented pronouns.

It wasn't that he would not, in some person-to-person contact, agree to use a new "pronoun" to a student who requested it. His objection came from deeper sources: that the concepts behind the practice emerged from a mode of politics he regarded as pernicious. He emphatically declared that as either professor or citizen he would never submit to "compelled speech."

Skipping over much, a band of fevered students charged him with "transphobia"—not incidentally yet another term that has leaped into news and academic discourse, though you will not hear it much, even now, outside these progressive vaults. They interrupted Peterson's lectures, assailed him with contempt and insult, harassed him when he attempted to argue his case, brought noise machines to drown him out, and asked—demanded—he be fired.

The attempts to silence and ostracize Peterson failed in a divinely spectacular fashion. The woke, identity-politics mob—I'm going vernacular here—got its politically correct fat ass bitten as with the teeth of a monster crocodile—as he ascended into fame with supersonic speed, wrote the book "12 Rules for Life" that sold millions, and became the most famous academic in the world—a heralded icon to masses of people grateful for his advice, his multitude of Biblical and other lectures, and his articulated defiance of the bullying tactics and ideology of left dogma.

They tried to smother Peterson, and even his own University of Toronto was complicit in the early effort. But to their woe and heartburn resentment, unwittingly fed him Grade A oxygen and launched him to undreamt of fame and access to a worldwide audience. They had attempted to crush a sparrow and lo, they set a dragon in flight against themselves.

Sapient beings take notice!

## More So Called 'Fact Checkers" Retract Their "Pants on Fire" Ratings

PolitiFact has quietly retracted a September 2020 fact check that labeled a Hong Kong virologist's claim that COVID-19 originated in a lab as inaccurate and a "debunked conspiracy theory" as reported by Isabel van Brugen of the *Epoch Times* in her May 2021 article "PolitiFact Quietly Retracts Fact Check Labeling COVID-19 Lab Origin Theory as 'Debunked Conspiracy.'"

"The claim is inaccurate and ridiculous," the now-archived fact check from PolitiFact previously stated. "We rate it Pants on Fire!" In an updated editor's note published on May 24, 2021, PolitiFact explained why it has now removed the label.

"When this fact-check was first published in September 2020, PolitiFact's sources included researchers who asserted the SARS-CoV-2 virus could not have been manipulated. That assertion is now more widely disputed," the note states. "For that reason, we are removing this fact-check from our database pending a more thorough review. Currently, we consider the claim to be unsupported by evidence and in dispute."

The original fact check from PolitiFact cited a Sept. 15, 2020, Fox News interview with Hong Kong virologist Yan Limeng, in which she said she has "solid scientific evidence" that COVID-19, the disease caused by the CCP (Chinese Communist Party) virus, is "not from nature."

"It is a man-made virus created in the lab," the virologist and former postdoctoral fellow at the University of Hong Kong told the news network at the time. She also claimed in the interview that the virus was intentionally released by the Chinese regime, without elaborating. Yan said the virus's genome indicates that it was modified.

"In a Sept. 15 interview, the most-watched program on cable network television aired a conspiracy theory that has been debunked since the beginning of the coronavirus pandemic," PolitiFact's fact check said of the virologist's claims. Social media sites such as Facebook and Instagram, which partner with PolitiFact, flagged posts containing Yan's claims as false.

### PolitiFact Awarded This Now Undisputed Fact as Their "2020 Lie of the Year"

The quiet retraction comes as Republican members of the House Intelligence Committee say they believe it to be more likely that the CCP virus originated within a Chinese laboratory than from an animal.

"There is overwhelming circumstantial evidence … to support a lab leak as the origination of COVID-19," stated a May 19 committee report, which was led by Rep. Devin Nunes (R-Calif.), the ranking member on the committee. "By contrast, little circumstantial evidence has emerged to support the PRC's [People's Republic of China] claim that COVID-19 was a natural occurrence, having jumped from some other species to humans."

COVID-19 first appeared in China's central city of Wuhan in late 2019, when a cluster of cases was linked to a local wet market. More than a year later, the origins of the virus remain unknown, though the focus has now shifted toward the theory that the virus was leaked from a laboratory at China's Wuhan Institute of Virology (WIV). Such a leaked virus could either be a naturally occurring virus or one that had been manipulated in the laboratory.

WIV is home to China's only P4 lab—the highest level of biosafety—and it's located not far from the city's wet market. A State Department fact sheet released in January stated that the WIV had been conducting experiments on bat coronavirus starting at least as far back as 2016. The institute also carried out "laboratory animal experiments" for the Chinese military since at least 2017.

More importantly, the department stated that it had reason to believe that "several researchers inside the WIV became sick in autumn 2019, before the first identified case of the outbreak, with symptoms consistent with both COVID-19 and common seasonal illnesses."

The Chinese regime has denied that the virus's origin is linked to the WIV and has pushed a natural zoonotic hypothesis—that the virus was transmitted to humans from an animal host. However, Beijing has so far failed to identify the original animal species that allegedly passed the virus on to humans.

According to the report, Beijing tested more than 80,000 animals and still couldn't identify the original species. PolitiFact didn't respond to requests for comment by press time. In December 2020, the fact-checking website named COVID-19 disinformation, including the claim that the virus was manipulated in a lab, as the "lie of the year."

## Viewpoint Diversity on Campus is Essential

Viewpoint diversity refers to the state of a community or group in which members approach questions or problems from multiple perspectives. When a community is marked by intellectual humility, empathy, trust, and curiosity, viewpoint diversity gives rise to engaged and civil debate, constructive disagreement, and shared progress towards truth. Viewpoint diversity enables colleges and universities to realize their twin goals of producing the best research and providing the best education.

As citizens who are counting on students' and researchers' future contributions to our shared social, civic, moral, and scientific endeavors, we all suffer when orthodoxies distort and limit understanding of the social, aesthetic, and natural world—or when institutions of higher learning are unable to draw in perspectives from the whole of society. To help  solve this problem we need heterodox academies.

To make headway on solving the world's most complex problems, scholars and policy makers must deploy the best ideas. This typically requires consulting a wide range of perspectives.

While a community of inquiry defined by intellectual humility, curiosity, empathy, and trust may hold many beliefs in common, few ideas will be beyond discussion, revision, or good-faith debate.

### The Surest Sign of an Unhealthy Scholarly Culture is the Presence of Orthodoxy

Orthodoxies are most readily apparent when people fear shame, ostracism, or any other form of social or professional retaliation for questioning or challenging a commonly held idea.

The best way to defend against orthodoxies—or to neutralize them—is to foster commitment to open inquiry, viewpoint diversity and constructive disagreement. When these elements are missing, orthodoxies can take root and thrive.

Viewpoint diversity occurs when members of a group or community approach problems or questions from a range of perspectives. Institutions of higher learning face several interrelated viewpoint diversity deficits including:

- Racial/Ethnic

- Socioeconomic

- Geographical

- Religious

- Political

- And in many fields, Gender

Academic freedom demanded a respect for a diversity of views. During the Vietnam War years, college campuses were alive with debates about the war and a host of other subjects. There was no effort to silence diverse points of view.

Per Haidt, the future of liberal democracy depends in no small measure on empathy—the ability to humanize and understand others and tolerance. Students need to see those with whom they disagree politically as people—or else they risk alienating and demonizing the other side, which only leads to further conflict and highly-limited understanding.

A culture that will not tolerate divergence of opinion harms students, but academic research is also at risk when dominant theories and opinions no longer encounter counterclaims that test their validity.

## Viewpoint Diversity Deficits Can Lead to Intolerance

When environments lack sufficient viewpoint diversity, problematic assumptions can go unchallenged, promising ideas and methods can go underexplored, and it can be difficult to effectively understand or engage with others who have different backgrounds, priors, and commitments.

For instance, to the extent that institutions of higher learning lack viewpoint diversity (and are thus not representative of the broader societies in which they are embedded), scholars may struggle to communicate the value and relevance of their work to people outside the academy in an accessible and compelling way.

Well-intentioned social programs can fail in their stated aims—or even cause harm—when the people designing policies are too far removed from the populations their interventions are intended to serve. Meanwhile, young people from underrepresented groups may come to feel as though they don't belong in the academy—and decline to apply to college, drop out midway through, or pursue non-academic paths if they push through to graduation.

In short, we would have reasons to recruit and retain a more diverse pool of faculty, staff, and students even if the lack of viewpoint diversity were purely the result of differences in interests and priorities among members of various groups.

However, we know that many disparities are also—at least in part—the result of a hostile atmosphere, discrimination, a lack of access or institutional dynamics that tend to privilege certain groups for reasons other than the quality of their research or ideas. It seems important to rectify these imbalances for moral as well as practical reasons.

**Political Intolerance Among University Faculty Highlights Need For Viewpoint Diversity**

Viewpoint diversity has become the bane of the academic elite per the "Political Intolerance Among University Faculty Highlights Need For Viewpoint Diversity" in the November 2016 *Forbes* article by Nathan Honeycutt:

It's an inconvenient reality: Universities are champions for diversity and inclusivity, except when it comes to viewpoint diversity. Supporting viewpoint diversity is certainly not "mainstream"— academics have proven predominantly resistant to research and discussions calling for this issue to be addressed.

Recently published research, though, suggests the lack of viewpoint diversity in our universities is neither a small nor trivial issue: It's widespread, impacting academia across disciplines. Further, the data clearly indicate that explicit political discrimination is widely endorsed.

Surveying faculty across all academic disciplines at four California State University campuses my coauthor and I found that overall 71% of respondents were liberal (15% moderate, 14% conservative). Liberals comprised an overwhelming majority in every academic area except for Agriculture where conservatives were a plurality, but not a majority.

Reporting on their experiences in the academy, conservative faculty were found to have experienced significantly more hostility than their more liberal colleagues. Additionally, nearly one-third of both liberals and conservatives expressed a willingness to discriminate in hiring decisions. These individuals explicitly reported that if presented with two equally qualified job candidates, they would choose the candidate that shared their political beliefs.

Given the symmetrical nature of expressed willingness to discriminate, it certainly would be inappropriate to label the liberal majority as the "bad guys" for not wanting to hire conservatives, as conservatives indicated they wouldn't be interested in hiring liberals. But stopping here and claiming there is no cause for concern is a tad too simplistic.

Conservatives clearly lack the means and opportunity to act upon their willingness to discriminate due to their small numbers. Given the sheer quantity of liberal faculty, and the willingness of a sizable number to make political ideology a "litmus test" for hiring, it's more realistic to expect that the number of politically conservative faculty on university campuses will continue to shrink.

This quickly becomes problematic on multiple fronts. As Jonathan Haidt of New York University has routinely argued, dismissing conservative (or non-liberal) views could lead scholars to overlook meaningful research questions, or even misinterpret the results of their research. Psychology and many other academic disciplines are working to maintain sure footing amidst a relative crisis of scientific integrity, characterized in part by incidences of fabricated data and influential studies failing replication. Scientific integrity has the potential to be bolstered by an increased commitment to viewpoint diversity.

Welcoming different perspectives allows ideas to be better refined, questions that may otherwise be avoided to be pursued, and data to have a better chance at being accurately analyzed and interpreted. It provides a natural check on research, preventing it from descending into what Philip Tetlock of the University of Pennsylvania dubbed "scientific hell," where scientific standards are clouded by political passions.

Volumes of research related to minority influence—such as that by Charlan Nemeth of the University of California, Berkeley—have demonstrated the benefits of welcoming divergent or underrepresented perspectives into the fold. Numerical minorities positively influence creativity and divergent thinking in problem solving and decision-making. Even if minority positions and ideas aren't adopted, their influence on the quality and quantity of thought still provides a positive boost for the quality of the group's end product.

Collaborations or coexisting with those who may see the world in a fundamentally different way is certainly not easy—it's a primary instinct to surround ourselves with like-minded individuals. Ultimately, though, it's counterproductive for academics to respond to research or ideas they don't agree with by stifling the research or the colleagues performing it. Rather, the best way academics can seek to most accurately answer difficult questions and understand perplexing phenomena is by openly debating the issues and conducting more research.

If universities and university faculty seek to support diversity and inclusivity, they cannot continue to apply it in selective or convenient ways. By welcoming those who think differently—perhaps coupled with a focus on superordinate goals such as the pursuit of truth—academics can become better stewards of the pluralistic tradition of our universities, and can correspondingly bolster scientific integrity in their work.

## A Plea for Civil Discourse: Needed, the Academy's Leadership

The United States of America—that inspiring experiment in democratic government—was founded on compromise; the Constitution, one of the greatest give-and-take documents, describes a government with multiple loci of power. The bicameral makeup of Congress ensures the rights of small and large states alike, a solution reached during the republic's creation.

The United States came into existence because of religious and heritage plurality. The country's plurality in the twenty-first century includes an entire spectrum of skin colors, ethnic groups, beliefs, languages, and cultures. In a pluralistic society, people hold varying views, and that very diversity is an inherent strength. In a country anchored in compromise and diversity, discourse among people of good faith should flourish.

*A Crucible Moment: College Learning and Democracy's Future*, commissioned by the US Department of Education, was published by the Association of American Colleges and Universities (AACU) in 2012.

Representing the work of the National Task Force on Civic Learning and Democratic Engagement (2012), the report builds a strong case for higher education's responsibility, in collaboration with the larger society, for assuring that all students have the skills and knowledge they need to become informed, civically engaged citizens. The section below is intended to complement *A Crucible Moment* by focusing in greater depth on civil discourse and the crucial need for colleges and universities to commit strongly to its survival.

### Wider partisan gaps emerge in trust of national and local news organizations, social media

*% of U.S. adults who say they have a lot or some trust in the information that comes from ...*

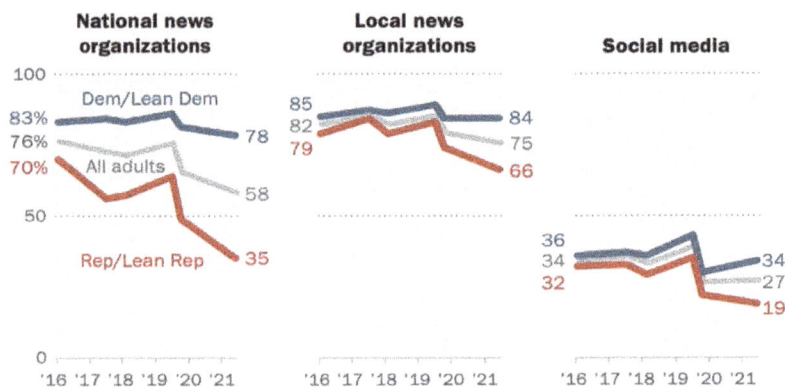

Note: In 2016, trust of information from social media was only asked of and based on internet-using U.S. adults.
Source: Survey of U.S. adults conducted June 14-27, 2021. For dates of other surveys, see the topline.

**PEW RESEARCH CENTER**

## Defining Civil Discourse

What is civil discourse? A 2011 conversation among national leaders from many fields, held at the US Supreme Court, defined civil discourse as "robust, honest, frank and constructive dialogue and deliberation that seeks to advance the public interest" (Brosseau 2011).

James Calvin Davis, in his book *In Defense of Civility*, proposes "the exercise of patience, integrity, humility and mutual respect in civil conversation, even (or especially) with those with whom we disagree" (2010, 159).

National Public Radio journalist Diane Rehm, during an event at Oberlin College, said simply: our ability to have conversation about topics about which we disagree, and our ability to listen to each other's perspectives (Choby 2011).

Civil discourse is discourse that supports, rather than undermines, the societal good. It demands that democratic participants respect each other, even when that respect is hard to give or to earn. Democratic societies must be societies where arguments are tolerated and encouraged, but this is not always easy.

"To engage in a healthy political argument is to acknowledge the possibility that one's own arguments could be falsified or proven wrong," says Thomas Hollihan, professor at the University of Southern California's Annenberg School of Communication. "This demands that citizens listen respectfully to the claims made by others. Name-calling, threats and bullying behaviors do not meet the demands of effective deliberation."

For the purposes of this article, discourse that is civil means that those involved:

- Undertake a serious exchange of views.

- Focus on the issues rather than on the individual(s) espousing them.

- Defend their interpretations using verified information.

- Thoughtfully listen to what others say.

- Seek the sources of disagreements and points of common purpose.

- Embody open-mindedness and a willingness change their minds.

- Assume they will need to compromise and are willing to do so.

- Treat the ideas of others with respect.

- Avoid violence (physical, emotional, and verbal).

While some consider politeness and good behavior as essential to civil discourse, Ahrens (2009) argues that civil discourse must accommodate offensive expression, with the latter term capturing the harshness of many public debate conflicts. Leach (2011) says that civility "is not simply or principally about manners. It doesn't mean that spirited advocacy is to be avoided. Indeed, argumentation is a social good.

Without (it) there is a tendency to dogmatism, even tyranny." Herbst (2010, 148) suggests that "even some incivility can move a policy debate along. Creating a culture of argument, and the thick skin that goes along with it, are long-term projects that will serve democracy well." One should not expect civil discourse to create a feeling of comfort; discord causes uneasiness, and a challenge to deeply held opinions induces pain.

Wegge (2013) distinguishes two elements in civil discourse: (1) the emotive, as expressed through manners and norms of behavior (moderating or failing to moderate self-control), and (2) "constructive confrontation" or civility demonstrated through argument and deliberation. In any case, civil discourse goes beyond courtesy. It involves committing to an informed, frank exchange of ideas, along with an understanding of complexity and ambiguity.

Koegler (2012) clarifies that "civil" refers not to mannered conduct but to membership in a civil society. He suggests that civil discourse has both a process ("a pragmatic and open dialogue of the issues themselves, based on evidence and argument, coupled with the willingness to learn from the other") and content ("serious conversation about public matters of common concern").

As used here, the term civil discourse includes speaking or writing knowledgeably about a topic and harkens back to the definition of discourse as the process or power of reasoning. It is this basis in reasoned inquiry that affords one essential hook for holding higher education accountable.

## Civil Discourse in Civic Learning

*A Crucible Moment* advocates for adding to college study a third nationwide educational priority, complementing those of increased access and career preparation: the graduation of responsibly engaged citizens.

These graduates will need to be informed through knowledge, including knowledge of the political process and the major issues of current and former times. They will also need to be empowered by possessing a range of intellectual and practical skills. Civil discourse, a central skill of such civic learning, itself rests on core intellectual abilities at the very heart of powerful education:

- Critical inquiry.

- Analysis and reasoning.

- Information retrieval and evaluation.

- Effective written communication.

- Effective oral communication that includes listening as well as speaking.

- An understanding of one's own perspectives and their limitations.

- The ability to interact constructively with a diverse group of individuals holding conflicting views.

Civil discourse also embodies the very values of civic learning: open-mindedness, compromise, and mutual respect.

Participants in civil discourse need to learn about the issue at hand, critically weigh the information's veracity and validity, build a logical argument, and present it in a convincing but nondoctrinaire manner to individuals who might not share the same views. They need to be respectfully attentive to alternative interpretations—weighing them, too, analytically—and be willing to alter positions based on convincing argument and evidence.

Educators will recognize these skills and values as those of any serious intellectual undertaking, which is why civil discourse is not limited to political science or the political arena. It figures as centrally in any field with controversies—science, art, or philosophy, for example—and, therefore, can be learned and practiced in most disciplines.

Just like the core intellectual and practical abilities of liberal learning, civil discourse is transferable across disciplines and outside the academy, to the workplace and civic life. While concern about the harsh tenor of interchanges in the political arena catalyzed this article, as a democratic approach to handling controversy, civil discourse has broad applicability. Referencing Diane Rehm again, civil dialogue and discourse begin at home.

## Promoting Civil Discourse in Undergraduate Education

Once we accept that students need to become adept civil discoursers—for their own and democracy's good—how can college education foster this important skill?

First, civil discourse must be addressed at the heart of undergraduate education. It cannot be relegated to student affairs or simply embodied in codes of conduct or speech, nor can it remain the purview of a department of politics or communications. Civil discourse needs to be addressed in general education for all students and embraced by the various majors, across the curriculum. Given the swirl of many students among institutions, commitment will be needed in all high schools, colleges, and universities.

Second, students need to be taught (and not simply exposed to or asked to use) civil discourse, which means giving them both a theoretical basis of the concept and practical tools for using it.

Theory could include, for example, definitions and rules, cultural variations, and norms, plus analysis of the consequences of dogmatism. Practical tools might involve applying to contentious issues skills learned elsewhere in the curriculum: active listening, debating techniques, public speaking, as well as the basics of persuasive writing (turning opinions into arguments, refuting the arguments of others).

Pedagogy is at least as important here as curricular design. Useful non-subject-specific classroom practices (discussed by Shuster but applicable to the university level) include intentionally teaching controversy or turning classroom discussion into a pedagogical strategy: consciously attending to the conduct of discussions, setting goals, having students summarize discussions, and requiring meta-analysis.

Third, we know from much formal research and informal observation that deep learning occurs cumulatively and progressively, whether the learning is of information or of skills. One-time exposure only initiates the process. Learners also progress better when exposed to multiple modalities, including active involvement.

Therefore, college curricula and cocurricula should provide students the opportunity to study about, reflect on, and practice civil discourse in a purposeful manner at several points and in increasingly sophisticated ways. The process might start in a first-year seminar, continue in an introduction to the major where civil discourse could be applied to the controversies of the field, and form part of a senior seminar or thesis defense.

Fourth, as with any important learning outcome, the ability to engage in civil discourse needs to be assessed at least at the individual student and the program levels, formatively and summatively. How well do students understand the concept? How skillfully do they practice discourse that is effective and responsible? How successfully does the program (be it for a degree or not) meet its objectives and in what ways can it be improved? For such assessment, rubrics for civil discourse would need to be developed.

Fifth, given that the ability to engage in civil discourse has rarely figured as an institutional learning outcome (Roger Williams University is one notable exception), most professors will be ignorant of ways to include it in their courses—or even how to model it. Therefore, faculty development will be vital; fortunately, most campuses have internal expertise upon which to draw (e.g., their own political scientists, linguists, philosophers, debate coaches, rhetoric teachers, and those from any field who teach controversy in the classroom).

## Ground Rules for Respectful Public Discourse & Behavior

Being concerned about growing incivility in our civic and public settings we can learn from the people of Utah to return to fundamental principles that will lead to greater civility and a new spirit of community. In 2008, they reaffirmed their "inherent and inalienable" Constitutional rights is the fundamental right "to communicate freely about our thoughts and opinions," and yet they are also "responsible for the abuse of that right" Constitution of Utah Article I Section 1. In that context they believe that there must be a renewal of respectful discourse and behavior in civic and public settings in Utah.

This is not an appeal for us all simply to get along. We recognize that there are profound differences among us, and that spirited debate is a vital part of American democracy. Participation in American civic and public life does not require us to sacrifice our deepest convictions; rather we best protect our own rights by protecting the rights of others and adhering to high ethical standards.

With that in mind lets propose the following ground rules of civic and public engagement that recognize the important place of the rights, responsibilities, and respect inherent in our civic and constitutional compact.

1. Remember the Importance of Rights and the Dignity of Each Individual. Our society is founded upon the proposition that all people are born free and equal in dignity and rights, and that freedom of conscience and expression are at the foundation of our rights.

2. Responsibly Exercise your Rights While Protecting the Rights of Others. Each of us should be responsible both in the exercise or our rights and in protecting the rights of others. Especially on matters of personal faith, claims of conscience, and human rights, public policy should seek solutions that are fair to all.

3. Respect Others. All people—especially our leaders and the media—should demonstrate a commitment to be respectful in discourse and behavior, particularly in civic and public forums. Respect should also be shown by being honest and as inclusive as possible, by mindfully listening to and attempting to understand the concerns of others, by valuing their opinions even when there is disagreement, and by addressing their concerns when possible.

4. Refrain from Incivility. Public discourse can be passionate while maintaining mutual respect that reaches beyond differing opinions. Intimidation, ridicule, personal attacks, mean spiritedness, reprisals against those who disagree, and other disrespectful or unethical behaviors destroy the fabric of our society and can no longer be tolerated.

Those who engage in such behavior should be brought to light, held accountable and should no longer enjoy the public's trust.

5. Rekindle Building Community. Our social compact "of the people" and "by the people" is "for the people." Each one of us has a responsibility to build community. On divisive issues, areas of common ground should first be explored. Effort should be given to building broad-based agreement, giving due regard to the concerns of minority points of view.

## Open Inquiry

A world-class academic community depends on an open society to thrive; it also models an ideal culture of discourse. Questioning and argument, weighing evidence and analyzing alternative interpretations—such values are at the core of teaching and scholarship.

Open Inquiry is the ability to ask questions and share ideas without risk of censure.

In an environment that is insufficiently open, facts can be corrupted or suppressed for the benefit of special interests. Important innovations can be set back or outright snuffed out. Avoidable problems can fester and spread. Personal and intellectual growth can be stunted.

Open inquiry is threatened on several fronts. Across the political spectrum there are people who make it their business to surveille and mob scholars who threaten their preferred narratives.

Expanding bureaucracies at many colleges and universities subject ever more of campus life to administrative oversight—and encourage people to resolve disputes through reporting, investigations, and academic reprisals rather than good-faith debate and discussion.

Concerns about placating donors, ensuring high enrollments or positive course evaluations can distort research and pedagogy—especially for the growing numbers of contingent faculty whose careers and livelihoods can be threatened by a single upset student, donor, or colleague.

And, of course, many fear losing the esteem of, or being ostracized by, one's peers for saying the "wrong" thing (a risk which is more pronounced in highly-homogenous environments). Even in the absence of formal sanctions, social and professional isolation can make academic life extremely difficult and unpleasant—and many reasonably prefer to self-censor rather than risk it. This is a significant concern among students, faculty, and administrators.

Academics worried about attacks on free speech have felt the need to respond, and they have articulated sound principles. Princeton professors Robert P. George and Cornel West recently attracted lots of supporters for a statement underscoring that "all of us should seek respectfully to engage with people who challenge our views" and that "we should oppose efforts to silence those with whom we disagree—especially on college and university campuses."

Trying to understand the logic of someone else's arguments is a core skill that schools should be paying more attention to, and it doesn't always require elaborate new programs. The group Heterodox Academy, which includes faculty from many universities and from across the political spectrum, has recently launched the "Viewpoint Diversity Experience," an online effort to combat "the destructive power of ideological tribalism." The aim is "to prepare students for democratic citizenship and success in the political diverse workplaces they will soon inhabit."

Such efforts are sorely needed, but they can succeed only if we do a better job of bringing underrepresented points of view into the mix. Simply relying on the marketplace of ideas isn't enough. We need an affirmative-action program for conservative, libertarian, and religious modes of thinking.

### Trump Media & Technology Group (TMTG) Counters the Mediacrats

From Alexander Hall's December 2021 "Rep. Devin Nunes to Resign from Congress, Join Trump Media & Technology Group (TMTG) as CEO" article in MRC's Newsbusters:, Rep. Devin Nunes (R-CA) to help break the destructive power of ideological tribalism when he resigns from his position as a congressman to join former President Donald Trump's burgeoning TMTG.

Trump is out of the presidency, but his company has the potential to be a major player in the social media sphere, and it just gained one major power-player.

TMTG  announced "that Congressman Nunes has been selected to join the Company as Chief Executive Officer," TMTG declared in a Dec. 6, 2021, press release. "Mr. Nunes will be leaving the U.S. House of Representatives and will begin his new role as Chief Executive Officer of TMTG in January 2022." Donald Trump commented in the press release that Nunes will be instrumental to making his grand designs a reality:

"Congressman Devin Nunes is a fighter and a leader. He will make an excellent CEO of TMTG. Devin understands that we must stop the liberal media and Big Tech from destroying the freedoms that make America great. America is ready for TRUTH Social and the end to censorship and political discrimination."

## 14 – Mill vs. Marx: Free Speech Champions Rise Up Against Free Speech Suppressors

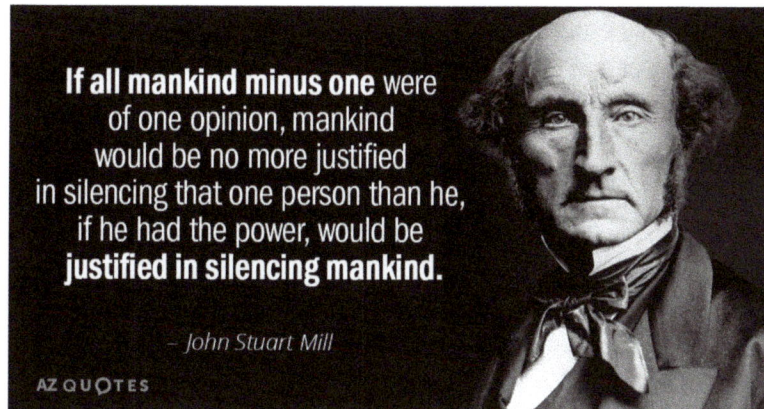

If all mankind minus one were of one opinion, mankind would be no more justified in silencing that one person than he, if he had the power, would be justified in silencing mankind.

*– John Stuart Mill*

Today, Americans are deeply divided about the meaning of their country, its history, and how it should be governed. This division is severe enough to call to mind the disagreements between the colonists and King George, and those between the Confederate and Union forces in the Civil War. They amount to a dispute over not only the history of our country but also its present purpose and future direction.

Comprising actions by imperfect human beings, the American story has its share of missteps, errors, contradictions, and wrongs. These wrongs have always met resistance from the clear principles of the nation, and therefore our history is far more one of self-sacrifice, courage, and nobility. America's principles are named at the outset to be both universal—applying to everyone—and eternal: existing for all time.

According to the October 2021 "What Happens When Free Speech Dies" article by Judson Berger in the *National Review:* In the past years, the political and intellectual energy has been with illiberal movements. Too often, the advocates of free speech and free institutions have been passive, even fatalistic. It is high time for those of us who believe in these enduring ideals to stand up for our convictions.

In September 2021, the *Economist* featured "the threat from the illiberal left" on its cover as well. One article included this haunting line: "Belief in foundations of liberalism such as free speech declines with each generation." This is a demonstrable trend in America's generations.

Pew found that 40 percent of Millennials (also referred to as Generation Y) "say the government should be able to prevent people publicly making statements that are offensive to minority groups." Compare that with 27 percent for Generation Xers and 24 percent for Baby Boomers.

Making the data even more alarming is that it was gathered in 2015; one can only presume that the percentage today, especially among Generation Z, is even higher.

What does our campus culture value? One recent survey found that a majority of college students support shouting down speakers with whom they disagree; 23 percent supported the use of violence toward this end. At some colleges, the percentage supporting such violence crept into the 40s.

That is not a culture that values free speech. It is a culture that values freedom from emotional, political, and intellectual disturbance of any kind. These shifts in attitude, which have escaped campus and are spreading quickly throughout America and the world —are a detriment to free speech and expression and an accelerant for free speech suppression and censorship.

### The Moral Authority of the Campus Left is Starting to Dwindle

The campus left, in particular, is fiercely determined to forestall any expression of views that run counter to its preferred narratives, and to punish those who disobey. Shout downs are a blend of forestalling and punishing as noted by Peter Wood's article that is part of the July 2018 "A Tide Flowing Toward Free Speech on Campus" article inside the report *Free Speech in Peril: College—Where You Can't Say What You Think* by Peter Wood of the Minding the Campus organization.

The tactics used against Charles Murray at Middlebury College and Heather Mac Donald at Claremont College, to cite two of the most famous instances, were aimed at preventing speech but also at humiliating the speakers. The spirit of such disruption is theatrical anger in service of what the protester takes to be righteous indignation.

Those feelings are not going to evaporate like the morning dew. They have become ingrained among the protesters. And yet the protesters are losing the dark glamour they enjoyed when shouting-down, taking over, and spitting outrage seemed somehow authentic and cool.

The protesters seemed for a while to be immune to all the rules because leftist administrators just couldn't bring themselves to impose serious consequences for lawlessness in the name of "social justice." But something has changed.

The moral authority of the campus left is starting to dwindle. We see that in the sudden emergence of the "walk away" movement. A gay New York hairdresser, Brandon Straka, has given the movement its manifesto in a YouTube video. Straka denounced what he calls "liberalism" as "tyrannical groupthink," and described it this way: "For years now, I have watched as the left has devolved into intolerant, inflexible, illogical, hateful, misguided, ill-informed, un-American, hypocritical, menacing, callous, ignorant, narrow-minded, and at times blatantly fascistic behavior, and rhetoric." It is a system, he says, that allows a mob "to suppress free speech, create false narratives, and then apathetically steamroll over the truth."

I can think of any number of conservatives who could say (and have said) much the same thing, though perhaps focusing more precisely on the progressive social justice zealots, rather than liberalism per se. But Straka brings to the message the burn of a Carolina Reaper chili pepper.

## Mill vs. Marx is a Battle for America's Soul

When it comes to preserving freedom of speech on campus, Dr. Jonathan Haidt explains eloquently why universities must choose one telos: truth or social justice. Furthermore, he elaborates that Aristotle often evaluated a thing with respect to its "telos"–its purpose, end, or goal. The telos of a knife is to cut. The telos of a physician is health or healing. What is the telos of university?

The most obvious answer is "truth"—the word appears on so many university crests. But increasingly, many of America's top universities are embracing social justice as their telos, or as a second and equal telos. But can any institution or profession have two teloses (or teloi)? What happens if they conflict?

Haidt believes that the conflict between truth and social justice is likely to become unmanageable. Universities will have to choose, and be explicit about their choice, so that potential students and faculty recruits can make an informed choice. Universities that try to honor both will face increasing incoherence and internal conflict.

To further illuminate his point, consider two quotations:

> *The philosophers have only interpreted the world, in various ways; the point is to change it.*–Karl Marx, 1845

> *He who knows only his own side of the case knows little of that. His reasons may be good, and no one may have been able to refute them. But if he is equally unable to refute the reasons on the opposite side, if he does not so much as know what they are, he has no ground for preferring either opinion...*–John Stuart Mill, 1859

As Haidt puts it: Marx is the patron saint of what he calls "Social Justice U," which is oriented around changing the world in part by overthrowing power structures and privilege. It sees political diversity as an obstacle to action. Mill is the patron saint of what he calls "Truth U," which sees truth as a process in which flawed individuals challenge each other's biased and incomplete reasoning. In this process, all become smarter. However, Truth U dies when it becomes intellectually uniform or politically orthodox.

### Progressivism Madness

Truth is paramount to sapience, and the antithesis to sapience is modern progressivism. Not only does progressivism deny commonly held truths across all cultures of the world, today's progressivism has evolved to many degrees into a twentieth century version of Marxism lite—without the horrific calories of human sacrifice, failed regimes, and economic ruin.

When progressivism madness is incubated in the right condition on campus, illiberalism will follow, and when illiberalism follows, so do social justice warriors and campus radicals. Put simply enough by Haidt, "no university can have Truth and Social Justice as dual teloses. Each university must pick one. He shows that Brown University has staked out the leadership position for Social Justice University (SJU), and the University of Chicago has staked out the leadership position for Truth U.

Throughout the Sapient Conservative Textbooks (SCT) Program series, we sometimes use the phrase "so called" progressive or "regressivism" or progressive regressive. The reason is because so many of the left's and "current" liberal platforms, policies, and agendas are actually regressive in regards to developing sapience. They are the antithesis to sapience! Please note this and the important distinction between progressive vs. progressivism as follows:

- **Progressive:** One favoring or advocating progress, change, improvement, or reform, as opposed to wishing to maintain things as they are, especially in political matters. Today, a conservative or Republican can be just as progressive as a liberal or a Democrat because they both advocate progress, change, improvement, or reform as well, but they have vastly different agendas and ideologies in this regard.

- **Progressivism:** A political philosophy in support of social reform based on the idea of progress in which advancements in science, technology, economic development, and social organization are vital to improve the human condition. It would be safe to say conservatives and Republicans favor addressing political matters vs. social ones so most who favor and/or part of the progressivism movement will be liberals and Democrats.

Furthermore, there's also a misconception that professors are leading their student disciples towards a path of Marxist indoctrination. That's partially true and a lessor of two influences. But if professors are not swaying student opinions in the classroom, and the lessor of two influencers, what is making them more sympathetic to socialism and less tolerant of conservative views about free markets and limited government?

Unknown to many, the greater influence is from college administrators which will be discussed later in this chapter. It's demonstrably true as the previous chapter has pointed out that professors are overwhelmingly liberal and have become more so in the past three decades. Some observers blame leftist professors for the socialist connection. This makes sense on the surface because the renewed sympathy for socialism seems most pronounced among recent college graduates.

However, it's far from conclusive that this kind of classroom and dormitory indoctrination is driving students to the far left. If it's not—what is?

## Generations X Y Z Are Less Politically Tolerant Than Their Parents

First, Kelly-Woessner makes the case that young people are less politically tolerant than their parents' generation and that this marks a clear reversal of the trends observed by social scientists for the past 60 years. Political tolerance is generally defined as the willingness to extend civil liberties and basic democratic rights to members of unpopular groups.

That is, in order to be tolerant, one must recognize the rights of one's political enemies to fully participate in the democratic process. Typically, this is measured by asking people whether they will allow members of unpopular groups, or groups they dislike, to exercise political rights, such as giving a public talk, teaching college, or having their books on loan in public libraries.

Americans have not, in fact, become more tolerant. Rather, they have shifted their dislike to new groups. For example, "Muslim clergymen who preach hatred against the United States" are now the least liked group included in the General Social Survey (GSS), followed by people who believe that "blacks are genetically inferior." Most importantly, compared to those in their 40s, people in their 30s and 20s actually show lower tolerance towards these groups.

According to the 2012 GSS, people in their 40s are the most tolerant of Muslim clergymen who preach anti-American hatred: 43% say a member of this group should not be allowed to give a public speech in their community. Among people in their 30s, the number who would prohibit this group from speaking climbs to 52%, and for those in their 20s it jumps to 60%.

Young people are also less tolerant than the middle aged groups toward militarists, communists, and racists. This is not true for tolerance towards gay people or atheists, because younger people simply like these groups more. Political tolerance is not a measure of liking someone, but the willingness to extend political freedoms to those one dislikes.

Second, Kelly-Woessner argues that youthful intolerance is driven by different factors than old fashioned intolerance, and that this change reflects the ideology of the New Left. Herbert Marcuse considered "The Father of the New Left," articulates a philosophy that denies political expression to those who would oppose today's progressive social agenda. In his 1965 essay "Repressive Tolerance," Marcuse (1965) writes,

"Tolerance is extended to policies, conditions, and modes of behavior which should not be tolerated because they are impeding, if not destroying, the chances of creating an existence without fear and misery. This sort of tolerance strengthens the tyranny of the majority against which authentic liberals protested … Liberating tolerance, then, would mean intolerance against movements from the Right and toleration of movements from the Left."

## The Illiberal and Orwellian Argument of 'Liberating Tolerance'

The idea of "liberating tolerance" then is one in which ideas that the left deems to be intolerant are suppressed. It is an Orwellian argument for an "intolerance of intolerance," and it appears to be gaining traction in recent years, reshaping our commitments to free speech, academic freedom, and basic democratic norms.

If we look only at people under the age of 40, intolerance is correlated with a "social justice" orientation. That is, I find that people who believe that the government has a responsibility to help poor people and blacks get ahead are also less tolerant. Importantly, this is true even when we look at tolerance towards groups other than blacks. For people over 40, there is no relationship between social justice attitudes and tolerance. I argue that this difference reflects a shift from values of classical liberalism to the New Left.

For older generations, support for social justice does not require a rejection of free speech. Thus, this tension between leftist social views and political tolerance is something new.

Third, Kelly-Woessner states that intolerance itself is being reclassified as a social good. For six decades, social scientists have almost universally treated intolerance as a negative social disease. Yet now that liberties are surrendered for equality rather than security, the Left seems less concerned about the harmful effects of intolerance. In fact, they have reframed the concept altogether. For example, political scientist Allison Harell (2010) uses the term "multicultural tolerance," which she defines as the willingness to "support speech rights for objectionable groups" but not for "groups that promote hatred."

In other words, multicultural tolerance allows individuals to limit the rights of political opponents, so long as they frame their intolerance in terms of protecting others from hate. This is what Marcuse refers to as "liberating tolerance."

In fact, the idea that one should be "intolerant of intolerance" has taken hold on many college campuses, as exemplified through speech codes, civility codes, and broad, sweeping policies on harassment and discrimination. Students now frequently lead protests and bans on campus speakers whom they believe promote hate.

While this may have the effect of creating seemingly more civil spaces, it has negative consequences. In fact, tolerance for all groups is positively correlated. It is not simply the fact that leftists oppose the expression of right-wing groups. Rather, those who are intolerant of one group tend to be intolerant of others and of political communication in general.

When colleges fail to represent the full measure of political ideas, students are less likely to learn to tolerate those unlike themselves. This combined with the New Left's legacy of "liberating tolerance," creates an environment that values anger and orthodoxy over inquiry, debate and viewpoint diversity.

## The Fight for Free Speech

While free speech has been under attack, we are beginning to see some pushback. More than 12,000 professors, free speech leaders, and conservative-leaning organization leaders have signed "The Philadelphia Statement."

The 845-word document, as reported in the October 2020 "The Fight for Free Speech" article in The Daily Signal by Walter E. William says in part:

Similarly, colleges, and universities are imposing speech regulations to make students 'safe,' not from physical harm, but from challenges to campus orthodoxy. These policies and regulations assume that we as citizens are unable to think for ourselves and to make independent judgments. Instead of teaching us to engage, they foster conformism ('groupthink') and train us to respond to intellectual challenges with one or another form of censorship.

A society that lacks comity and allows people to be shamed or intimidated into self-censorship of their ideas and considered judgments will not survive for long. As Americans, we desire a flourishing, open marketplace of ideas, knowing that it is the fairest and most effective way to separate falsehood from truth.

Accordingly, dissenting and unpopular voices—be they of the left or the right—must be afforded the opportunity to be heard. They have often guided our society toward more just positions, which is why Frederick Douglass said freedom of speech is the 'great moral renovator of society and government.'

The recognition of the intellectual elite attacking free speech is not new. In a 1991 speech, Yale University President Benno Schmidt warned:

The most serious problems of freedom of expression in our society today exist on our campuses. The assumption seems to be that the purpose of education is to induce correct opinion rather than to search for wisdom and to liberate the mind

Tyrants everywhere, from the Nazis to the communists, started out supporting free speech rights. Why? Because speech is important for the realization of leftist goals of command and control. People must be propagandized, proselytized, and convinced.

Once leftists have gained power, as they have in most of our colleges and universities, free speech becomes a liability. It challenges their ideas and agenda and must be suppressed.

Attacks on free speech to accommodate multiculturalism and diversity are really attacks on Western values, which are superior to all others. The indispensable achievement of the West was the concept of individual rights, the idea that individuals have certain inalienable rights that are not granted by government. Governments exist to protect these inalienable rights.

It took until the 17th century for that idea to arise and mostly through the works of English philosophers such as John Locke and David Hume. And now the 21st-century campus leftists are trying to suppress these inalienable rights.

Don't let it happen. Resist at all costs. America's future depends on it.

### Wesleyan President Roth Calls on Universities to Promote Intellectual Diversity

On May 11, 2017, Wesleyan President Michael Roth's statement about heterodoxy was published in *The Wall Street Journal* regarding the need for colleges and universities to proactively cultivate intellectual diversity on campus. While student protests over controversial speakers have dominated headlines of late, he writes:

The issue, however, isn't whether the occasional conservative, libertarian or religious speaker gets a chance to speak. That is tolerance, an appeal to civility and fairness, but it doesn't take us far enough. To create deeper intellectual and political diversity, we need an affirmative-action program for the full range of conservative ideas and traditions, because on too many of our campuses they seldom get the sustained, scholarly attention that they deserve.

Our present political circumstances should not prevent us from engaging with a variety of conservative, religious, and libertarian modes of thinking, just as they shouldn't prevent us from engaging with modes of thinking organized under the banner of progressivism or critical theory. Such engagement might actually lead to greater understanding among those who disagree politically, and it might also allow for more robust critical and creative thinking about our histories, our present and the possibilities for the future.

**President Trump Signs 2020 Executive Order Protecting Freedom of Speech on College Campuses**

One of those other critics is President Trump signed an executive order protecting freedom of speech on college campuses. At the signing, he was surrounded by student activists who have said conservative views are suppressed at universities.

Trump said he was taking "historic action to defend American students and American values that have been under siege" when he announced March 21, 2019 that he would make federal funding for universities contingent on assurances of free speech. Trump: 'People who are confident in their beliefs do not censor others'.

Trump strongly defended free speech on campus two years earlier after police at the University of California, Berkeley canceled a talk by the far-right agitator Milo Yiannopoulos amid intense protests by masked Antifa activists, who set fires and threw stones.

The order does not, on its face, make dramatic changes. But it was welcomed by people who say universities are fostering an unbalanced, liberal indoctrination of students—and condemned by those who say freedom of inquiry is a fundamental tenet of higher education, one the government should not be defining.

The president declared it the first in a number of steps the administration would take to defend students' rights. Universities have tried to restrict free thought and impose conformity, he said. "All of that changes right now," he added. "We're dealing with billions and billions and billions of dollars." Trump told the students that people can have different views, "but they have to let you speak."

**What We Can Learn From the Campus Free-Speech War**

Friends of liberty are few. But not as few as we might think according to the August 2021 "What We Can Learn from the Campus Free-Speech War" article by Isaac Willour in the *National Review*:

In July, free-speech advocates at the University of Connecticut took on a student body hellbent on destroying free speech on campus. A group of students pushed the university's student government to adopt the "UConn Statement," a petition for the university to uphold civil discourse on campus. According to the statement, UConn "has a solemn responsibility not only to promote a lively and fearless freedom of debate and deliberation, but also to protect that freedom when others attempt to restrict it."

Such attempts at restriction came swiftly and viciously. The simple move to promote the First Amendment on campus was met with stunning bigotry and intolerance from UConn's student body, and with it a barrage of hateful and violent threats. Students hurled accusations of white supremacy at UConn's student body president, an immigrant from Honduras. One of UConn's First Amendment advocates was harassed with racial slurs and even received a video of an ISIS beheading.

These students stared down an entire campus culture that had turned against them for their devotion to free speech. Though public sentiment remained negative and combative, people began voicing private support for UConn's free-speech warriors. Both faculty and students expressed agreement with the UConn Statement, and the First Amendment coalition on campus is moving forward with speaker events and increased activism. Free-speech debacles such as UConn's illustrate valuable lessons that advocates of conservatism would do well to bear in mind.

In my discussions with UConn students, both conservatives and those on the Left, I heard one description of the current political climate that piqued my interest. "Liberals give in to radicals too easily, and conservatives have some racism problems."

Innumerable members of the political Right cheer on the former characterization — the latter is met with defensiveness, skepticism, and a hearty chorus of "but look at the Left." This is why conservatives lose on the culture side. We know that the stereotype isn't true. But the culture doesn't, and we won't fix it by yelling. Segments of the modern American Right have embraced a reactionary response to conservatism's unwarrantedly negative cultural portrayal. But this tactic is not going to win over political moderates.

Visceral reactions are perfectly understandable in response to the far Left's blatant lies about conservatives. But we must change that tactic to persuade the persuadable. Moderates with deeply held biases against conservatism won't be won over by our most extreme and caustic voices and arguments. If we are to make cultural headway, our strategy must be responsive, not reactionary.

College students who advocate free speech are willing to do so with their ideological opponents, working with members of the opposite political party at institutions like UConn to advance the First Amendment. So should the movement more generally.

That's how we can fight back: With many allies by our side.

## Citizen Trump Announces 'Major' Class-Action Lawsuits Against Twitter, Facebook, Google

Former President Donald Trump announced on July 7, 2021 that he's filing lawsuits against Twitter, Facebook, and Google after the firms suspended his social media accounts six months ago over his comments after the Jan. 6 Capitol incident.

As per the July 2021 "Trump Announces 'Major' Class-Action Lawsuits Against Twitter, Facebook, Google" article by Jack Phillips of the *Epoch Times*: Trump and his team said the lawsuits are about protecting the First Amendment right to free speech. They argued that his rights were denied when the three big tech companies banned him.

Trump described the "major" lawsuits as a "very beautiful development" to protect free speech in the United States. The suits will be filed in the U.S. District Court in the Southern District of Florida and will ask a judge to order an immediate halt to social media companies' alleged shadowbanning, censoring, blacklisting, and canceling of people who express political viewpoints outside the mainstream.

"It's destroying the country," Trump said of social media's alleged control over political discourse.

Twitter, Facebook, and Google stated in January that they had banned Trump over his claims that the Nov. 3 election was stolen and alleged that he contributed to the Jan. 6 violence. Twitter executives have said Trump's ban will be permanent, Facebook imposed a two-year ban on the former president's account, and Google-owned YouTube has said it would curtail his suspension until it determines that "the risk of violence has decreased."

Facebook CEO Mark Zuckerberg, Google CEO Sundar Pichai, and Twitter CEO Jack Dorsey were named in the lawsuits—as well as the companies themselves. Trump said the lawsuits will seek a court award of punitive damages over the suspension.

Trump argued that social media companies have "ceased to be private" companies and cited the Section 230 protection shield that such firms employ to protect themselves from liability. Republicans have argued that the federal rule has allowed big tech firms to censor their political opponents—while some have gone further, arguing that social media giants should be regulated as utilities.

### "This Lawsuit is Just the Beginning," Trump Said

Section 230 of the 1996 Communications Decency Act allows internet companies to be generally exempt from liability for the material that users post. The law, which provides a legal "safe harbor" for internet companies, also allows social media platforms to moderate their services by removing posts that, for example, are obscene or violate the services' own standards, so long as they're acting in "good faith."

Trump's lawyers said the lawsuit will focus on provisions in Section 230, which they argue was created in the 1990s to protect children from harmful content online. The way big tech firms currently use the law as a shield, his team argued, oversteps what it was originally intended to do. "They are not immune anymore," lawyer Pam Bondi said.

Meanwhile, the former president also appeared to preempt his opponents' criticism of his lawsuit, arguing that mainstream media outlets and Democrat politicians are the "biggest spreaders of disinformation." Trump described mainstream narratives around Republicans wanting to "defund the police," the Russia collusion claims, and COVID-19 as false.

During his July 7 news conference, Trump accused the federal government of using Facebook, Twitter, and Google as its "de facto censorship arm" during the COVID-19 pandemic. One claim that was censored, he said, was the assertion that COVID-19 emerged from a Wuhan virology lab in 2019. But earlier this year, President Joe Biden said many members of the U.S. intelligence community now view the theory as viable.

"This was especially true during the pandemic when social media companies began censoring information" based on federal health guidance, the former president said.

Since leaving office, Trump has opted to release statements via his Save America PAC and through a now-defunct section of his website. The former president, who hasn't signed up for any upstart social media sites like Parler or GETTR, said on July 7 that he isn't sure whether he'll join Twitter, Facebook, or YouTube if the lawsuit is successful.

Trump announced that the legal effort is supported by the America First Policy Institute, adding that he believes thousands of other people may join his lawsuit.

## How To Keep Your Corporation Out of the Culture War

Dr. Jonathan Haidt and Dr. Greg Lukianoff wrote an afterword for *The Coddling of the American Mind* in the summer of 2021 with eight steps business leaders can take to prevent ideological pressure and political conformity in the workplace because business leaders from the corporate and non-profit sectors began contacting them about internal issues they are having with recent hires.

According to their December 2020 "How To Keep Your Corporation Out of the Culture War" article by Dr. Jonathan Haidt and Dr. Greg Lukianoff in Persuasion:

They told them that their youngest employees show increased levels of anxiety, depression, and fragility; a tendency to turn ordinary conflicts between co-workers into major issues requiring the attention of the Human Resources Department; and greater insistence that the organization must share and express their personal political values related to social justice.

Beginning around 2018, parts of the corporate world began to experience the same changes we saw in universities from around 2014. This makes sense once you realize that members of Gen Z began to arrive on campuses in 2013 and 2014—they spent four years within institutions that largely catered to their new needs and demands, and began to graduate from four-year colleges around 2017 or 2018.

A 2021 survey found that 48% of Gen Z respondents reported feeling stress all or most of the time, and the top source of worry among them was career prospects. As for the increased internal conflicts and tensions among employees, the title of a 2021 article on the front page of the business section of The New York Times sums it up well: "The 37-Year-Olds Are Afraid of the 23-Year-Olds Who Work for Them." Friction and punishment campaigns in the corporate world seem to be hyper-charged by Slack and other internal company messaging platforms.

The biggest change in the corporate world has been the explosion of social justice movements, employee political activism, and internal conflict about that activism since 2017, all playing out on social media.

### Why Would Gen Z Have Any Meaningful Influence On Corporations?

But why would Gen Z have any meaningful influence on corporations during this turbulent period—2017 to 2020—when they had just arrived in the workplace and were present only in small numbers? The primary reason comes back, again, to social media.

Gen Z is the first generation where a critical mass of young people grew up as social media natives (with a 2018 survey finding 97% on at least one social media platform). This allowed them to organize and mobilize in a way that was simply not available to previous generations.

A single employee who is adept at using social media can create a PR nightmare for employers, often leading to nearly instantaneous public capitulation accompanied by a formulaic apology. Social media played a key role in the ouster of James Bennet from *The New York Times* in the summer of 2020, when many NYT staffers tweeted that he "[put] Black @nytimes staff in danger" by running an op-ed by U.S. Senator Tom Cotton in favor of deploying military force during civil unrest—phrasing they were advised to use by their union due to the existence of employment protections for speech relating to workplace safety.

Five years ago, about three-quarters of Millennials said business was a force for good; at the time, Gen Z made up about five percent of the workforce. Today, Gen Z makes up about a quarter of the workforce, and fewer than half of Millennials say that business is a force for good—bringing them roughly in line with Gen Z. Whether the convergence came about by Gen Z influencing Millennials or because both generations responded in similar ways to the avalanche of social unrest since 2017 is unclear. But either way, Millennials seem to share Gen Z's skepticism about capitalism, and many of them share a willingness to prioritize social causes over company goals—to the detriment of free speech and expression.

Ever since they entered the corporate world in the early 2000s, some members of the Millennial generation (born 1982 to 1996) have pushed for being able to "bring their whole selves to work." Companies in the creative industries encouraged this shift, erasing boundaries between work life and private life. But as America became ever more politically polarized, the problem with this policy became evident: Some whole selves cannot tolerate working alongside other whole selves that have different political beliefs and voting patterns.

## Corporate Social Justice and Cancel Culture Issues

On an everyday level, the move towards corporate social justice and the expectation of company-wide solidarity with specific causes can lead to what has (controversially) been dubbed "cancel culture." One of its defining patterns is that employees face calls for discipline or termination for expressing non-conforming opinions, even when those opinions are expressed away from the workplace or with no hostile intent.

Corporations, of course, have the First Amendment right of association and therefore can decide whom they employ—at least insofar as they comply with anti-discrimination law. Our fear, however, is that if too many corporations see themselves both as businesses and as participants in social movements, then employees who disagree face a stark choice: Keep your mouth shut, or express yourself and face possible termination.

For companies that wish to hire talent of all political stripes, or to reduce the frequency of campaigns to fire employees for political nonconformity, we offer the following advice.

- Expand your definition of diversity.

- Reconsider what colleges you hire from.

- Orientation: Be direct with candidates and new hires.

- Have a talk with the human resources department.

- Survey employees to see if there's a problem.

- If a social media firestorm demands that you fire an employee, slow down.

- Don't make firing a first or preferred punishment.

- Ask yourself "where does this end?

In conclusion: Many of the dynamics we described in *The Coddling of the American Mind*, which transformed college campuses beginning in 2014, are now spreading rapidly through the corporate world in the U.S.

## The Free Speech Alliance

From L. Brent Bozell III, President, Media Research Center: "Voices are being silenced, opinions are being censored and conservative media are being suppressed. These tech companies claim they provide platforms to connect people and share ideas. However, when the only ideas permitted are from one side, any prospect of intellectual discourse dies. If these platforms merely serve as an echo chamber of liberal talking points, everyone loses."

And therein lies problem—conservatives, their ideals, and constitutional rights are under attack and are being sidelined on the intellectual playfield and marketplace of ideas. In today's America, conservatives face an existential crisis as social media giants in collusion with the radical left root out and silence conservative speech on their platforms and across the Internet.

This is the worst threat to free speech our country has ever faced and Dr. Michael Poliakoff, president of the American Council of Trustees and Alumni (ACTA), which also focuses on free speech and academic freedom, said he was happy the alliance was taking a stand.

The future of the conservative movement depends on our ability to communicate our message. If Facebook, Twitter, and Google censor conservatives on the Internet, the modern day public square, everything conservatives have fought for is at risk. The Left will control the narrative. The Internet is truly the new battleground for liberal media bias.

In April 2018, the Media Research Center released a groundbreaking report exposing efforts to censor conservatives and silence conservative speech from major online platforms. Our report was so impactful that US Representatives on the House Judiciary Committee cited it four separate times during a July 17, 2018 congressional hearing.

Our project reveals two concerns:

Online censorship is a very real and dangerous problem, the ramifications of which are far more troubling than many conservatives realize.

The problem is so dangerous that the MRC must take a stand against it.

Now—together with a Coalition of more than 90 conservative organizations—the MRC is letting tech giants know that we will not be silenced. We need the force of the entire conservative movement to win this battle.

The Free Speech Alliance protects the free speech of conservatives online. We fight for transparency on social media and demand equal footing for conservatives on Twitter, Facebook, Google and the other platforms. We defend the incredible and revolutionary ideal of free speech in which American democracy is rooted.

We actively work with tech companies to ensure that they are protecting conservative speech online and that the radical left does not contaminate the national online dialogue with their bias. For more information on how to join the alliance, please visit the Appendix under Free Speech Alliance.

The Alliance is calling on social media companies to address four key issues in order to begin to rectify their credibility problem and rebuild trust with conservatives:

**1) Provide Transparency:** We need detailed information so everyone can see if liberal groups and users are being treated the same as those on the right. Social media companies operate in a black-box environment, only releasing anecdotes about reports on content and users when they think it necessary. This needs to change. The companies need to design open systems so that they can be held accountable, while giving weight to privacy concerns.

**2) Provide Clarity on 'Hate Speech':** "Hate speech" is a common concern among social media companies, but no two firms define it the same way. Their definitions are vague and open to interpretation, and their interpretation often looks like an opportunity to silence thought. Today, hate speech means anything liberals don't like. Silencing those you disagree with is dangerous. If companies can't tell users clearly what it is, then they shouldn't try to regulate it.

**3) Provide Equal Footing for Conservatives:** Top social media firms, such as Google and YouTube, have chosen to work with dishonest groups that are actively opposed to the conservative movement, including the Southern Poverty Law Center. Those companies need to make equal room for conservative groups as advisers to offset this bias. That same attitude should be applied to employment diversity efforts. Tech companies need to embrace viewpoint diversity.

**4) Mirror the First Amendment:** Tech giants should afford their users nothing less than the free speech and free exercise of religion embodied in the First Amendment as interpreted by the U.S. Supreme Court. That standard, the result of centuries of American jurisprudence, would enable the rightful blocking of content that threatens violence or spews obscenity, without trampling on free speech liberties that have long made the United States a beacon for freedom.

The Free Speech Alliance is made up of more than 90 organizations and individuals who oppose the silencing of conservative voices on social media. Members of the Free Speech Alliance are not affiliated with MRC and the MRC does not endorse any of the positions or opinions of the other members of the FSA.

You can also look into MRC NewsBusters Censorship Project in the Appendix.

## 15 – Freedom of Speech Models & Policies for America's Public-Private Institutions

*Credit: Wallpaper Cave.*

Though the Cold War ended 30 years ago, our nation is still in a war that has been brewing for decades—a war for America's soul. Nikita Khrushchev, who ran the Soviet Union from 1958 to 1964, openly predicted the destruction of the United States and said it would happen in the way that every society eventually collapses.

"We will take America without firing a shot," he said. "We do not have to invade the U.S. We will destroy you from within." He was talking about an entire system of Marxist indoctrination and takeover that had been refined and executed in country after country during the 20th century.

Soviet defector Yuri Bezmenov, a former KGB operative and high-level Russian propagandist, escaped to the West in 1970. He warned the United States about the KGB tactics used to subvert a nation that he witnessed firsthand in the Soviet Union. Those tactics amounted to a planned process of altering the way people think for a particular purpose, which is to affect a regime change.

Per the September 2021 "We Are in a War for America's Soul" article by Michele R. Weslander Quaid of the *Epoch Times*: It's effectively the brainwashing of society—a slow, methodical transformation. Those who conduct that ideological subversion are very patient to employ the tactics over decades. This ideological subversion has four stages and follows the Hegelian dialectic, a tactic long exploited by Marxists and Fascists to control people.

187

**Stage 1: Demoralization.** This is the destruction of faith in the government and society. Believing that society is broken, systems are failing, and patriotism is evil are three key beliefs that are promoted to create guilt. This leads to the acceptance of radical new ideas, because the current structure is believed to be harmful. Traditional Judeo-Christian morality, classical education, and U.S. patriotism are discarded.

**Stage 2: Destabilization.** With the decision-making ability of Americans negatively affected through demoralization, the next step takes a foothold—destabilization of the nation's foundations. Destabilization causes citizens to believe the worst of what they hear about their nation and form of government. Supporters of traditional values and foundational structures in the nation are ostracized and even demonized.

**Stage 3: Crisis.** The altered values of Americans cut to the root of the current systems. Upheaval presents opportunities for change. Once a society is destabilized, it begins to collapse into chaos. At that point, citizens want the government to provide stability.

We saw that recently as a demoralized and destabilized society responded with fear and panic when a "pandemic" faced our nation. Americans are willingly trading civil rights and freedoms for authoritarianism and overreach that they believe will keep them safe. The messaging in all of this is key. The mainstream media and their "tell-a-vision" programming play a key role in framing the prescribed narrative as truth.

**Stage 4: Normalization.** The "new normal" is a term we've heard constantly lately, and it's an accurate description of what the normalization stage is all about. When the government and societal structures have changed to restrict liberty, citizens are told the radical transformation is "the way it has to be." Ironically, it's described as normal when it's not normal at all. Normalization creates a new baseline for what a nation will accept, value, and promote. The cycle is complete.

## The United States Could Be On the Verge of Collapse

Those steps are repeated over and over, bringing a greater result with each cycle, until there's a controlled collapse. The United States could be on the verge of collapse right now unless we collectively wake up to reality and take a stand to stop tyranny.

The Hegelian dialectic is the framework for guiding people's thoughts and actions into conflicts that lead them to a predetermined solution. The enemies of the United States are using that tactic to create fear, turn citizen against citizen, and divide our nation. A house divided can't stand.

If people don't understand how the Hegelian dialectic shapes their perceptions of the world, then they don't know how they're helping to implement the agenda, which ultimately is to advance humanity into a dictatorship—whether by the fascists, the communists, or the globalists and their New World Order. We must step outside the dialectic so that we can be released from the limitations of controlled and guided thought.

The most important thing about America is liberty. America is what has stood between power-hungry people and their goals of world domination. The true enemies of the United States are trying to convince us that we're each other's enemies and that big government and control of the lives of the many by a few is the cure for what ails us.

We must all recognize that they're weaponizing the crisis and that this narrative is a lie. Government bureaucrats are now labeling anyone who thinks that they've overstepped their constitutional bounds as enemies of the state—"patriot terrorists." What liberty-loving people are now combating is pure evil.

All it takes for evil to prosper is for good people to do nothing. As we reflect back on Sept. 11, 2001, one thing that stands out about that time following the terrorist attacks is that we forgot about the things that divided us. We united as Americans. There's no better example than what we saw in New York. We were united together in support of one another fighting a common enemy.

So many have sacrificed so much to secure our liberty and preserve it for future generations. Many of us have lost a loved one on a foreign battlefield or from a service-connected illness after they had returned, or in the line of duty here at home. How do we honor their sacrifice and that of so many others in our nation's 245-year history? We stand and fight to uphold liberty and our unalienable rights enshrined in America's founding documents. If liberty is to be lost, it won't be on our watch.

## Free Speech Suppression Thrives Without Civics Literacy

It should be mandatory for all students to take courses relating to civic education and the U.S. Constitution. According to a recent study, only 18% of American colleges and universities require their graduates to take a foundational course in U.S. history or U.S. government.

But civic education should accompany these other mandatory courses. By the time they've graduated, all college students should have analyzed the text and history of the Constitution. They should have read the Federalist papers, Alexis de Tocqueville's "Democracy in America," and other important foundational documents: It's a matter of empowering our citizens by teaching them their rights and responsibilities.

"Knowledge will forever govern ignorance," said James Madison, "and a people who mean to be their own Governors, must arm themselves with the power which knowledge gives." We are failing to educate our students about American institutions and self-government. And this failure, if uncorrected, will lead to greater political ignorance, greater political polarization, and a greater disconnect between those with power and those without.

And as long as we fail to provide young people with a civics education, we are what we teach.

## The First Amendment and Public Schools

Public schools embody a key goal of the First Amendment: to create an informed citizenry capable of self-governance and political debate. As many commentators have observed, a democracy relies on an informed and critical electorate to prosper.

On the eve of the Constitutional Convention in 1787, Benjamin Rush stated that "to conform the principles, morals, and manners of our citizens to our republican form of government, it is absolutely necessary that knowledge of every kind should be disseminated through every part of the Unites States."

Not surprisingly, universal access to free public education has long been viewed as an essential to realize our democratic ideals. According to the Supreme Court in *Keyishian v. Board of Education,* 1967:

> *The classroom is peculiarly the "marketplace of ideas." The Nation's future depends upon leaders trained through wide exposure to that robust exchange of ideas which discovers "truth out of a multitude of tongues, (rather) than through any kind of authoritative selection."*

Schools must, of course, convey skills and information across a range of subject areas for students of different backgrounds and abilities. They must also help students learn to work independently and in groups and maintain a safe environment that promotes learning. Given the complexity of these responsibilities, school officials are generally accorded considerable deference in deciding how best to accomplish them.

Modern Supreme Court decisions have made it clear that the right to free speech and expression can sometimes be subordinated to achieve legitimate educational goals. (See discussions of *Hazelwood School District v. Kuhlmeier* and *Bethel School District v. Fraser*.)

A school is not comparable to a public park where anyone can stand on a soapbox or a bulletin board on which anyone can post a notice. While students and teachers do not "shed their constitutional rights to freedom of speech or expression at the schoolhouse gate" (*Tinker v. Des Moines*), speech is not quite as free inside educational institutions as outside.

This does not mean that students and teachers have no First Amendment rights at school. Quite the contrary. But within the educational setting, the right to free speech is implemented in ways that do not interfere with schools' educational mission. Students cannot claim, for instance, that they have the right to have incorrect answers to an algebra quiz accepted as correct, nor can teachers claim a right to teach anything they choose.

## Restoring Free Speech on Campus

Restrictions on free expression on college campuses are incompatible with the fundamental values of higher education. At public institutions, they violate the First Amendment; at most private institutions, they break faith with stated commitments to academic freedom. And these restrictions are widespread.

The good news is that the types of restrictions discussed in this section can be reformed. A student or faculty member can be a tremendously effective advocate for change when he or she is aware of expressive rights and is willing to engage administrators in defense of them. Public exposure is also critical to defeating speech codes since universities are often unwilling to defend their speech codes in the face of public criticism.

Unconstitutional policies also can be defeated in court, especially at public universities, where speech codes have been struck down in federal courts across the country. Many more such policies have been revised in favor of free speech as the result of legal settlements.

Any speech code in force at a public university is vulnerable to a constitutional challenge. Moreover, as speech codes are consistently defeated in court, administrators cannot credibly argue that they are unaware of the law, which means that they may be held personally liable when they are responsible for their schools' violations of constitutional rights.

Censorship in the academic community is commonplace. Students and faculty are increasingly being investigated and punished for controversial, dissenting or simply discomforting speech. It's time for colleges and universities to take a deep breath, remember who they are and reaffirm their fundamental commitment to freedom of expression.

The suppression of free speech at institutions of higher education is a matter of great national concern. However, by working together with universities to revise restrictive speech codes and to reaffirm commitments to free expression, we can continue to stride toward campuses that truly embody the "marketplace of ideas" that such institutions must be in our society.

With these issues and goals in mind, in 2015, the University of Chicago convened a Committee on Freedom of Expression to do exactly that. The committee issued a statement identifying the principles that must guide institutions committed to attaining knowledge through free and open discourse. Guaranteeing members of the academic community "the broadest possible latitude to speak, write, listen, challenge, and learn," the statement guarantees students and faculty the right "to discuss any problem that presents itself."

**The Chicago Statement (Committee on Freedom of Expression)**

How should students and scholars respond when challenged by speech with which they disagree, or that they even loathe? The Chicago Statement (Committee on Freedom of Expression) sets forth the answer: "by openly and vigorously contesting the ideas that they oppose." Anticipating the push and pull of passionate debate, the statement sets forth important ground rules: "Debate or deliberation may not be suppressed because the ideas put forth are thought by some or even by most members of the University community to be offensive, unwise, immoral, or wrong-headed."

Perhaps most important, the Chicago statement makes clear that "it is not the proper role of the University to attempt to shield individuals from ideas and opinions they find unwelcome, disagreeable, or even deeply offensive." Laura Kipnis, Alice Dreger, and Teresa Buchanan would have benefited from this frank and necessary recognition.

"Because the University is committed to free and open inquiry in all matters, it guarantees all members of the University community the broadest possible latitude to speak, write, listen, challenge, and learn."–The Chicago Statement.

Since last year's report, FIRE has observed an increase in the adoption of free speech statements at colleges and universities inspired by the "Report of the Committee on Freedom of Expression" at the University of Chicago (better known as the "Chicago Statement"). As of May 2019, 63 institutions or faculty bodies have adopted or endorsed the Chicago Principles or a substantially similar policy statement.

Thousands more need to follow!

## Adopting the Chicago Statement

All colleges that are seriously committed to free inquiry and robust debate should consider adopting a version of the Chicago Statement. In doing so, the college not only reaffirms its core purpose as a place for discourse and debate, but also encourages the campus community to engage in such expression. By actively prioritizing free speech in this manner, universities can outline a set of principles that will become the hallmark of the community they aspire to build.

As eloquently described in the Chicago Statement, "fostering the ability of members of the University community to engage in such debate and deliberation in an effective and responsible manner is an essential part of the University's educational mission." That is the type of campus community FIRE and HxA hope all colleges will aim to cultivate.

When institutional leaders wait until controversy erupts on campus to publicly endorse free speech, detractors often accuse well-meaning administrators of favoring one side over the other. A proactive endorsement of free expression principles effectively shuts down any criticism that the university is picking sides in the latest campus controversy. Why wait until a controversial speaker comes to campus or racist posters fill your residence halls to take a principled stand on free speech? Instead, consider adopting a free expression statement today.

## The Chicago Statement Can Take Three Different Forms

As tracked by FIRE, endorsement of the Chicago Statement may take three different forms: official adoption by a university, approval by a governing board, or endorsement by a faculty body. Additionally, to ensure campus-wide engagement with the free speech issues raised by the Chicago Statement, many institutions choose to include several other stakeholders in the process, such as the student government and other campus community members.

Backed by a strong commitment to freedom of expression and academic freedom, faculty could challenge one another, their students, and the public to consider new possibilities, without fear of reprisal. Students would no longer face punishment for exercising their right to speak out freely about the issues most important to them.

Instead of learning that voicing one's opinions invites silencing, students would be taught that spirited debate is a vital necessity for the advancement of knowledge. And they would be taught that the proper response to ideas they oppose is not censorship, but argument on the merits. That, after all, is what a university is for.

Free speech and academic freedom will not protect themselves. With public reaffirmation of the necessity of free speech on campus, the current wave of censorship that threatens the continuing excellence of U.S. higher education can be repudiated, as it should be, as a transitory moment of weakness that disrespects what our institutions of higher learning must represent.

## Say "No!" to Campus Mob Fascism

In response to the Berkeley riot incident in 2017, FIRE issued this statement:

No university may be considered "safe" if speakers voicing unpopular ideas on its campus incur a substantial risk of being physically attacked. A university where people or viewpoints are likely to be opposed with fists rather than argumentation is unworthy of the name. Granting those willing to use violence the power to determine who may speak on campus is an abdication of UC Berkeley's moral and legal responsibilities under the First Amendment.

Strong-arming one's belief onto others is just a form of mob fascism—no matter what side of a political spectrum you are coming from.

If the Chicago Principles support allowing any invited speaker, as the statement does, then great. We must value our wonderful educational space, framed by laws and policies on one side and supported by documents like the Chicago Principles on the other. We need students to feel free to offer any viewpoint and likewise to offer any challenge, both within the context of our curriculum and on campus, to open up a discourse, and to learn from the engagement.

Let's underscore that point at the beginning: the Chicago principles envision and protect both controversial viewpoints and protests against those viewpoints, with the proviso that protesters "may not obstruct or otherwise interfere with the freedom of others to express views they reject or even loathe."

## How Can I Bring the Chicago Statement to My Campus?

Any statement or policy that supports students' freedom of speech rights is welcomed. Below is an excerpt from the Chicago Statement as a reference if there is ever a question or push-back about allowing a controversial speaker on campus because someone finds some topic of inquiry distasteful.

> "Because the University is committed to free and open inquiry in all matters, it guarantees all members of the University community the broadest possible latitude to speak, write, listen, challenge, and learn . . . . it is not the proper role of the University to attempt to shield individuals from ideas and opinions they find unwelcome, disagreeable, or even deeply offensive."

The "Chicago Statement" refers to the free speech policy statement produced by the Committee on Freedom of Expression at the University of Chicago. In July of 2014, University of Chicago President Robert J. Zimmer and Provost Eric D. Isaacs tasked the Committee with "articulating the University's overarching commitment to free, robust, and uninhibited debate and deliberation among all members of the University's community." The Committee, which was chaired by esteemed University of Chicago Law School professor Geoffrey Stone, released the report in January of 2015.

Here are several tips for ensuring that your university will be the next institution to stand in solidarity with the Chicago Statement's principles:

- Work to pass a student government resolution calling on the university to adopt its own version of the Chicago Statement.

- Reach out to faculty members and work with faculty governing bodies on campus.

- Build a broad coalition of students and groups, particularly across the ideological spectrum, to support the Chicago Statement and raise awareness on campus.

- Publish articles and op-eds in student newspapers and other outlets.

- Host events on campus, such as debates, speakers, and panels to discuss the principles supported by the Chicago Statement.

- Communicate and collaborate with members of your university's administration.

- Host a petition drive, asking students to pledge their support for the Chicago Statement's principles in a petition that will go to the administration.

- Work with other freedom of speech groups like the SAPIENT Being.

## Every University Should Adopt the University of Chicago's Academic Freedom Statement

The statement, which can be adapted to all universities—not just your high school, college, or university—guarantees "all members of the University community the broadest possible latitude to speak, write, listen, challenge, and learn." Most importantly, it makes clear that "it is not the proper role of the University to attempt to shield individuals from ideas and opinions they find unwelcome, disagreeable, or even deeply offensive."

### Showing Your Commitment to Campus Freedom of Speech

The Chicago statement is one of the best, most inspiring declarations of the critical importance of free speech on college campuses. They have become a gold standard among institutions that wish to show their commitment to American higher education's core principle of freedom of expression, argues Dr. Michael Poliakoff, ACTA President. And make no mistake about it, if universities reaffirm the necessity of free speech on campus, our students will enjoy better educations.

FIRE's often quoted author Will Creeley and University of Chicago Law Professor Geoffrey Stone write in their 2015 *Washington Post* op-ed:

Backed by a strong commitment to freedom of expression and academic freedom, faculty could challenge one another, their students, and the public to consider new possibilities, without fear of reprisal. Students would no longer face punishment for exercising their right to speak out freely about the issues most important to them.

Instead of learning that voicing one's opinions invites silencing, students would be taught that spirited debate is a vital necessity for the advancement of knowledge. And they would be taught that the proper response to ideas they oppose is not censorship, but argument on the merits. That, after all, is what a university is for.

### Get Your University or Alma Mater to Endorse the Chicago Statement

If you want your high school, college, or university *alma mater* to endorse the Chicago statement, I encourage you to sign FIRE's pledge and write to your *alma maters* or local institutions. The 931-word statement is balanced and nuanced, protecting both those articulating unpopular viewpoints and the rights of protesters.

It is, moreover, all too short a step from that to Herbert Marcuse's theory that tolerance of viewpoints that diverge from liberalism is itself repressive, and from there to the contemporary meme that speech that departs from the perceived interests of the oppressed is a form of violence that justifies physical violence to counter it.

At institutions throughout America, the fruit of that ideology has stained the reputation of higher education. The clarity of the Chicago principles is urgently needed to clean up the mess of freedom of speech suppression.

The worst irony of all is that the world of higher education, which should be eager for vigorous debate and challenge, often lags behind the diverse leaders who embrace free speech as the engine of progress. U.S. congressman and civil rights leader John Lewis asserted, "Without freedom of speech and the right to dissent, the civil rights movement would have been a bird without wings."

And, in a more recent struggle, Jonathan Rauch, senior fellow at the Brookings Institution and LGBTQ advocate observed, "Not long ago, gays were pariahs. We had no real political power, only the force of our arguments. In a society where free exchange is the rule, that was enough. We had the coercive power of truth."

## Campus Free Speech: A Legislative Proposal

In her 2016 convocation speech, Brown University President Christina Paxson explained that a re- porter had recently asked school officials if Brown had established any "safe spaces" on campus. "What on earth are they referring to?" Paxson said. "Idea-free zones staffed by thought police, where disagreement is prohibited?"

Yes, precisely such spaces as detailed in the "Campus Free Speech: A Legislative Proposal" by Stanley Kurtz, James Manley, and Jonathan Butcher of the Goldwater Institute.

Sadly, this kind of challenge to campus free speech is now widespread. Surveys show that student support for restrictive speech codes and speaker bans is at historic heights. As both a deeply held commitment and a living tradition, freedom of speech is dying on our college campuses, and is increasingly imperiled in society at large.

Nowhere is the need for open debate more important than on America's college campuses. Students maturing from teenagers into adults must be confronted with new ideas, especially ideas with which they disagree, if they are to become informed and responsible members of a free society.

In order to protect the increasingly imperiled principle and practice of campus free speech, this brief offers model legislation designed to ensure free expression at America's public university systems. It is hoped that public debate over these legislative proposals will strengthen freedom of speech at private colleges and universities as well. The key provisions in this model legislation are inspired by three classic defenses of campus free speech: Yale's 1974 Woodward Report, The University of Chicago's 1967 Kalven Report, and the University of Chicago's 2015 Stone Report.

The model legislation presented and explained in this brief does several things:

- It creates an official university policy that strongly affirms the importance of free expression, nullifying any existing restrictive speech codes in the process.

- It prevents administrators from disinviting speakers, no matter how controversial, whom members of the campus community wish to hear from.

- It establishes a system of disciplinary sanctions for students and anyone else who interferes with the free-speech rights of others.

- It allows persons whose free-speech rights have been improperly infringed by the university to recover court costs and attorney's fees.

- It reaffirms the principle that universities, at the official institutional level, ought to remain neutral on issues of public controversy to encourage the widest possible range of opinion and dialogue within the university itself.

- It ensures that students will be informed of the official policy on free expression.

- It authorizes a special subcommittee of the university board of trustees to issue a yearly report to the public, the trustees, the governor, and the legislature on the administrative handling of free-speech issues.

Taken together, these provisions create a system of interlocking incentives designed to encourage students and administrators to respect and protect the free expression of others.

### Free Speech is Under Siege on America's College Campuses

Freedom of speech, that cornerstone of our liberty and most fundamental constitutional right, is under siege on America's college campuses. Speakers who challenge campus orthodoxies are rarely sought out, are disinvited when called, and are shouted down or otherwise disrupted while on campus. Speech codes that substantially limit First Amendment rights are widespread. New devices like "trigger warnings" and "safe spaces" shelter students from the give-and-take of discussion and debate.

When protestors disrupt visiting speakers, or break in on meetings to take them over and list demands, administrators look the other way. Students have come to take it for granted they will face no discipline for such disruptions. Administrators themselves often disinvite controversial speakers and limit the exercise of liberty to narrow "free speech zones." Administrators also focus enforcement on silencing "offensive" speech and give short shrift to due process protections for students accused of saying the wrong thing to the wrong group.

University governing boards (boards of trustees) rarely act to curb these administrative abuses. Substantial sections of the faculty have abandoned the defense of free speech. The classic advocates of liberty of thought and discussion are rarely taught. Surveys show that student support for restrictive speech codes and speaker bans is at historic heights.

In short, as both a deeply held commitment and a living tradition, freedom of speech is dying on our college campuses, and is increasingly imperiled in society at large.

The Goldwater Institute has partnered with Stanley Kurtz of the Ethics and Public Policy Center to craft a model bill that will allow state legislatures to restore freedom of speech to our public university systems. As legislators introduce this bill across the country, a national debate on preserving campus free speech should influence both private colleges and the broader culture.

In 2016, the Goldwater Institute helped design a policy protecting free speech on Arizona campuses. Under HB 2615, community colleges and universities cannot create "free speech zones" that relegate free expression to narrow areas of campus. Rather, there is a presumption in favor of free speech and tailored restrictions to address legitimate time, place, and manner concerns are the exception.

The bill also "removes permissive language" in existing Arizona law that allows a "university or community college to restrict a student's speech in a public forum."

The model legislation presented in this white paper is patterned on recommendations contained in three reports widely regarded as classic statements on campus free expression: Yale's Woodward Re- port of 1974, the University of Chicago's Kalven Report of 1967, and the University of Chicago's Stone Report of 2015.5

**Model Bill is Designed to Change the Balance of Forces**

The model bill offered herein is designed to change the balance of forces contributing to the current baleful national climate for campus free speech. Administrators generally feel pressured to placate demonstrators who interfere with the free expression of others, so as to move campus controversies as quickly as possible out of the public eye.

Students who know they have little to fear in return for shouting down visiting speakers or interfering with public meetings feel free to protest in highly disruptive ways. In this atmosphere, students or faculty who disagree with current campus orthodoxies are left intimidated and uncertain of administrative support for their rights. Meanwhile, all students suffer for want of opportunities to hear the very best arguments on opposing sides of public questions.

The model legislation offered here challenges this balance of forces in several ways:

- First, it creates an official university policy that strongly affirms the importance of free expression, while formally nullifying any existing restrictive speech codes.

- Second, it establishes a system of disciplinary sanctions for students and others who interfere with the free-speech rights of others, while strongly protecting the due-process rights of those accused of such disruption.

- Third, it empowers persons whose free-speech rights have been infringed to seek legal recourse and recover court costs and attorney's fees.

- Fourth, it ensures that students will be informed of their university's commitment to free expression, and of the penalties for the violation of others' free-speech rights, during a special section of freshman orientation.

- Fifth, it authorizes a special subcommittee of the university governing board to issue a yearly report to the board itself, the public, the governor, and the legislature on the administrative handling of free-speech issues, including the application of disciplinary sanctions.

In sum, the model bill is designed to encourage public and institutional oversight of administrators' handling of free-speech issues, thus counterbalancing pressures on administrators to overlook interference with the free-speech rights of others.

Students will know from the moment they enter the university that they must respect the free expression of others, and will face significant consequences if they do not. An annual report on the administrative handling of these issues will either hold university presidents accountable, or be subject to public criticism for failing to do so. The overall effect will be to break the vicious cycle that has placed campus free speech in increasing peril.

## The Model Bill Affirms Institutional Neutrality on Issues of Public Controversy

In addition to these provisions, the model bill affirms the principle of institutional neutrality on issues of public controversy. As articulated by the University of Chicago's Kalven Report of 1967, the institutional neutrality of universities on controversial public issues is the surest guarantee of intellectual freedom for individuals within the university community. When a university, as an institution, takes a strong stand on a major public debate, this inherently pressures faculty and students to toe the official university line, thereby inhibiting their freedom to speak and decide for themselves.

We see this issue at work today in the campaigns to press universities to divest their endowments of holdings in oil companies or companies based in the state of Israel. At any university, such divestment would tend to inhibit intellectual freedom. This is particularly true for state universities, which should reflect the diverse views of the entire population of the state that provides the university funding.

It's important to note, however, that the model bill's provision bearing on institutional neutrality is aspirational in character. Rather than undertaking the difficult task of identifying a clear boundary in law between issues on which there is social consensus and issues of public controversy, the bill simply affirms the basic principle of institutional neutrality and leaves its application in the hands of the university governing board.

Considered as a whole, the model bill presented in this report constitutes the most comprehensive legislative proposal ever offered to restore and protect campus free speech.

## A Far Reaching Conclusion

Freedom of speech in America is facing the greatest threats since the Alien and Sedition acts of 1798, which unconstitutionally punished "false, scandalous, or malicious writing" against the United States.

Taken from Alan Dershowitz's "America's New Censors" Horizons: Journal of International Relations and Sustainable Development Summer 2021 article comes a sobering warning: Today's threats are even greater than during McCarthyism. This is true for three important reasons.

Today's censorship comes, for the most part, from so-called progressives, who are far more influential and credible than the reactionaries who promoted and implemented McCarthyism.

The current efforts to censor politically incorrect and "untruthful" views are led by young people, academics, high tech innovators, and writers—yes, writers! These self-righteous and self-appointed Solons of what is and is not permissible speech represent our future, whereas the McCarthyite censors were a throwback to the past—a last gasp of repression from a dying political order.

The new censors (Generations X Y Z) are our future leaders. They are quickly gaining influence over the social media, the newsrooms of print and TV, the academy, and other institutions that control the flow of information that impacts all aspects of American political life.

These censorial zealots will soon be the CEOs, editors-in-chief, deans, and government officials who run our nation. They are destined to have even more influence over what we can read, see, and hear.

If today's attitudes toward freedom of speech by these unsapient freedom of speech suppressors become tomorrow's rules, our nation will lose much of its freedom of thought, expression, and dissent. Those of us who cherish these freedoms must become more proactive in their defense.

# Appendix

**50 *MADNESS* Textbook Titles:** https://www.fratirepublishing.com/madnessbooks

- *Fake News Madness*

- *Crime Rate Madness*

- *Voting Madness*

- *California Madness*

**Annual Media Fibbys – Top Mainstream Media Fails of 2021:**
https://www.youtube.com/watch?v=3T5De2S2luw

**Freedom Forum Institute:** https://www.freedomforuminstitute.org/

**Freedom to Read Foundation:** https://www.ftrf.org/page/About

**Free Speech Alliance – Media Research Center (MRC):** https://www.mrc.org/freespeechalliance

**Goldwater Institute – Campus Free Speech: A Legislative Proposal:**
https://goldwaterinstitute.org/article/campus-free-speech-a-legislative-proposal/

**Institute For Free Speech:** https://www.ifs.org/cases/marshall-v-amuso/

**Judicial Watch:** https://www.judicialwatch.org/jwtv/

**Minding The Campus:** https://www.mindingthecampus.org/author/pwood/

**MRC NewsBusters Censorship Project:** https://www.newsbusters.org/other-topics/censorship-project?page=1

**No U.S. History? How College History Departments Leave the United States out of the Major:**
https://www.goacta.org/wp-content/uploads/2021/11/No.-U.S.-History_2.pdf

**American Council of Trustees and Alumni (ACTA):**

https://www.realclearpublicaffairs.com/public_affairs/2021/12/16/no_us_history_how_college_history_departments_leave_the_united_states_out_of_the_major_807864.html#!

**Pennsbury School Board Aggressive Censorship of CRT Debate:** https://www.ifs.org/wp-content/uploads/2021/10/PennsburySchoolBoard.mp4

**Pew Research Center:** https://www.pewresearch.org/about/

**Retraction Watch:** https://retractionwatch.com/retracted-coronavirus-covid-19-papers/

**The Joy of Being Wrong – Video by the John Templeton Foundation:** https://youtu.be/mRXNUx4cua0

**SAPIENT BEING PROGRAMS:**

- **Make Free Speech Again On Campus (MFSAOC) Program:**

- https://www.sapientbeing.org/programs

- **Sapient Conservative Textbooks (SCT) Program:** https://www.sapientbeing.org/programs

- **World Of Writing Warriors (WOWW) Program:** https://www.sapientbeing.org/programs

- **World Of Writing Warriors (WOWW) Journalism Code of Ethics, Practical Logic & Sapience Guidelines:** https://www.sapientbeing.org/resources

**Student Press Law Center:** https://splc.org/about/

*The S.A.P.I.E.N.T. Being:* https://www.fratirepublishing.com/books

**Vote Integrity – Data Analytics For Election Integrity by Vote P. Analysis:** https://votepatternanalysis.substack.com/people/20957397-vote-integrity

# Glossary

**Algorithmic Unfairness –** A social media term describes systematic programing and repeatable errors that create unfair outcomes, such as privileging one arbitrary group of users over others.

**Arguments –** Should have three parts: an assertion, reasoning, and evidence (easily remembered with the mnemonic ARE).

**Big Tech –** Refers to the major technology companies such as Twitter, YouTube, Apple, Google, Amazon, Facebook and Microsoft, which have inordinate influence.

**Bill of Rights –** Comprises the first ten amendments added to the United States Constitution in 1791 that clarify the specific guarantees of personal freedoms and rights, clear limitations on the government's power in judicial and other proceedings, and explicit declarations that all powers not specifically granted to the federal government by the Constitution are reserved to the states or the people.

**Content Discrimination –** A law that discriminates based on the content of a message — as opposed to the time, place or manner in which that message is made, or the reactions it incites in people — is considered presumptively unconstitutional.

**Critical Legal Theory (CLT) –** A progressive movement that challenges and seeks to overturn accepted norms and standards in legal theory and practice.

**Critical Race Theory (CRT) –** A progressive movement that is "a collection of activists and scholars interested in studying and transforming the relationship among race, racism, and power."

**Critical Theory (CT) – A** Marxist-inspired movement in social and political philosophy originally associated with the work of the Frankfurt School.

**Deep State –** Is a type of governance made up of potentially secret and unauthorized networks of power operating independently of a state's political leadership in pursuit of their own agenda and goals.

**DEI –** Diversity, equity, and inclusion: a conceptual framework that promotes the fair treatment and full participation of all people, especially in the workplace, including populations who have historically been underrepresented or subject to discrimination because of their background, identity, disability, etc.

**Democracy –** A government in which the supreme power is vested in the people and exercised by them directly or indirectly through a system of representation usually involving periodically held free elections; a political unit that has a democratic government.

**Diversity –** Diversity is desirable when it obtains organically as a result of meritocracy. Numerous reports show that companies with women and people from various demographic backgrounds in leadership out-earn companies without them. In one such report this year, McKinsey & Company found that "the relationship between diversity on executive teams and the likelihood of financial outperformance has strengthened over time."

**Equity –** The Merriam-Webster Dictionary defines equity as "justice according to natural law or right, specifically: freedom from bias or favoritism." This meaning has been completely inverted in today's usage. Today, equity has come to mean the opposite of equality.

**False Light –** A form of invasion of privacy in which a person is presented in a way that leaves a negative and inaccurate impression about that person.

**Fascism –** A political philosophy, movement, or regime (as that of the Fascisti) that exalts nation and often race above the individual and that stands for a centralized autocratic government headed by a dictatorial leader, severe economic and social regimentation, and forcible suppression of opposition; a tendency toward or actual exercise of strong autocratic or dictatorial control.

**First Amendment –** States that "Congress shall make no law respecting an establishment of religion, or prohibiting the free exercise thereof; or abridging the freedom of speech, or of the press; or the right of the people peaceably to assemble, and to petition the government for a redress of grievances" and applies to every American citizen.

**Heckler's Veto –** A heckler's veto occurs when government attempts to suppress speech (usually of an inflammatory nature) in order to avoid an undesirable reaction. Such suppression is generally a violation of the First Amendment.

**Identity Politics –** Is a political approach wherein people of a particular gender, religion, race, social background, social class or other identifying factors, develop political agendas that are based upon these identities.

**Idiocracy –** An idiocracy is a disparaging term for a society run by or made up of idiots (or people perceived as such). Idiocracy is also the title of 2006 satirical film that depicts a future in which humanity has become dumb.

**Illiberalism –** The 21st century term is used to describe an attitude that is close-minded, intolerant, and bigoted.

**Incitement –** The act of one person causing another to consider committing a crime, regardless of whether in fact the crime was committed. Incitement is the attempt to draw in another person as a conspirator or an accomplice.

**Inclusion –** The practice or policy of providing equal access to opportunities and resources for people who might otherwise be excluded or marginalized, such as those who have physical or mental disabilities and members of other minority groups.

**Indecency –** "Indecent" speech usually receives First Amendment protection, except when it is broadcast over the airwaves.

**Indirect Burden –** The standard of review used in both free-speech and free-exercise cases is the determination of whether the regulation in question poses a direct or indirect burden upon the right in question.

**Intellectual Humility –** A mindset that encompasses empathy, trust, and curiosity, viewpoint diversity gives rise to engaged and civil debate, constructive disagreement, and shared progress towards truth.

**Intersectionality –** A term that refers to the "multiple social forces, social identities, and ideological instruments through which power and disadvantage are expressed and legitimized."

**Jim Crow –** Racial segregation laws up to 1965, that were enacted and enforced in the South in the late 19th and early 20th centuries by white Southern Democrat-dominated state legislatures to disenfranchise and remove political and economic gains made by blacks during the Reconstruction period.

**Judicial Fiat –** Refers to an order or a decree especially an arbitrary one.

**Libertarian** – An advocate of the doctrine of free will; a person who upholds the principles of individual liberty especially of thought and action; a member of a political party advocating libertarian principles.

**Limited Open Forum** – Under the Equal Access Act, a limited open forum is created whenever a public secondary school provides an opportunity for one or more "noncurriculum-related student groups" to meet on school premises during noninstructional time.

**Locke, John** – Often credited as a founder of modern "liberal" thought, Locke pioneered the ideas of natural law, social contract, religious toleration, and the right to revolution that proved essential to both the American Revolution and the U.S. Constitution that followed.

**Madison, James** – Known as the Father of the Constitution because of his pivotal role in the document's drafting as well as its ratification. Madison also drafted the first 10 amendments -- the Bill of Rights.

**Mainstream Media (MSM)** – Traditional forms of mass media, as television, radio, magazines, and newspapers, as opposed to online means of mass communication.

**Marxism** – The political, economic, and social principles and policies advocated by Marx and a theory and practice of socialism including the labor theory of value, dialectical materialism, the class struggle, and dictatorship of the proletariat until the establishment of a classless society.

**Mill, John Stuart** – Was a champion of diverse opinions since they stem from individuality. Even false ideas, he suggests, benefit the common good because they contribute to thoughtful discussions that might result in valuable truths.

**Minorities** – This term has evolved to include now the idea of "collective victimization" and is intricately tied to identity politics, which is a political project of the Left. This was not always the case, however. The modern-day usage of this word does not appear in a dictionary until 1961.

**Open Inquiry** – Is the ability to ask questions and share ideas without risk of censure.

**Overbreadth Doctrine** – This doctrine holds that a regulation of expression that curtails protected speech, even if it also restricts unprotected speech, can be challenged as invalid.

**Political Correctness** – A term used to describe language, policies, or measures that are intended to avoid offense or disadvantage to members of particular groups in society.

**Progressivism** – A political philosophy in support of social reform based on the idea of progress in which advancements in science, technology, economic development, and social organization are vital to improve the human condition.

**Public Forum** – Under the public-forum doctrine, government officials have less authority to restrict speech in places that by tradition have been open for free expression.

**Qualified Immunity** – A doctrine that protects government officials from liability in civil rights actions when they do not violate clearly established principles of law.

**Reckless Disregard** – In *New York Times Co. v. Sullivan* (1964), the Supreme Court defined actual malice as a state of mind in which a person or publication makes an untrue and defamatory statement about a person "with knowledge that it was false or with reckless disregard of whether it was false or not."

**Reporters' Privilege** – Reporters are protected, on a state-by-state basis, by statutory law or constitution, from testifying about confidential information or sources at trial.

**Sapience** – Also known as wisdom, is the ability to think and act using knowledge, experience, understanding, common sense and insight. Sapience is associated with attributes such as intelligence, enlightenment, unbiased judgment, compassion, experiential self-knowledge, self-actualization, and virtues such as ethics and benevolence.

**Sedition** – Generally seen as expression with the intent to incite rebellion against the government, sedition is constitutionally protected unless it falls outside the "clear and present danger" test.

**Social Justice** – A political and philosophical theory which asserts that there are dimensions to the concept of justice beyond those embodied in the principles of civil or criminal law, economic supply and demand, or traditional moral frameworks.

**Social Media** – Websites and other online means of communication that are used by large groups of people to share information and to develop social and professional contacts.

**Tort liability** – A tort is a wrong done to someone, a civil cause of action for which a standard remedy is monetary damages or an injunction.

**Useful Idiot** – Is attributed to Vladimir Lenin. It describes naïve people who can be manipulated to advance a political cause.

**Viewpoint Discrimination** – A regulation is considered to discriminate on the basis of viewpoint when it attacks a particular individual's or group's message, as opposed to the mode in which that message is conveyed.

**Viewpoint Diversity** – Viewpoint diversity occurs when members of a group or community approach problems or questions from a range of perspectives.

**White Supremacy** – The term "white supremacy" can be confusing because it can mean an actual belief in the superiority of white people, in which case it is despicable. However, it is nearly always employed to mean something much larger—anything from classical philosophers to Enlightenment thinkers to the Industrial Revolution.

# References

Arnn, Larry P. "Orwell's 1984 and Today." *Imprimis.* December 2020, Volume 49, Number 12. https://imprimis.hillsdale.edu/orwells-1984-today/.

Berger, Dr. Raymond M. "Marxism and Progressivism: A Play in Two Acts" *The Times of Israel*, Jun 2, 2018. https://blogs.timesofisrael.com/marxism-and-progressivism-a-play-in-two-acts/.

Berger, Judson. "What Happens When Free Speech Dies." *National Review.* October 29, 2021. https://www.nationalreview.com/the-weekend-jolt/what-happens-when-free-speech-dies/.

Berstein, Brittany. "Support for Shouting Down Speakers on Campus Spikes after Political Chaos of 2020." September 22, 2021. *National Review.* https://www.nationalreview.com/news/support-for-shouting-down-speakers-on-campus-spikes-after-political-chaos-of-2020/.

Bokhari, Allum. "Who Is in Control? The Need to Rein in Big Tech. *Imprimis.* January 2021, Volume 50, Number 1. https://imprimis.hillsdale.edu/control-need-rein-big-tech/.

Butcher, Jonathan and Mike Gonzalez. "Critical Race Theory, the New Intolerance, and Its Grip on America." Heritage Foundation. December 7, 2020. https://www.heritage.org/civil-rights/report/critical-race-theory-the-new-intolerance-and-its-grip-america.

Democrats' Weaponization of the DOJ. Republican National Committee. June 25, 2021. https://gop.com/rapid-response/democrats-weaponization-of-the-doj/.

Dershowitz, Alan. "America's New Censors." Horizons: Journal of International Relations and Sustainable Development, No. 19 (2021): 202–21. https://www.jstor.org/stable/48617365.

Dershowitz, Alan. *Cancel Culture: The Latest Attack on Free Speech and Due Process.* Hot Books: New York. 2020.

Dershowitz, Alan. *Case Against the New Censorship: Protecting Free Speech from Big Tech, Progressives, and Universities.* Hot Books: New York. 2021.

Dice, Mark. *The True Story of Fake News: How Mainstream Media Manipulates Millions.* The Resistance Manifesto: San Diego. 2017.

Djordjevic, Milos. "27 Alarming Fake News Statistics on the Effects of False Reporting [The 2021 Edition]." LETTER.LY. April 1, 2021. https://letter.ly/fake-news-statistics/.

Free Speech Alliance. Media Research Center (MRC). https://www.mrc.org/freespeechalliance.

Guelzo, Allen C. "Free Speech and Its Present Crisis: In today's America, the right to express one's opinion is threatened by activists and authorities alike." *City Journal.* Autumn 2018. https://www.city-journal.org/free-speech-crisis.

Haidt, Dr. Jonathan and Dr. Greg Lukianoff. "How To Keep Your Corporation Out of the Culture War." Persuasion. Dec. 3, 2020. https://www.persuasion.community/p/haidt-and-lukianoff-how-to-end-corporate.

Haidt, Dr. Jonathan and Lukianoff, Dr. Greg. *The Coddling of the American Mind: How Good Intentions and Bad Ideas Are Setting Up a Generation for Failure*, Penguin Random House: New York. 2018.

Haidt, Dr. Jonathan and Lukianoff, Dr. Greg. *The Righteous Mind: Why Good People Are Divided by Politics and Religion*, Vintage Books: New York. 2012.

Haidt, Dr. Jonathan. "Viewpoint Diversity in the Academy." www.righteousmind.com. 2019.

Hall, Alexander. "Rep. Devin Nunes to Resign from Congress, Join Trump Media & Technology Group as CEO." MRC: Newsbusters. December 7th, 2021. https://www.newsbusters.org/blogs/free-speech/alexander-hall/2021/12/07/rep-devin-nunes-resign-congress-join-trump-media.

Hemingway, Mollie. *Rigged: How the Media, Big Tech, and the Democrats Seized Our Elections*. Regnery Publishing: Washington, D.C. 2021.

Holmes, Dr. Kim R. "Intolerance as Illiberalism." The Heritage Foundation. July 16, 2014. https://www.heritage.org/political-process/commentary/intolerance-illiberalism.

Holmes, Dr. Kim R. *Rebound: Getting America Back to Great*. Rowman & Littlefield Publishers: Lanham. 2013.

Honeycutt, Nathan. "Political Intolerance Among University Faculty Highlights Need For Viewpoint Diversity." Forbes. https://www.forbes.com/sites/realspin/2016/11/21/political-intolerance-among-university-faculty-highlights-need-for-viewpoint-diversity/?sh=578e68a214b5.

Hudson Jr., David L. and Mahad Ghani. "Clubs." Freedom Forum Institute. September 18, 2017. https://www.freedomforuminstitute.org/first-amendment-center/topics/freedom-of-speech-2/k-12-public-school-student-expression/clubs/.

Jilani, Zaid. "Forward Most Americans are now self-censoring. We're regressing." July 23, 2020. https://forward.com/opinion/451361/most-americans-are-now-self-censoring-were-regressing/.

Kan, Janita. "Biden Revokes Trump Order Protecting Users From Censorship on Social Media." Epoch Times. May 17, 2021. https://www.theepochtimes.com/biden-revokes-trump-order-on-protecting-censorship-on-social-media-platforms_3817163.html.

Kurtz, Stanley, James Manley, and Jonathan Butcher. "Campus Free Speech: A Legislative Proposal." Goldwater Institute. https://goldwaterinstitute.org/wp-content/uploads/cms_page_media/2017/2/2/X_Campus%20Free%20Speech%20Paper.pdf.

Levin, Mark R. *Unfreedom of the Press*. Threshold Editions. 2019.

Lindsay, Tom. "New Report: Most College Students Agree that Campus Free Speech is Waning." Forbes. May 31, 2019. https://www.forbes.com/sites/tomlindsay/2019/05/31/new-report-most-college-students-agree-that-campus-free-speech-is-waning/.

Lukianoff, Dr. Greg. "The Second Great Age of Political Correctness." Reason. January 2022 Issue. https://reason.com/2021/12/13/the-second-great-age-of-political-correctness/.

Luo, Irene, and Jan Jekielek. "Robert Epstein: How Big Tech Bias Threatens Free and Fair Elections." *Epoch Times*. October 5, 2019. https://www.theepochtimes.com/robert-epstein-how-big-tech-bias-threatens-free-and-fair-elections_3077681.html.

Marshall v. Amuso. Institute For Free Speech. October 1, 2021. https://www.ifs.org/cases/marshall-v-amuso/.

McWhorter, John. "Taking on the Woke Movement." *Newsmax*. November 12, 2021. https://www.newsmax.com/george-j-marlin/wokism-john-mcwhorter-antiwoke/2021/11/12/id/1044432/.

Murphy, Rex. "How the 'Cancel Culture' Mob's Attempt to Silence Jordan Peterson Backfired." *Epoch Times*. December 14, 2021. https://www.theepochtimes.com/rex-murphy-how-the-cancel-culture-mobs-attempt-to-silence-jordan-peterson-backfired_4153530.html?utm_source=ai_recommender&utm_medium=a_bottom_above_etv.

Niemiec, Emilia. "COVID-19 and Misinformation." EMBO Reports. October 26, 2020. https://www.embopress.org/doi/full/10.15252/embr.202051420.

Pavlich, Katie. "Pavlich: Democrats' Weaponization of the DOJ is Back." EMBO Reports. Oct. 27, 2021. https://thehill.com/opinion/education/578622-pavlich-democrats-weaponization-of-the-doj-is-back.

Phillips, Jack. "Parler Files New Lawsuit Against Amazon, Says Tech Giant Tried to 'Destroy' App." March 4, 2021. *Epoch Times*. https://www.theepochtimes.com/parler-files-new-lawsuit-against-amazon-says-tech-giant-tried-to-destroy-app_3720632.html.

Phillips, Jack. "Trump Announces 'Major' Class-Action Lawsuits Against Twitter, Facebook, Google." *Epoch Times*. July 12, 2021. https://www.theepochtimes.com/trump-announces-major-class-action-lawsuits-against-twitter-facebook-and-google_3890863.html.

Phillips, Jack. "Trump Takes Aim at Critical Race Theory, Signs Executive Order on 'Patriotic Education.'" *Epoch Times*. September 17, 2020. https://www.theepochtimes.com/trump-takes-aim-at-critical-race-theory-proposes-patriotic-education-commission_3504254.html?utm_source=ai&utm_medium=search.

Republicans Are Right to Push Back Against CRT in the Classrooms. National Review. July 10, 2021. https://www.nationalreview.com/2021/07/republicans-are-right-to-push-back-against-crt-in-the-classrooms/.

Shapiro, Ben. "Ben Shapiro Breaks Down the Top Mainstream Media Fails of 2021." Daily Wire. Dec. 23, 2021. https://www.youtube.com/watch?v=3T5De2S2luw.

Shapiro, Ben. "Viewpoint Discrimination with Algorithms." National Review. March 7, 2018. https://www.nationalreview.com/2018/03/social-media-companies-discriminate-against-conservatives/.

Smith, Bradley A. "Democrats Propose a Federal Speech Czar." The Hill. October 20, 2021 https://www.nationalreview.com/2021/10/democrats-propose-a-federal-speech-czar/.

Soave, Robby. "At Universities Across the Country, Liberalism is Going Extinct." *The Daily Caller*. Nov. 22, 2013. https://dailycaller.com/2013/11/22/the-death-of-liberalism-on-college-campuses/.

Spotlight on Speech Codes F.I.R.E. 2022. Foundation for Individual Rights in Education (F.I.R.E.). https://www.thefire.org/resources/spotlight/reports/spotlight-on-speech-codes-2022/.

Stepman, Jarrett. "Social Justice Warriors Taking Over and Purging Newsrooms." June 10, 2020. The Daily Signal. https://www.cnsnews.com/index.php/commentary/jarrett-stepman/social-justice-warriors-taking-over-and-purging-newsrooms.

Stieber, Zachary. "NIH: Check Out Wikipedia to See Why Great Barrington Declaration is 'Dangerous.'" *Epoch Times*. December 24, 2021. https://www.theepochtimes.com/nih-check-out-wikipedia-to-see-why-great-barrington-declaration-is-dangerous_4176405.html?utm_source=mr_recommendation&utm_medium=left_sticky.

Stone, Geoffrey R. and Creeley, Will. "Restoring Free Speech on Campus." *The Washington Post*. Sep. 25, 2015.

Talgo, Chris. "Big Tech's Assault on Free Speech." *The Hill*. August 4, 2020. https://thehill.com/opinion/technology/510367-big-techs-assault-on-free-speech.

Tierney, John. "Journalists Against Free Speech." *City Journal*. Autumn 2019. https://www.city-journal.org/journalists-against-free-speech.

Turley, Jonathan. "The Dangerous Liberal Ideas For Censorship in the United States." May 2, 2020. *The Hill*. https://thehill.com/opinion/civil-rights/495788-the-dangerous-liberal-ideas-for-censorship-in-the-united-states.

Vadum, Matthew. "Prager U Censored by Video Platform." June 9, 2021. *Epoch Times*. https://www.theepochtimes.com/prageru-censored-by-video-platform_3852182.html?utm_source=pushengage.

van Brugen, Isabel and Joshua Philipp. "Dangerous New Wave of Censorship Culminating in the US: Dershowitz." May 26, 2021. Epoch Times. https://www.theepochtimes.com/dangerous-new-wave-of-censorship-culminating-in-the-us-dershowitz_3831339.html.

van Brugen, Isabel. "PolitiFact Quietly Retracts Fact Check Labeling COVID-19 Lab Origin Theory as 'Debunked Conspiracy.'" *Epoch Times*. May 25, 2021. https://www.theepochtimes.com/politifact-quietly-retracts-fact-check-labeling-covid-19-lab-origin-theory-as-debunked-conspiracy_3824881.html.

Weslander Quaid, Michele R. "We Are in a War for America's Soul." *Epoch Times*. September 21, 2021. https://www.theepochtimes.com/we-are-in-a-war-for-americas-soul_4001263.html?utm_source=ai_recommender&utm_medium=a_bottom_above_etv.

Williams, Walter E. "The Fight for Free Speech." The Daily Signal. October 07, 2020. https://www.dailysignal.com/2020/10/07/the-fight-for-free-speech/.

Willour, Isaac. "What We Can Learn from the Campus Free-Speech War." National Review. August 22, 2021. https://www.nationalreview.com/2021/08/what-we-can-learn-from-the-campus-free-speech-war/.

Wood, Peter. A Tide Flowing Toward Free Speech on Campus. Minding the Campus. July 16, 2018 (from Free Speech in Peril: College—Where You Can't Say What You Think – Minding the Campus). https://www.mindingthecampus.org/wp-content/uploads/2020/01/MTC-e-book.pdf.

# Index

# C

# G

# H

## U

## V

## W

# Author Bio

*Author: Corey Lee Wilson.*

Corey Lee Wilson was raised an atheist by his liberal *Playboy* Bunny mother, has three Anglo-Latino siblings, a brother who died of AIDS, a biracial daughter, baptized a Protestant by his conservative grandparents, attended temple with his Jewish foster parents, baptized again as a Catholic for his first Filipina wife, attends Buddhist ceremonies with his second Thai wife, became an agnostic on his own free will for most of his life, and is a lifetime independent voter.

Corey felt the sting of intellectual humility by repeating the 4th grade and attended eighteen different schools before putting himself through college at Mt. San Antonio College and Cal Poly Pomona University (while on triple secrete probation). Named Who's Who of American College Students in 1984, he received a BS in Economics and won his fraternity's most prestigious undergraduate honor, the Phi Kappa Tau Fraternity's Shideler Award, both in 1985. In 2020, he became a member of the Heterodox Academy and in 2021 a member of the National Association of Scholars and 1776 Unites.

As a satirist and fraternity man, Corey started Fratire Publishing in 2012 and transformed the fiction "fratire" genre to a respectable and viewpoint diverse non-fiction genre promoting practical knowledge and wisdom to help everyday people navigate safely through the many hazards of life. In 2018, he founded the SAPIENT Being to help promote freedom of speech, viewpoint diversity, intellectual humility and most importantly advance sapience in America's students and campuses.

The SAPIENT Being has three programs: Make Free Speech Again On Campus (MFSAOC), World of Writing Warriors (WOWW) and the Sapient Conservative Textbooks (SCT) all working together to promote its mission and vision of sapience. The WOWW program plans to self-publish 50 *MADNESS* non-fiction textbooks in partnership with Fratire Publishing over the span of the 2020 decade in alliance with the MFSAOC program to start 50 chapters on America's high school and college campuses by 2030.

If you're interested in the MFSAOC Program and starting a S.A.P.I.E.N.T. Being club, chapter, or alliance please go to https://www.SapientBeing.org/start-a-chapter, e-mail SapientBeing@att.net, or call (951) 638-5562 for more information.

If you're interested as an author or journalist in the WOWW Program and their 50 MADNESS series of textbooks from the S.A.P.I.E.N.T. Being, please check them out at https://www.FratirePublishing.com/madnessbooks, e-mail SapientBeing@att.net, or call (951) 638-5562 for more information.

If you're interested as an educator or marketer in the SCT Program and their 50 MADNESS series of textbooks from the S.A.P.I.E.N.T. Being, please check them out at https://www.FratirePublishing.com/madnessbooks, e-mail SapientBeing@att.net, or call (951) 638-5562 for more information.

Hopefully, this book was enlightening and your journey through it—along with mine—made you aware of the issues and challenges ahead of us. If it has, your quest and mine towards becoming a sapient being has begun. If it hasn't, there's no better time to start than now. Come join us in creating a society advancing personal intelligence and enlightenment now together (S.A.P.I.E.N.T.) and become a sapient being.

www.ingramcontent.com/pod-product-compliance
Lightning Source LLC
Chambersburg PA
CBHW051555030426
42334CB00034B/3448